Foundations

LAYING THE GROUNDWORK FOR A LIFETIME OF SPIRITUAL GROWTH

by Vince Vaughan

FOUNDATIONS

LAYING THE GROUNDWORK FOR A LIFETIME OF SPIRITUAL GROWTH

Copyright © 2015 by Vince Vaughan

Cover & interior design by: Mandy Flateland

ISBN-13: 978-0-692-51810-6
ISBN-10: 0-692-51810-X

www.vincevaughan.com
Email: vince@vincevaughan.com

Printed in U.S.A.

Contents

Acknowledgements

I would like to thank the many people at Quarry Community Church who have been discipled and have discipled others using the Foundations materials. Your enthusiasm for discipleship is inspiring to me!

I would also like to thank Michael Grose, lead pastor of the Quarry, for his support when I first felt called to pursue discipleship in a focused way. His encouragement and "getting" the importance of discipleship was pivotal for me.

I am grateful to Deb Goldberg, my dear friend and ministry partner, who was very helpful in the early stages and along the way in bringing these materials together.

I am also grateful to Mandy Flateland, designer extraordinaire, for her many hours of work in taking this from a boring looking old thing, and making it look like a real book!

Thanks to Kristy McEathron Nordeen for your amazing editing skills and for making this book readable!

I want to thank my wonderful family who helped me come to Christ at an early age and continue to model what it means to know and follow him.

I also want to thank Nick Taylor, a key mentor and friend for much of my life who has significantly influenced my understanding of Jesus and his grace.

And lastly, I want to thank my amazing wife, Jacki, who is my greatest cheerleader and one of the best mentors I have ever known. And my awesome, crazy kids, Tucker and Abbie: I hope you will always know the Father's deep love for you, and that I model that for you!

The fact that you are considering being discipled or discipling others is very exciting! It says that you have a heart that is seeking after more of God. When we enter an intentional discipleship process, it sets up a great environment to experience significant growth in our life with God.

Foundations is a set of materials and approach designed to help you in this process. It can be used individually, but is ideally suited for mentors and those they are discipling. In addition, Foundations is set up to help those being discipled go on to disciple others in the future. This is Jesus' command to us, and also happens to be one of the most exciting things we can do in our lives.

I would encourage you to read more about the discipleship process itself, especially if you are in a leadership role in a church. A particularly helpful resource is Transforming Discipleship by Greg Ogden. Ogden explores Jesus' approach to discipleship in detail and suggests strategies for the church to implement. Some of the concepts within Foundations have been based on Ogden's ideas, making it a helpful companion to the Foundations materials.

It is exciting to see God moving upon the hearts of leaders and individuals in many parts of his Church across the U.S. and the world in the area of personal discipleship. Many are reconnecting with Jesus' strategy of pouring deeply into a few, who in turn go on to disciple others, resulting in Jesus' transforming power rippling throughout the world.

Expect him to do great things in your life as you take this exciting step!

When you see professionals at the top of their fields, whether it is a successful business owner, government leader, or accomplished athlete, you will often find something else: a mentor who has significantly impacted their careers and their lives. It is no different in our spiritual lives. If we want to be effective and fulfilled in our relationship with God, we need the help of others who can share from their lives and experiences. That is the purpose of Foundations—joining people with mentors and fellow journeyers to help establish a solid spiritual base. This base can then become a launching pad for growth throughout our lives as disciples of Jesus.

Foundations is designed to offer disciples and mentors a combination of elements to help them in their journey. The first element is what God is currently doing through the disciples' everyday lives. When disciples have someone assisting them in understanding how God may be teaching them through the challenges, joys, and questions that life is bringing them, then real-life growth can take place quickly.

A second element is a more structured set of materials that intentionally cover key themes of the Christian faith. When covered in a purposeful way, these themes begin to form a strong foundation that the disciples can build on for the rest of their lives. The hope is that the structured elements of the materials provided in this course would merge with the real-life situations of the disciples to become a rich mix of fertile soil for growth.

The last key element is community. When we meet with a fellow disciple and a mentor, we can learn from their perspectives and journeys. When combined with the first two elements, we have a great recipe for significant spiritual growth.

The following description of a typical group time will give you a good idea of what is involved in the Foundations discipleship process. *If you are leading a Foundations group, it will also be important to read Session #29, "Discipling Others" before you begin, to gain a broader perspective and practical help in leading a Foundations group.*

If you would like to be *discipled*, ask God to lead you to someone who you could ask to disciple you (and others) and share this material with them. If no one is available, consider asking a fellow disciple to go through the process with you. Lastly, although Foundations is best experienced in community, you could also benefit from pursuing it individually.

A Closer Look at a Typical Group Time

Supporting One Another

Each week, the disciples (two or three people of the same gender) and the mentor will meet for an hour and a half. Having groups be the same gender and smaller in size allows people to share more openly. The first part of the group time will be spent in supporting one another in any of the following ways:

○ Sharing the significant things that have been happening in our lives that week. This could include the challenges as well as the ways God may be working in different areas of our lives, such as relationships in marriage, with children, and at work.

○ Confessing any sins we have committed or may be struggling with and receiving support. While confession is encouraged, it will be shared as group members feel comfortable and in an environment of grace.

○ Praying for specific friends in our lives who do not know Christ. This is done throughout the life of the group, because building relationships and sharing our faith with others is such a core part of being a disciple. Ideally, we would have the opportunity to disciple these friends in the future.

○ Prayer for one another for any of the above that has been shared with the group.

This will typically take 30-45 minutes of the group time. There may be weeks, however, when someone in the group has something pressing to share, which requires most or all of the group time. This is fine, because this discipleship process is designed to flow out of our lives; that is where God often does his best work in us. In other words, while discussion of the materials is important, it is secondary to what God is doing in the midst of our lives.

Obviously, a key aspect of supporting one another in these ways is a willingness to be open and vulnerable. Again, this will not be forced, but will deepen naturally over time.

Discussing the Materials

The second half of the group time each week will focus on discussing the theme for the week. Group members will spend time on their own during the week with the materials and then discuss with the group what has been helpful to them and what questions have been raised.

The mentor leading the group will prepare during the week just as the disciples do. Although the mentor will facilitate discussion, the goal is for all participants—disciples and mentor—to learn from one another. Later in the course, disciples will be asked to begin leading discussions to help prepare them to lead future discipleship groups.

○ **Themes**

Each session will address a theme that is core to our lives as disciples. Each theme falls under one of three categories: *Beliefs, Spiritual Practices,* and *Inner Transformation.* These categories have been adapted from the *The Christian Life Profile Assessment Tool Workbook: Discovering the Quality of Your Relationships with God and Others in 30 Key Areas,* a resource written by Pastor Randy Frazee.

Beliefs focuses on issues that are important, particularly in terms of **knowledge**. We need to have a clear understanding, for example, of what the Bible has to say about the nature of God, salvation, and eternity. Having an accurate understanding of these issues will significantly impact our lives and our relationship with God.

Spiritual Practices focuses on what we can **do** to foster our relationship with God and others. These are skills we learn, such as prayer, reading and studying Scripture, and understanding and using our spiritual gifts. Much like learning to drive a car, the hope is that by becoming comfortable with these practices, they can help us for a lifetime.

Inner Transformation focuses on who we are **becoming** as disciples of Jesus. This is the transformation of our hearts: what the apostle Paul calls the fruit of the Spirit. These new attitudes and behaviors impact our relationships and our decisions. We will look at what some of the key areas of transformation are and what they look like in relationships, how our culture impacts our character, and the role of emotional healing in our transformation process.

Know, do, become. See how simple it is? Okay, maybe not so simple to do, but at least it's nice to know that most of our journey as disciples will fall into one of these categories. This gives us a helpful handle for thinking about our process.

In addition to these broad categories, a key goal in the choosing of these themes was to be as comprehensive as possible in order to lay a strong foundation for the disciples. In pursuing this goal, themes emphasized in Scripture and expressed through the various rich traditions of the Church have been chosen.

If you have some church background, some of these themes may be familiar, but some less so depending on your tradition. For example, some of the following themes may be newer to you depending on your background: the Bible as the authority and guide for our lives, evangelism as a high priority, God's heart for compassion and justice, experiencing emotional health, ministering in the power of the Holy Spirit, and practicing a breadth of spiritual disciplines. If some or many of these are new for you, then God has some interesting things in store for you!

○ **Exploring Each Theme**

We will approach each theme from four different angles. The hope is that the combination of these approaches will help the truth of that particular theme begin to take root in our minds and hearts, as well as foster our relationships with God. In other words, this is not intended to be an academic exercise, but one that helps us connect what we are learning to our relationships with God.

The various elements are to be completed one per day, during our time with God for that day, as opposed to cramming them all into one time like homework. Prayer should also accompany each element whenever possible. For example, if you are doing some reading for the Spiritual Reading section, it would also be good to follow up this time with prayer related to the exercise and other aspects of your relationship with God. On average, it will take 30-45 minutes to complete each element, along with prayer.

Here are the 4 elements or sections we will use each week to explore each theme:

Digging into Scripture

Each week, a study of one or more key passages will be provided to help us understand God's truth and perspective on the theme. The type of study used is called the inductive study method. It is a study method designed to help you discover what God may be showing you in the passage, rather than a fill-in-the-blank approach. We will explore the inductive method more closely early on in the course.

Spiritual Practices

Because there are so many helpful practices, we will explore different ones each week throughout the discipleship process. The practice will be explained in the materials, and in most cases will tie into the theme being discussed. During the group time, participants will discuss their experience of trying out that particular practice. As you explore, you will discover that some practices will appeal to you more than others, which is part of the idea! Although you will take advantage of most of these practices in the future, there will be some that you will utilize more frequently.

Soaking in Scripture

Because we want God's truth to "seep" into our hearts and not just remain in our heads, we will take a short passage of Scripture—usually one verse—and reflect on it more closely. The goal here is not so much to analyze, but to let God speak to us through the passage and to store it away in our hearts by memorizing it. This allows God to speak to us again and again through his Word as it lodges in our hearts and minds.

Spiritual Reading

This will be a brief reading related to the theme, followed by questions for reflection and discussion. The goal of this section is to flesh out the theme to help us see what it might look like in our lives.

Themes

One theme will be covered each week, unless the group decides to add additional weeks.

Keys to Getting Started
- The Big Picture
- Who are We? Our Identity as Beloved Children of the Father
- Authority and Overview of the Bible
- How to Study the Bible
- Prayer
- Prayer, Part 2: Listening to God
- God's Guidance

Key Beliefs

- The Trinity: The Three-Personal God
- Jesus
- Know Your Enemy: Understanding Satan and His Tactics
- Being Sure of Our Salvation
- The Cost and Adventure of Being a Disciple
- The Holy Spirit
- Eternity: Understanding Heaven and Hell

Key Areas of Inner Transformation

- Developing the Fruit of the Spirit
- Becoming a Peacemaker: Handling Conflict
- Sexual Wholeness
- Emotional Health
- Spiritual Health: Avoiding the Pharisee Trap
- Spiritual Health: Living in Grace and Truth

Key Spiritual Practices

- Sharing Jesus with Others, Part 1: Being Connected to the World
- Sharing Jesus with Others, Part 2: Following the Lead of the Holy Spirit
- Compassion and Justice
- The Church
- Worship
- Discovering Spiritual Gifts and Passions
- The Voice and Power of the Holy Spirit
- Discovering God's Perspective on Money
- Discipling Others
- Celebration

Foundations Covenant

In order to provide the greatest opportunity for growth for myself and my Foundations group, I make the following commitments to myself, my group members, and to God.

1. I will make the weekly meeting with my Foundations group a high priority and attend if at all possible.

2. I will consistently complete the individual exercises and do so as a part of my time with God.

3. I will strive to share openly and honestly about what is happening in my life and how God is at work.

4. In order to foster a climate of trust I commit to keep all things shared in the group confidential.

5. I will regularly contribute to the discussion but be careful not to dominate so that everyone has the opportunity to share.

6. I will give strong consideration to discipling others in a Foundations group upon completion of the current group, and I see this as a part of my own discipleship process.

Signed_____

Dated_____

Personal Sharing Questions

One of the key goals of Foundations is to support and encourage one another as God works through our everyday lives to help us grow and transform more and more into his likeness. The aim is not only to learn more through the materials, but to change in the various areas and roles of our lives—as husbands and wives, as workers, as students, as friends, as parents—to become more like Jesus.

An important opportunity to do this is through our personal sharing time with the group, as we share about what has happened in our lives during this past week. Here, we can talk about what God has been doing in our lives, what challenges we have faced, and the small and large victories we have experienced. Of course, we can also carry this into the discussion of the materials and how God is using what we are learning in the midst of our lives.

The questions below are intended to be a help for the personal sharing time. These do not have to be completed each time, but they may be a helpful resource to refer to, especially in the early weeks. From there, it will probably become natural to share in this way. On any of these questions, you can feel free to share at a level that feels comfortable for you. Hopefully, that comfort level will increase as trust deepens. Feel free to add other questions that may be helpful to the group.

- Is there anything encouraging that God is doing in some area of your life—work, family, friendships, marriage, school, your relationship with him—that you want to share with the group? This may include the ways God is changing your attitudes and actions in these relationships and settings as he reveals his heart and wisdom to you.

- Is there any challenge or concern in an area of your life that you would like to share for support or prayer?

- Are there any ways you have stumbled in sin that you would like to share so the group can support you? These are often ongoing challenges/patterns of sin that we are trying to overcome. Also, while some sin is more individual in nature, many expressions are in the context of relationships; for example, the way we treat others, such as our spouses, children, and friends.

- Have there been any victories you have experienced this week in overcoming temptation or an ongoing challenge?

- Is there something going on in the spiritual journey of someone in your life who doesn't know Christ that you would like to share with the group for input, prayer, or celebration?

In this first week, we will step back and take a look at the big picture of our journey with God. What can we expect? What are we shooting for? We will also take stock of where we are at right now, spiritually speaking. What are our strengths and what are our areas of growth? Look at this first week as a kind of orientation to help set our course for the months ahead and our lifetime journey with God.

Soaking in Scripture

Jesus' words below sum up our goal as disciples. They are short and simple concepts, but with depths that require a lifetime to truly understand and live out.

Matthew 22:34-40

34Hearing that Jesus had silenced the Sadducees, the Pharisees got together. 35One of them, an expert in the law, tested him with this question: 36"Teacher, which is the greatest commandment in the Law?"

37Jesus replied: "'Love the Lord your God with all your heart and with all your soul and with all your mind.'38This is the first and greatest commandment. 39And the second is like it: 'Love your neighbor as yourself.'40All the Law and the Prophets hang on these two commandments."

- Write down vv. 37-39 word for word in the space below, and then spend some time repeating the passage in an effort to memorize it.

- The passage emphasizes the word "all." Why do you think that is? What does that mean to you?

- What might it look like if someone only did one of the two commandments?

- As a part of your prayer time, express your love to God. What is it about him or the things he has done for you that might prompt your love for him?

Digging into Scripture

Jesus often used parables as a teaching device. Parables are simple stories used to teach one or more truths. In the parable below, Jesus takes a big picture view of discipleship and describes the various responses that people have to God's truth in their lives. This is a great passage for us to look at as we begin this discipleship journey.

First, read through the passage in your own Bible. Then read through it again, using the text below. As you read it the second time, mark any words, phrases, or ideas that you find interesting or that raise questions. Often, repeated words or phrases or contrasting ideas will be helpful in understanding the main messages of the passage. After you read the passage the second time and mark your thoughts, respond to the questions following the passage.

Mark 4:1-20 *The Parable of the Sower*

1Again Jesus began to teach by the lake. The crowd that gathered around him was so large that he got into a boat and sat in it out on the lake, while all the people were along the shore at the water's edge.

2He taught them many things by parables, and in his teaching said: 3"Listen! A farmer went out to sow his seed. 4As he was scattering the seed, some fell along the path, and the birds came and ate it up. 5Some fell on rocky places, where it did not have much soil. It sprang up quickly, because the soil was shallow. 6But when the sun came up, the plants were scorched, and they withered because they had no root. 7Other seed fell among thorns, which grew up and choked the plants, so that they did not bear grain. 8Still other seed fell on good soil. It came up, grew and produced a crop, multiplying thirty, sixty, or even a hundred times."

9Then Jesus said, "He who has ears to hear, let him hear."

10When he was alone, the Twelve and the others around him asked him about the parables. 11He told them, "The secret of the kingdom of God has been given to you. But to those on the outside everything is said in parables 12so that,

"'they may be ever seeing but never perceiving,
and ever hearing but never understanding;
otherwise they might turn and be forgiven!'"

13Then Jesus said to them, "Don't you understand this parable? How then will you understand any parable? 14The farmer sows the word. 15Some people are like seed along the path, where the word is sown. As soon as they hear it, Satan comes and takes away the word that was sown in them. 16Others, like seed sown on rocky places, hear the word and at once receive it with joy. 17But since they have no root, they last only a short time. When trouble or persecution comes because of the word, they quickly fall away. 18Still others, like seed sown among thorns, hear the word; 19but the worries of this life, the deceitfulness of wealth and the desires for other things come in and choke the word, making it unfruitful. 20Others, like seed sown on good soil, hear the word, accept it, and produce a crop—thirty, sixty or even a hundred times what was sown."

- Overall, what stood out to you as interesting? What questions came up for you?

- What significance, if any, does the fact that Jesus is speaking to a large crowd have in regards to what he is teaching them?

- Why do you think he spoke to them in parables (v. 2)? Also, what do you think he meant by, "He who has ears to hear, let him hear" (v. 9)?

- What repeated words/ideas do you see in vv. 3-8? Contrasts?

- Which of the four situations that Jesus describes in vv. 14-20 can you identify with as you look at your past?

- What are specific things from your life that could be examples of what Jesus is describing in v. 19 as the thorny soil?

- What do you think it looks like to "produce a crop—thirty, sixty, or even a hundred times what was sown" (v. 20) in our lives? What does it take for this to become a reality?

Take some time to pray about whatever you are connecting with the most on a personal level from this passage. This may include expressing some of your desires to God, asking for his help, or asking for his forgiveness.

Spiritual Practices
Reflecting on Growth Opportunities

This is a simple practice that should be helpful during this discipleship process. Take a look back at the list of topics in the table of contents. As you look at the topics, place a check mark by the ones that you think will be especially helpful to you. These may be areas that you are less familiar with or know you would like help with. Feel free to select as few or many as you would like.

During your group time, share about these topics and why you selected them. This will be helpful to you and your mentor as you go through Foundations. This will ensure that the group takes the necessary time (including extra weeks, if necessary) on a given topic to help group members feel confident in the areas selected.

As a part of your prayer time, share any of your desires with God concerning the areas you have selected.

Spiritual Reading
A Map for Our Spiritual Journey

Where's the Map?

When we take a trip, it is usually helpful to have a good idea of where we want to end up and an understanding of how we are going to get there. We may not know all of the details of what the journey will look like (that's half the fun), and we may take some detours from our original plan, but it's helpful to have an idea of the big picture.

This is true of our discipleship journey—our journey with God throughout our lives. Where are we headed? What does this journey usually look like? What can we expect? It's helpful to know some of these answers early on in the journey.

Where are We Headed?

A big question concerns the ultimate destination. What is the end goal of this lifetime journey? One could, of course, write books in response to that question, but when asked a similar question, Jesus answered it in a few sentences:

> *Love the Lord your God with all your heart and with all your soul and with all your mind...and love your neighbor as yourself. All the Law and the Prophets hang on these two commandments.* **Matthew 22:37-40**

At the end of our journey—the end of our lives—we want to love God more than ever and know how deeply he loves us. We want to express that love by enjoying him, worshipping him, thinking like him, and loving others like him. And we want to do this in increasing measure throughout our lives. Another way of saying it is: we are becoming more and more transformed into his likeness over our lifetime out of our love for him.

How Long Does It Take?

While some journeys take a few days and some a few weeks, this journey takes a lifetime. It is not a quick process. If it were only about gaining knowledge, we might be able work really hard and cram for the exam. But, as stated earlier, discipleship is about ongoing change. Whether we are seventeen or seventy, we should be growing and changing because of our love for God.

The good news is that we can get off to a strong start, which will make the rest of our journey much more fruitful and enjoyable. Just like a trip, if you get headed in the right direction in the beginning, it helps throughout the journey. This intentional discipleship process that you are now entering plays a vital part in getting off to that strong start.

Do Most Journeys Look the Same?

Yes and no. Every person's journey looks different; you and your relationship with God are unique. However, there are some similarities that emerge. Typically, there are different stages of the journey that we all go through. In much the same way that we all experience the stages of childhood, adolescence, and adulthood, we also experience different stages in our spiritual development.

- **Stage 1: Finding God** (Spiritual Explorers)

  This is the stage of discovering God for the first time or coming back to him. We may have been experiencing emptiness or chaos in our lives and began reaching out to God. Often, through the help of others, we begin to discover that God cares for us and can provide the help and answers we need. It is in this stage that we take the step of surrendering our lives to Christ and choose to follow him as one of his disciples.

- **Stage 2: Getting Grounded in God** (New Disciples)

  All disciples, if they are going to grow, begin with a phase of the discipleship journey that includes a great deal of initial learning and growth, because there are so many new things to explore. This is where an intentional discipleship process like the one you are beginning can be so helpful. This stage includes gaining knowledge about important truths about God and the Christian faith, as well as practices that help us know God and live out our lives as his disciples.

  In this stage, we also begin to discover our spiritual gifts and how we can use them in our churches, and we begin to experience Christian community as we get more involved in the life of the church.

- **Stage 3: Deepening Our Lives with God** (Deeper Disciples)

  In this stage, we begin to build on the things we have learned in the previous stage. Because there is so much to learn and experience in our lives with God, there is always opportunity to go deeper in the areas we have been introduced to. This may happen through individual study, small groups, classes, sermons, or retreats.

We also begin to take on more responsibility in our church communities in this stage. We begin to disciple others, take on significant roles in the areas in which we are serving, and see ourselves as part of the core of the church, which may include other steps, such as church membership.

- **Stage 4: Rediscovering God** (Confused Disciples)

  In this stage, those who have been following Christ for some time may experience some confusion or frustration in their spiritual lives. This can be due to difficult life circumstances, a sense of stalling out or getting stuck in their relationship with God, or a sense of God letting them down. This stage often includes a time of healing. Often, one of the greatest discoveries through this confusing time is the awareness that God loves us as we are, not based on how well we are doing spiritually or how much we are producing in our spiritual lives. He loves us simply because we are his children.

- **Stage 5: Living Out of God's Love** (Beloved Disciples)

  Once we begin to understand the depth of God's love for us, we begin to live out of this love. Living this way usually produces greater joy and a childlike freedom in our lives. It also results in a deeper trust in God that brings greater peace. In addition, this love often moves us to love others on a deeper level.

Moving through these stages doesn't happen automatically. We must have the desire to continue growing throughout our lives. Otherwise, we will get stuck in any one of these stages. We will also need the help of others in each of the stages.

Who Will Be Joining Us?

This is the best part: we don't have to take this journey alone. Thank goodness—how confusing and boring that would be!

First of all, we need personal guides. This is important throughout our journey, but is particularly critical in the early stages, such as the second stage mentioned above. There is so much to learn and so many potential dangers and unnecessary detours that we need someone to personally help us navigate this spiritual terrain. We need someone to lead us in our discipleship journey and help us in a very hands-on way.

As we move into the "deepening" stage (Stage 3), these guides can act more as coaches, supporting us on an as-needed basis. They can be available to answer questions that arise, point out helpful resources, and support us as we begin to disciple others and step into new ministry opportunities.

Finally, during the latter stages of our journey, it is helpful to have a mentor who can help us understand the deeper things God wants to do in our lives and in our relationships with him. Sometimes, this will be the key person who has already been helping us. At other times, it may be someone who has a special gifting and sometimes training in helping those of us who are going through challenging times in our spiritual lives. This may be a wise friend, a pastor or leader at church, or a spiritual director.

In addition to the various types of mentors mentioned above, there are also fellow journeyers—our peers. Whether it's a friend, a small group member, or someone in our family, if they are on the same journey, then they will be a huge help in this adventure. This is not an individual pursuit; we need them, and they need us.

Lastly, there are those we will help guide. Sadly, many Christians think about their own growth, but don't have a vision for discipling others. Jesus' last words to his disciples before returning to heaven were, "Go and make disciples" (Matthew 28:19). **From the very beginning of their journey, a disciple needs to know that part of being a disciple is the expectation that they will disciple others.** This is not something that has to take years, either. If someone is intentionally discipled in the first phase of their journey and has good coaching as they begin the second phase, they can begin discipling others. In fact, this will continue to accelerate their personal growth.

What Elements Produce the Most Fruitful Journey?

There are different elements that can help us move forward in our journey in a fruitful way. The combination of the following elements will usually provide momentum in our journey:

- **People**

   This is what we just discussed. Having mentors and supportive peers who are also growing will go a long way in helping us continue to grow. Again, this is important throughout our lives, not just in the beginning of our journey. The key here is that we have those with whom we can share openly and who can speak into our lives.

- **Truth**

   Consistently receiving truth, especially from the Bible, is critical. Because we live in a world that largely does not live according to God's ways, we need to regularly be exposing ourselves to his truth through the study of Scripture, reading, and teaching. Again, early on this will be aided by an intentional discipleship process, but this will need to continue on throughout our lives.

- **Life**

   One of the best growth opportunities is life itself. It's usually through the challenges and confusion of everyday life that God does his best work in us. This is where he teaches us and shapes us. This simple idea is helpful to be aware of so that we can be cooperating with God's efforts. Also, it adds a purposeful quality to what otherwise could be seen simply as frustrating circumstances we have to endure. God uses it all!

   The key here, though, is that we need to combine the three elements above to learn what God is teaching us through our daily lives. When we bring the messiness of life to mentors and friends who care about us and can guide and support us, and when God's truth is informing us, then we can truly experience growth and transformation. Without people and truth, they just remain frustrating situations.

It's an Adventure!

When we know where we are headed and have the right elements in place, our journey with God can truly be an adventure. We don't always know what's coming around the next turn—that's the adventurous part—but we know that God, through his Holy Spirit, will be guiding us and helping us. We do not serve a boring God, so this journey shouldn't be boring either!

Questions for Reflection and Discussion

- What did you find helpful in this overview of our spiritual journeys?

- How do the descriptions of the stages of our journey help you in understanding the "big picture" of our journeys?

- Which of the three elements (People, Truth, Life) has been especially helpful in your journey? How have you seen these three elements working together?

During your prayer time, share with God your hopes, as well as any concerns you have about the discipleship process you are beginning.

The picture we hold of God, and the picture we believe he holds of us, is of critical importance to our relationship with him and to the overall discipleship process. If our picture of God is skewed, then everything we do in trying to relate to him or follow him can be skewed.

This week's passages, practices, and readings will all point to one important truth: that we are children deeply loved by our Father, and nothing can ever change that. This truth can take some time to take hold in our hearts, but when it does, it begins to bring everything else into proper focus. Because understanding our identity as beloved children is often a long journey, we will return to it again and again as we discuss the many themes throughout this discipleship process.

Soaking in Scripture

One of the amazing truths we can hold on to is that the Father loves us in the way that he loves Jesus, his Son. In one of his final prayers before his arrest and crucifixion, Jesus prayed that his disciples would be unified so that "the world will know that you sent me and *have loved them even as you have loved me.*" (John 17:23).

With this in mind, it is appropriate and helpful to reflect on the Father's love for his Son and receive that same love for ourselves as the Father's sons and daughters. Using the Father's words to Jesus below can be a helpful way to do that.

This passage takes place at the time of Jesus' baptism; they are words that come directly from the heart of the Father to his Son.

> **Mark 1:11** (NLT)
>
> *You are my dearly loved Son, and you bring me great joy.*

As you read this passage, read it as a prayer, hearing these words spoken from the Father to you.

- A great way to use this passage as a prayer is to hear your Father saying these words to you over and over, each time emphasizing a different word to you:

  "YOU are my dearly loved son/daughter, and you bring me great joy."

  "You are MY dearly loved son/daughter, and you bring me great joy."

  And so on. Each time, briefly reflect on what each word expresses from his heart to you. We can be confident that the Father feels this way about us, because Jesus has made that truth clear.

Using the passage in this way is a great way to start every prayer time you have with your Father. Really experiencing God as our Father who sees us as his precious children can be difficult. This type of regular prayer exercise can help this reality "seep" into our hearts.

Digging into Scripture

First, read the passage in your Bible. Then read it again, using the printed text below to note interesting ideas, repeated words/themes, contrasting thoughts, or questions you have. After you have read and reflected, respond to the questions that follow the text.

Through this famous parable, Jesus reveals the distorted pictures many people have of the Father and his true heart toward us.

Luke 15:1-2, 11-32

¹Now the tax collectors and sinners were all gathering around to hear Jesus. ²But the Pharisees and the teachers of the law muttered, "This man welcomes sinners and eats with them."

¹¹Jesus continued: "There was a man who had two sons. ¹²The younger one said to his father, 'Father, give me my share of the estate.' So he divided his property between them.

¹³"Not long after that, the younger son got together all he had, set off for a distant country and there squandered his wealth in wild living. ¹⁴After he had spent everything, there was a severe famine in that whole country, and he began to be in need. ¹⁵So he went and hired himself out to a citizen of that country, who sent him to his fields to feed pigs. ¹⁶He longed to fill his stomach with the pods that the pigs were eating, but no one gave him anything.

¹⁷"When he came to his senses, he said, 'How many of my father's hired men have food to spare, and here I am starving to death! ¹⁸I will set out and go back to my father and say to him: Father, I have sinned against heaven and against you. ¹⁹I am no longer worthy to be called your son; make me like one of your hired men.' ²⁰So he got up and went to his father.

"But while he was still a long way off, his father saw him and was filled with compassion for him; he ran to his son, threw his arms around him and kissed him.

²¹"The son said to him, 'Father, I have sinned against heaven and against you. I am no longer worthy to be called your son.'

²²"But the father said to his servants, 'Quick! Bring the best robe and put it on him. Put a ring on his finger and sandals on his feet. ²³Bring the fattened calf and kill it. Let's have a feast and celebrate. ²⁴For this son of mine was dead and is alive again; he was lost and is found.' So they began to celebrate.

²⁵"Meanwhile, the older son was in the field. When he came near the house, he heard music and dancing. ²⁶So he called one of the servants and asked him what was going on. ²⁷'Your brother has come,' he replied, 'and your father has killed the fattened calf because he has him back safe and sound.'

²⁸"The older brother became angry and refused to go in. So his father went out and pleaded with him. ²⁹But he answered his father, 'Look! All these years I've been slaving for you and never disobeyed your orders. Yet you never gave me even a young goat so I could celebrate with my friends. ³⁰But when this son of yours who has squandered your property with prostitutes comes home, you kill the fattened calf for him!'

³¹"'My son,' the father said, 'you are always with me, and everything I have is yours. ³²But we had to celebrate and be glad, because this brother of yours was dead and is alive again; he was lost and is found.'"

- Who is Jesus telling this parable to (vv. 1-2)?

- How would you describe the attitude of the son in vv. 11-16?

- How would you describe his attitude in vv. 17-19? What kind of response from his father does he seem to be expecting?

- What strikes you about the father's response in v. 20? In vv. 22-24?

- What do you think Jesus is trying to tell his listeners and us about the heart of the Father through the father's response in the story?

- Based on v. 29, how do you think the older son would describe his relationship with his father? Why do you think Jesus includes the character of the older son in his story?

In your relationship with God, which picture of the father do you relate to more: the picture of the father as experienced by the younger son in v. 20 or the picture of the father held by the older son in v. 29?

Spiritual Practices
Picturing the Scene

Have you ever watched a movie about some part of the Bible, maybe about the life of Moses or Jesus, and found parts of the story you have read before coming alive for you in a new way? Maybe it's experiencing the storm, or hearing the crowds, or seeing the anguish in someone's face that helps you encounter a biblical scene in a new way.

We can do something similar through the use of our imagination, which is what movie makers are using, of course. By picturing in our mind a story that is being told or event that takes place, we can interact with Scripture in some new way. We can see, hear, feel—even smell—the scene as it unfolds. We can observe the scene as an onlooker or take on the role of someone in the scene and experience it from his vantage point. What might we notice as we watch Jesus tenderly touching a leper? What would it have felt like to try to walk on the water as Peter did? What might Jesus say to us in that moment?

This simple practice is a wonderful way to not only encounter Scripture, but to encounter Jesus and the Father in new ways. Through the use of the imagination he gave us, we can imagine what he might want to say to us, how he may want to express his love to us, and how he shows his love to others.

The story of the prodigal son is a good opportunity to use this practice. Give it a try!

- Read Luke 15:11-20 once again so the story will be fresh in your mind.

- Close your eyes and take a moment to quiet yourself. Taking a few deep breaths can be helpful.

- Slowly picture the story unfolding in your mind like a movie. Picture the story as if you were the younger son (or daughter) and imagine the father as your heavenly Father.

- What do you see and experience as you go away from your Father? What do you see and feel as you return to your Father and experience his response as described in the story? Imagine what he might say to you as his son or daughter and what you may want to say to him. Take your time.

- After you are done with this exercise, take a few moments to thank him and express anything else on your heart. If you keep a journal, you may want to write down any reflections you have from this exercise.

📖 Spiritual Reading
Boss or Father?

God as Boss

Mrs. Stout. What a perfect name. Four foot nothin' and tough as nails. She could have been a drill sergeant, but instead she was my seventh-grade Social Studies teacher.

Her gaze was like one of those roving security cameras that track your every move. She never missed anything. If you ever tried to deny doing something wrong, she would bellow, "Trying to hang your halo on your horns, are ya?" It took me awhile to figure that one out.

How could someone so small be so scary? I'm twitching a little bit right now just thinking about her...

Did you ever have a teacher, boss, or manager like that? Someone who seemed mostly to be focused on watching to see if you would mess up? They were ready to pounce; eager to share their disappointment in you. Good times, right?

Unfortunately, this is how many, many people see God. Often it is on an unconscious level—they don't even realize that they are seeing him in this way. But if you poke around a little bit, it will start coming out. They believe that God is watching them in the same way: looking for ways that they are falling short, not measuring up, or messing things up—again.

And then they think, "Why don't I feel close to God?" which would be like me asking, "Now why don't I feel closer to Mrs. Stout?"

God as Father

If you talked to my mom, you would think I should be nominated for a Nobel Prize or something. Who knows, maybe I should. Take that, Mrs. Stout. Growing up, she would give me hugs that left me gasping for air and "love pats" on the back that would leave me wincing a bit. She couldn't help it! She was so full of love for me!

Even today, if you ask my mom how she feels about me, she wouldn't rattle off a list of what I had done wrong that day or how I was disappointing her. She would tell you about me. What she loves about who I am: my personality, the good qualities she sees in me, and what she loves about our relationship.

She might tell you about some of what she sees as accomplishments in my life—Eagle Scout, brain surgeon, compulsive liar. But even that wouldn't really be the main thing she would focus on. It wouldn't be about what I had or had not done, it would be me. She loves me. Not in some abstract way. She loves me—likes me—as a person.

If you're a parent, you get this, right? Are there times you want to strike your forehead repeatedly against a hard surface? Sure. Do you get frustrated and have to discipline your kids? Of course. But don't you think they are pretty freaking amazing?

Don't you love the funny, clever little things they say and do? Don't you love watching their talents and gifts emerge? Don't you love watching as their friendships grow? Don't you hurt with them when they experience pain in those same relationships?

When you are disciplining them, isn't even that out of your love for them and hope that they will grow into people of character, at least on your good days?

So here's the million-dollar question: is God more like a menacing boss looking for ways you've disappointed him or a parent who is crazy about you? This is a very important question.

Jesus' Picture

In our passage for study this week, Jesus created a parable to reveal what his Father was truly like. When you think back to that story, what would you say God is like? Think about the scene of the prodigal son's return. What does the father do? Fold his arms, wait for his "employee" to get to the house, and then recount all of his mistakes? Interestingly, that's pretty much exactly what the son expects to happen. And it's what many of us expect to happen to us.

Jesus' picture shatters that false picture of God. In the scene, the father looks like a... father. He is a loving, affectionate father who is crazy about his son. As soon as he sees his son from afar, he takes off running toward him. Before his son can say much of anything, the father hugs him (probably like one of my mom's bear hugs) and kisses him. Is this a cold, distant, disapproving, boss-like father? Doesn't sound like it, does it?

So the question is, which picture of God are we going to believe is true?

The one we may have picked up somewhere, from our own assumptions about him or out of our own insecurities about ourselves or from church leaders that may see God this way?

Or the one we see from Jesus, who actually knows the Father up close and personal? Many people, even well intentioned people, *think* they know him, but Jesus actually does. This is the picture he gives us; he gave it to us on purpose, because he knew that we needed to have a true picture of our Father.

It doesn't mean that our Father won't correct us or discipline us. I mention this, because some people worry that this picture is too "soft." The reality is that sometimes God can be disappointed in our actions; sometimes, he needs to discipline us or challenge us to grow. The key is in knowing that this all comes out of the Father's love for us. The Bible says that "the LORD disciplines those he loves" (Proverbs 3:12). He isn't looking for our mistakes; he's looking for ways to love us and help us grow.

But he's not only interested in our growth. He's interested in us as people. Much like we feel toward our children, he *enjoys* watching us and being with us as we express ourselves: through our personalities, our gifts, our relationships. Remember that he created us as the people we are. Imagine the joy it must bring him to see us live out who he has made us to be—especially when we are living in relationship with him—and realize how much he loves us.

Ironically, our awareness of his love and affection for us is a way of loving *him*. Imagine if your children didn't think you really loved them or thought you were simply disappointed in them most of the time. Not good! We want them to know how we truly feel about them, and so does our Father.

A Pretty Big Deal

It's hard to express how important having this true picture of our Father is. When we have a false picture, such as the disappointed boss picture, it has a chilling effect on our relationship with God. We become focused on our mistakes and shortcomings, because we think that's what he is focused on. We can be robbed of our joy and find ourselves on an endless treadmill of trying to please him and feeling like we are never doing enough. This can lead to burnout as we try to do more and more to please God.

It can also distort our understanding of circumstances in our lives. Something good happens: "God must love me! He must be pleased with me!" Something bad happens or a prayer seems to go unanswered: "What did I do wrong? Why is God upset with me?" This is a recipe for a roller coaster life.

These events are not based on the Father's love for you any more than the ups and downs of your children's life are based on your love for them. Can you imagine: "I was thinking about giving you a gift, but I'm just not loving you as much today."

The reality is that we live in a broken world, and ups and downs are going to happen. The only constant is our Father's deep love for us, on the good days and the bad.

When we really begin to believe that God is an affectionate Father who loves us and enjoys us, we begin to experience increased joy and freedom. We become more of who he made us to be. We begin to love others more freely. It's interesting—when you stop focusing on your own shortcomings, you focus less on others', too.

Understanding and believing in the Father's love for us is like a key that unlocks many good things. However, it usually takes people a period of time—a process—to begin to truly believe that this is how their Father really feels about them.

A good place to start is to ask God to reveal his true heart to you, to show you in ways that you can relate. A big help is being around people who get it. You can find these people by looking for the clue: you sense a joy and peace about them that may be different than what others have. Watch how they live and how they talk about their relationship with God. This is one of those things that is caught more than taught.

In addition, using practices like the one we used in our Soaking in Scripture section this week can be helpful. Doing this every day for a number of weeks can help the reality of God's love begin to soak into us, like a sponge that begins to soften as the water is absorbed.

Allow your Father's love to begin to seep into your heart and mind. Nothing would make him happier.

Questions for Reflection and Discussion

- What are some ways that you have viewed God as a boss?

- What stood out to you as the things God might appreciate about someone as his child?

- Do you have someone in your life that sees God as his/her Father? What do you notice about him/her?

How should we view the Bible? As an interesting read? An important book? Something more? The belief we have in the Bible will have a direct impact on the place it holds in our lives. In the upcoming weeks, we will look at *how* to read and study the Bible, but this week, we will focus on the *nature* of the Bible and what that means for our lives.

In our Spiritual Reading section, we will look at an overview of the Bible to help us become more comfortable navigating Scripture.

Soaking in Scripture

It is very easy to depend on many things other than the wisdom and guidance of God through his Word (the Bible) and the words he speaks through his Holy Spirit. This is a wonderful passage to store in our hearts to remind us when we are relying only on our own wisdom or on the things of this world.

Deuteronomy 8:3

Man does not live on bread alone but on every word that comes from the mouth of the LORD.

- Repeat this passage a number of times until it becomes a part of your memory.

- Post it somewhere that you can see during the week. One idea would be to place it where you keep your bread or on the bread itself as a reminder of the role of God's Word in your life.

- What "bread" in your life might you be tempted to live on more so than the words of the LORD?

- During your prayer time, share your thoughts with God related to these potential substitutes.

Digging into Scripture

First, read the passage in your Bible. Then read it again, using the printed text below to note interesting ideas, repeated words/themes, contrasting thoughts, or questions you have. After you have read and reflected, respond to the questions that follow the text.

In his mentoring of Timothy, the apostle Paul discussed the nature and role of the Bible.

2 Timothy 3:14-17

14 But as for you, continue in what you have learned and have become convinced of, because you know those from whom you learned it, 15 and how from infancy you have known the Holy Scriptures, which are able to make you wise for salvation through faith in Christ Jesus. 16 All Scripture is God-breathed and is useful for teaching, rebuking, correcting and training in righteousness, 17 so that the servant of God may be thoroughly equipped for every good work.

- What do you see that has been important and helpful to Timothy in his spiritual journey (vv. 14-15)?

- What do you think Paul means by "holy" and "God-breathed" in describing Scripture?

- What, if anything, makes it difficult for you to believe that the Bible is inspired (God-breathed)?

- The four terms in v. 16—teaching, rebuking, correcting and training in righteousness—can be a bit confusing. Take a shot at putting each term in your own words.

- Do you think the Bible would be useful in these ways in our lives if we didn't see it as God-breathed? Why or why not?

- Give an example of how the Bible has helped you in your life. Then give an example of how the Bible has challenged you in some area of your life.

- During your prayer time, express any desires, requests for help, gratitude, or confessions you may have related to God's Word.

Spiritual Practices
Using Biblical Tools

If the Bible is going to be useful in our lives like 2 Timothy 3:16 tells us, we need to learn how to use various resources and tools that can help us in navigating and understanding the Bible. Because the Bible is such a large book—actually a collection of books, like a small library—we often need assistance, particularly if we are trying to find out what the Bible has to say about a specific theme or topic.

Let's say you wanted to see what the Bible had to say about hope. Maybe you or a friend of yours is feeling discouraged or you heard a message on hope and wanted to find out more. First, you could turn to the back of most Bibles and find a *concordance*. A concordance is a list of passages containing the word you are looking for. Under the word hope, you would find passages with that word in it.

Another tool found in the back of most Bibles is a *topical index*. Here you would also look up the word and find passages that discuss that topic, but may or may not use the actual word. This can be a very helpful tool.

Both of these tools can also be found online on sites such as www.biblestudytools.com and www.biblegateway.com. For online sites, the concordance is simply a key word search.

Other tools that can be helpful when studying the Bible are commentaries that scholars have written to help explain the Bible and Bible dictionaries that define words and places found in the Bible. These can be found in print form at bookstores or online at websites like those mentioned above. Study Bibles, which have notes that explain passages and give background information, can also be very helpful. Two good examples are the NIV Study Bible and the Life Application Study Bible.

Trying It Out

All right, let's give this a shot. Find two passages on hope from a concordance (where the word is in the passage itself). Then find two different passages on hope from a topical index (where the word may or may not be in the passage). You can use the tools from the back of your Bible or from one of the websites provided above. Write down the passages with their references, that is, where the passage is found in the Bible.

When you are done, choose one passage and include it in your prayer time, sharing any thoughts and desires with God that came from reflecting on that passage.

There you go. Happy hunting!

Spiritual Reading
Spiritual Reading: A Brief Overview of the Bible

Occasionally, I am forced to go into The Home Depot. I say forced, because I'm not what you might call handy. I always have the same feeling every time I walk in there: overwhelmed. Everything is huge. The shelves, the aisles, the carts, the whole store—huge, huge, huge. I don't have a clue where to find anything, and half the time I don't even really know what I'm looking for to begin with. It's pretty fun.

I have friends who *love* to go to The Home Depot. I'm not sure why they're my friends. They know exactly what they need, how the store is laid out, where to find things, and they love that there is so much to choose from. They go there as often as they can. Weird.

Many people feel about the Bible like I do about The Home Depot: overwhelmed. They don't know how it all fits together, where to start, or where to find what they need. And it's huge!

The goal here is to help you become like my friends. To help you feel comfortable with the Bible and able to use it easily. To want to come back to it again and again. Specifically, my goal is to give you some handles so that you have an overarching view of the Bible and the various parts, or acts, as in a play. Once we get this bigger picture in our minds, the Bible can become less intimidating to us. Ultimately, we want to be able to use the Bible in a way that helps us grow closer to God and follow him and his ways in our lives.

The Big Picture

Although the Bible is broken into different sections and books, the main storyline—the plot—is God's relentless pursuit of us, his creation, and his desire to bring us back into relationship with him. The central character of this story is Jesus Christ, the one who comes to rescue us and restore our relationship with himself and God the Father. All the parts of the Bible are drawn into this storyline.

The tricky part about the Bible is that it is not like picking up a typical book from one genre, written by one author. The Bible is really a collection of books that has been put into one volume; a collection that is remarkably diverse.

The Bible includes sixty-six books written over a span of 1,500 years by forty authors, ranging from kings to peasants, statesmen to fishermen, doctors to businessmen. It includes history, poetry, wisdom writings, prophetic literature, teaching-focused letters (epistles), and more. And yet, with all of this diversity, the story—the message— remains remarkably unified. This, in fact, is one of the supports for believing that there is ultimately one Author guiding this multitude of human authors.

Breaking it Down

How does it all fit together? We will start with the major themes of the story found in the Bible and then break it down further.

Four Major Acts

The story of the Bible and of God can be broken down into four major acts:

Act 1: Creation (Genesis 1-2)
God creates the world, including human beings made in his image. There is no sin and no relational barriers between God and humans.

Act 2: Fall (Genesis 3 through the rest of the Old Testament)
Beginning with Adam and Eve, human beings choose to disobey God (sin), causing relational separation between God and mankind.

Beginning with Abraham, God forms a nation of people (Israel, also known as the Jews) that he promises to lead and care for. Through the Jewish people, God will make himself known to the rest of the world.

Act 3: Rescue (Matthew, Mark, Luke, and John)
God the Father sends his son, Jesus, into the world to be born as a human. Through Jesus' death, humanity's sin is paid for; when we accept his sacrifice, we can be reunited relationally with God.

Act 4: Restoration (Acts through the rest of the New Testament)
God forms followers of Jesus into a community—a family—called the Church. The Church's mission is to partner with God in restoring the world and its people to its original condition before the fall.

Ultimately, Jesus will return to establish a new earth, fulfilling God's original plan of a kingdom in which he is with his people and there is no sin or the consequences of sin, such as pain and death.

Understanding the Major Sections of the Bible

As we move forward, it might be helpful to open up your Bible to the table of contents to follow along. As we discuss the major sections of the Bible, we will reference how they relate to the main acts of the story above, as well as the chronology of each section.

Understanding a few terms may be helpful. The Bible is broken down into books (for example, Genesis). Each book has chapters (for example, Genesis 2 means Chapter 2 of Genesis). Lastly, each chapter is broken down into verses (for example, Genesis 2:12 means the twelfth verse in the second chapter of Genesis). A verse is usually a sentence or two in length. The purpose of using verses is to make it easier to reference a specific passage within a chapter.

Old and New Testaments

The Bible is divided into two main sections—the Old Testament (OT; also called the Hebrew Scriptures) and the New Testament (NT). The word "testament" means agreement or covenant. The OT is the covenant between God and the Jews, while the NT is the covenant between God and all of humanity through the life and death of Jesus.

The OT spans from creation to 400 BC. The NT covers 6 BC to 100 AD. Looking at the table of contents, you will see that the OT books go from Genesis to Malachi. The NT books go from Matthew to Revelation.

Old Testament Sections (Act 1: Creation and Act 2: Fall)

Below you will find the major sections within the OT. It is important to note that, within the Bible, the sections are formed by type of writing (genre). For instance, you will see that the first fourteen books of the OT are historical; that is, they are the history of the Jewish people, Israel. Later on, under Chronological Overview, you will find more details of this history.

History of Jews: Creation to approximately 550 BC

Genesis	Exodus	Leviticus	Numbers
Deuteronomy	Joshua	Judges	Ruth
1 & 2 Samuel	1 & 2 Kings		1 & 2 Chronicles
Ezra	Nehemiah		Esther

Next are poetry and wisdom writings. These are poems, songs, and practical wisdoms written by King David and his son, Solomon, with the exception of Job. These writings have provided comfort and insight to people over the centuries.

Poetry and Wisdom: Approximately 1000 BC

Job	Psalms	Proverbs	Ecclesiastes	Song of Songs

The rest of the OT consists of books written by prophets. Prophets were people chosen by God to give a special message from him to his people. Typically, these were warnings to the Jewish people and their leaders when they had strayed from the path of following God, as well as reminders of God's love for his people.

It is important to note that the timing of these writings overlaps with the historical books earlier in the OT. For example, some of the kings of Israel discussed in 1 & 2 Kings were warned by various prophets listed below.

Prophets: 800-400 BC (overlaps with historical books)

Isaiah	Jeremiah	Lamentations	Ezekiel
Daniel	Hosea	Joel	Amos
Obadiah	Jonah	Micah	Nahum
Habakkuk	Zephaniah	Haggai	Zechariah
Malachi			

New Testament Sections (Act 3: Rescue and Act 4: Restoration)

The NT begins with a focus on the birth, life, death, and resurrection of Jesus. The term gospel means "good news." These first four books focus particularly on the message or good news that Jesus brought, as well as the miracles that demonstrated his power. They are not biographies in the typical sense of describing each era of someone's life.

Gospels : Life and teachings of Jesus, approximately 6 BC-33 AD

Matthew	Mark	Luke	John

The next book, sometimes shortened to Acts, is historical. It is a history of the first disciples of Jesus and the churches they formed after Jesus returned to heaven.

Acts of the Apostles: History of the early Church from 30-100 AD

Epistles are letters written to encourage and teach the early churches in various cities in the Roman world (for example, Ephesians is written to Christians in Ephesus). Many of these letters were written by the apostle Paul, one of the key leaders in the early Church.

Epistles: Letters from Paul and others to support and teach the early Church

Romans	1 & 2 Corinthians	Galatians	Ephesians	Philippians
Colossians	1 & 2 Thessalonians			
1 & 2 Timothy	Titus	Philemon	Hebrews	
James	1 & 2 Peter	1, 2 & 3 John	Jude	

The Book of Revelation is referred to as apocalyptic literature, because it is a vision of what will happen at the end of this world and the beginning of the new world and new era. This type of writing is very symbolic in nature, making it challenging at times to fully understand or interpret.

Book of Revelation: God reveals what will happen at the end of the world

Creation → Flood · Abraham → 12 Tribes · Enslaved in Egypt · Moses & Exodus · 1st Kings of Israel · Civil War · N. Kingdom Exiled · S. Kingdom in Captivity

①—//—② ┼ ┼ ③a ┼ ┼ ③b ┼ ④ ┼ ⑤ ┼ ⑥a ⑥b ┼ ┼ ┼ ┼ ┼ ┼ —//—

2,000 BC · 1,700 BC · 1,290 BC · 1,100 BC · 1,000 BC · 900 BC · 722 BC · 590 BC

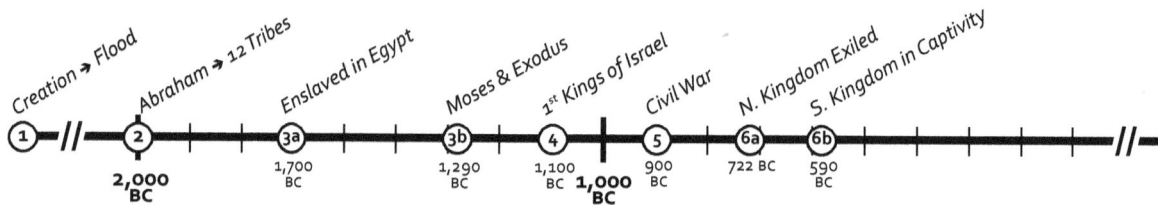

Chronological Overview or "Top 10 Eras of Biblical History"

Now that we have broken down the Bible into its major sections, it may be helpful to go back and look at the overall story from a chronological viewpoint with some details and major characters added in, along with where the events are located in the Bible. Most dates are approximate, noted by the "~" symbol.

1. **The Beginnings: Events in Prehistory** (Genesis)
   - Creation, Adam and Eve, Cain and Abel, Noah and the flood

2. **Abraham and the Beginning of the Jewish Nation** (2000 BC; Genesis)
   - Abraham; Isaac, son of Abraham; Jacob, son of Isaac
   - Jacob's twelve sons become the leaders of the twelve tribes of Israel

3. **The Israelites in Egypt and the Promised Land** (Genesis/Exodus)
   - Descendants of Jacob enslaved in Egypt (~1700-1290 BC)
   - Moses leads Israelites out of Egypt (~1290-1250 BC)
   - Moses receives the Law (The Ten Commandments) on Mount Sinai and leads Israelites through the desert
   - Joshua leads Israelites into the Promised Land (territory for the new nation of Israel)

4. **First Kings of Israel** (~1100-1000 BC; 1 & 2 Samuel, 1 Kings)
   - Saul, David, Solomon become the first kings of Israel

5. **Civil War in Israel** (900 BC)
   - Israel becomes two kingdoms: Judah in the south, Israel in the north

6. **Northern Kingdom Taken into Exile** (~722 BC)
   - They never return to homeland
   - Southern Kingdom taken into captivity (~590 BC) & return to homeland (~550 BC)

7. **Jesus Born** (~6 BC; Matthew, Mark, Luke, John)
   - Jews under Roman rule—Caesar Augustus

8. **Jesus Crucified** (~33 AD; Matthew, Mark, Luke, John)

9. **Early Church Begins** (~33-100 AD; Acts, the epistles)

10. **End of World/New World Begins** (Revelation)

Jesus Born / Jesus Crucified / Early Church Begins

6 BC   33 AD   100 AD   1,000 AD   2,000 AD   New World

Help for Our Lives

It may still take some time to find your way around the Bible, but this can be a reference for you in the future. When we begin to get oriented to the Bible and learn some tools for making personal discoveries, which we will look at next week, then the Bible can come alive for us. We can begin to learn more about who God is, gain wisdom for our life, and begin to experience God speaking to us through the Scriptures.

Now if someone could just do the same for me at The Home Depot!

Questions for Reflection and Discussion

- What has been confusing about the Bible for you?

- What did you find helpful in this reading about understanding the Bible?

Often people feel confused about the purpose of studying the Bible and how to go about doing it. This is a critical skill to develop that will benefit us throughout our lives. The purposes for Bible study are threefold:

1. To deepen our understanding of God and his ways (knowledge)
2. To learn how to use this knowledge in our everyday life (application)
3. To draw closer to God (relationship)

The primary method we will look at is called the inductive study method. This method gives us the tools for digging into Scripture, understanding what it says, and applying it to our lives. The inductive study method will be explained in the reading and then practiced. Also, because the practice may take more time, there will be no Soaking in Scripture section this week.

Digging into Scripture

First, read the passage in your Bible. Then read it again, using the printed text below to note interesting ideas, repeated words/themes, contrasting thoughts, or questions you have. After you have read and reflected, respond to the questions that follow the text.

In this passage, the writer shares about his attitude and need for God's Word.

Psalm 19:7-11

7The law of the Lord is perfect, refreshing the soul.
The statutes of the Lord are trustworthy, making wise the simple.
8The precepts of the Lord are right, giving joy to the heart.
The commands of the Lord are radiant, giving light to the eyes.
9The fear of the Lord is pure, enduring forever.
The decrees of the Lord are firm, and all of them are righteous.

10They are more precious than gold, than much pure gold;
they are sweeter than honey, than honey from the honeycomb.
11By them your servant is warned; in keeping them there is great reward.

- Who wrote this psalm? What significance does this have, if any?

- What are the characteristics used to describe God's Word?

- What strikes you about David's attitude or heart toward God's Word?

Continued...

- What are the benefits of following God's Word described by David?

- Which of these benefits have you experienced in the past from reading and applying God's Word?

- Which benefit could you use right now? Spend some time reflecting and praying on how God might want to use that benefit in something you are currently experiencing. It might help to do this through journaling.

Spiritual Reading
The Inductive Study Method

One of the best approaches for individual Bible study is called the inductive study method. It might also be called the detective method, because this method teaches you how to look closely at a passage and discover what the author intended to say, why he said it, and what it means to your life. Some methods basically *tell* you what the passage says, means, and how it applies to your life. While these methods are simpler, they are also often something else: boring. It's often more interesting to discover something for yourself rather than have someone tell you what something means. It also allows God to speak to you in personal ways concerning what he wants to show you in Scripture for your lives.

The inductive study method is not the only effective approach to learning from Scripture. Other approaches include reading larger portions of Scripture and are especially good for gaining a broader exposure to the Bible. Some methods, such as *lectio divina*, which means "divine reading," are good at incorporating prayer into Scripture reflection. We will explore these approaches as well in future weeks.

The discovery process for the inductive study method consists of three steps: observation, interpretation, and application. The ultimate goal is to discover how to *apply* what you're studying to your life. You're not just looking for additional knowledge, but life changes based on reliable knowledge.

Observation

In this first step of discovery, you take a close look at a section of Scripture. Most people are used to quickly reading a portion of Scripture like they would read a novel. When approaching Scripture this way, they usually end up feeling like they don't understand it or get much out of it. This is because they need the tools to *closely observe* the passage rather than simply read it. This helps you begin to understand what the author or speaker intended to communicate. Here are some tools for close observation:

- First, it is important to select a brief section of Scripture to study, typically twelve verses or less. These sections will often be natural breaks within a chapter. For this type of study, passages much longer than this include too much information, making it difficult to come away with a focused application for your life, which is the goal of the study. If you are studying a book of the Bible (often a good approach), you can simply move on to the next section.

- Next, you will want to briefly look at the context of the passage, that is, what is happening before and after the section you are studying. This will give you a sense of how this section fits into the broader thinking of the author.

- Now you are ready to dig into the section itself. Read over the section quickly to familiarize yourself with it—a first pass, you might say. Then go over the section again slowly, asking the following questions and noting your responses. To do this, it is very helpful to print out the passage and write on the page itself.

Questions to ask:

- *What statements or ideas strike me as interesting?*
 When you slow down and look closely at a passage, some thoughts or concepts will strike you as interesting or thought provoking. Make note of these.

- *What are key words or themes?*
 This is one of your best tools. Look for words or phrases that are repeated in the section. Sometimes they will be repeated word for word, and sometimes with slightly different wording but on the same theme. By discovering these repetitions and noting them, you will begin to pick up on the key theme(s) of the passage.

- *Are there any contrasts or similarities?*
 In some passages, the author or speaker will contrast two or more people, groups, or ideas. Or they may highlight the similarities between people or groups. This is another good clue to understanding the heart of the passage.

- *Who is involved in the passage?*
 Note any individuals or groups referenced in the passage. This begins to give you a sense of who the author is writing about or who the speaker in the account is addressing.

- *Where is the event taking place?*
 Note any locations mentioned. This often helps you understand more about the event taking place.

–   *When do the events take place?*
    Note any mentions of time of day, time of year, whether it is about the past, present, or future, or mentions of place in history (during a king's reign, for example).

•   Out of your observations, identify one that stands out to you personally. This may be because you find it intriguing or because it raises questions for you or because it has some relevance for your life.

Interpretation

After observation, where you are trying to have a good understanding of *what* the author or speaker is saying, you move on to interpretation, where you try to make sure you know the *meaning* of what the author or speaker is saying and *why* he is saying it. You are ensuring that you are drawing the right conclusions about what you are reading. Here are some tools for interpretation:

•   *Clarifying my understanding*

Some observations that you make will be pretty obvious as to their meanings. Some may be a little less clear as to exactly what the author intended. It helps to look at the passage as a whole and look at the context to try to gain a better understanding. Discussing a challenging passage with a group or another individual can also be helpful. If you are still feeling confused, it would be better to wait before basing application on that particular observation.

•   *Defining terms*

Some words are less familiar or are technical in nature; for example, "sanctification." It can help to look these words up in a dictionary or Bible dictionary to give you a clearer or fresher understanding of what the author is trying to say through these terms.

•   *Asking "why?"*

This is the key question for interpretation. Ask questions that get at why the author or speaker is making this particular point or why a certain action is taking place. For example: *why did Jesus take Peter, James, and John up the mountain to witness his transfiguration— why not the other disciples?* Learning to ask, "Why?" and then wrestling with the answers can open up some interesting ideas. Just as with clarifying your understanding, in trying to answer the "why" questions, you need to look at the entire passage and context.

Application

Once you have identified key themes and ensured that you understand the meaning and purpose of the writer or speaker concerning those themes, you can ask the key questions: What does this mean for my life? How might God want me to apply this truth to my life?

Typically, you will want to choose one or possibly two observations that are catching your attention on a personal level; one that you are sensing that God may want you to reflect on further. You may have made a number of observations, but, by narrowing it down, it helps you to focus and apply it to your life.

This type of life application can come in many forms. Here is what some possible next steps might look like (you would normally choose one of these):

- Thanking or praising him for how this truth has helped you in your life recently or in the past.
- Confessing ways that you have not been living according to a particular truth and receiving your Father's loving forgiveness.
- Seeking to change a behavior or attitude in your life, which may include doing something specific you sense God leading you to do.
- Praying about God's truth concerning a situation where the enemy's lies have come in.
- Reflecting more deeply on an issue through talking to a friend or through further reading.
- Pursuing an idea that God is prompting in you based on your observations.
- Taking a moment to rest in his love for you.

Obviously, there are numerous ways to respond, but the key is to ask God to lead you by his Spirit and to have a heart to change—a desire to bring the truth of Scripture into your everyday life. Not every day will feel like a major breakthrough, but over time, God's truth will take root in your day-to-day world.

Sample Passage

To get a feel for this process, look at the example on the following page from Luke 5:1-11. Various markings have been used on the text to note different observations, such as interesting ideas, repeated words/phrases, people, and locations. In addition to markings or symbols, you could also apply various colors using highlighters.

The different observations, interpretations, and applications are then listed below the passage. You will note that one of the key tools of observation used is identifying aspects of the passage that strike the reader as interesting for one reason or another. You will also notice that the application step is focused and connects with prayer. During the Spiritual Practice section for this week, you will have a chance to practice the inductive study method on a different passage.

Luke 5:1-11

¹One day as (Jesus) was standing by the <u>Lake of Gennesaret</u> with the people crowding around him and listening to the word of God, ²he saw <u>at the water's</u> edge two boats, left there by the fisherman, who were washing their nets. ³He got into one of the boats, the one belonging to (Simon,) and asked him to put out <u>a little from shore</u>. Then he sat down and taught (the people) from the boat.

⁴When he had finished speaking, he said to Simon, "Put out <u>into deep water</u>, and let down the nets for a (catch)"
⁵(Simon) answered, "|Master,| we've <u>worked hard all night</u> and <u>haven't caught anything</u>. But because you say so, I will let down the nets."
—CONTRAST—
⁶When they had done so, they <u>caught such a large number of fish</u> that their nets <u>began to break</u>. ⁷So they signaled their (partners) in the other boat to come and help them, and they came and filled both boats <u>so full</u> that they began to sink.

⁸When (Simon Peter) saw this, he fell at Jesus' knees and said, "Go away from me |Lord,| I am a sinful man!" ⁹For he and all his companions were astonished at the (catch) of fish they had taken, ¹⁰ and so were (James & John,) the sons of Zebedee, (Simon's partners.) Then Jesus said to Simon, "Don't be afraid; from now on you will (catch) men." ¹¹So they pulled their boats up <u>on shore</u>, [<u>left everything</u> and followed him.]

Observation

- **Who:** Jesus; people listening to Jesus teach; Simon (later renamed Peter by Jesus); Peter's partners, James and John (these three later become Jesus' inner circle).
- **Where:** By the lake, then a little from shore, then out into deep water.
- **Interesting observation:** Simon and others are washing their nets—done with fishing for the day (v. 2)?
- **Interesting observation:** Simon has exhausted all of his ideas and seems frustrated and discouraged: "We've worked hard all night and haven't caught anything" (v. 5).
- **Repeated words:** Jesus, Peter, nets, boats, fish, catch.
- **Contrast:** Tremendous contrast between results of Peter and his partners and Jesus' results (vv. 5-7).
- **Interesting observation:** Simon is both astonished and convicted (vv. 8-9).
- **Contrast:** Simon refers to Jesus as "Lord," as compared to "master" earlier (v. 5, v. 8).
- **Interesting observation:** Simon and partners leave everything, boats, nets, livelihood, and a huge catch, to follow Jesus (v.1 1).

Interpretation

- Why does Jesus choose this kind of miracle with these men (Peter, James, and John)? *Probably because something related to their livelihood would really impact them.*
- Why does Jesus wait until they have worked all night? *Most likely to make it clear that he could do something that was beyond their own natural abilities.*
- Why is Peter convicted ("I am a sinful man!")? *The miracle seems to have made it clear to Peter that he is in the midst of someone who is holy.*

Application

- **Key observation for me to focus on**: Peter has exhausted all of his efforts and ideas. He thinks it is hopeless. Jesus shows him that he has ideas and power that are beyond Peter's limited resources.
- **Application step:** I will ask God to show me if there is a current situation in my life where I might be tempted to be discouraged or think that there's not much hope, because I've exhausted all of my ideas. I will ask him for his ideas, resources, and power for that situation. I will see if he brings any ideas to mind at this time.

Spiritual Practices
Practicing the Inductive Study Method

For our Spiritual Practice this week, you will give the inductive method a try for yourself. Below, you will find the text for Mark 1:29-39, which is a good passage for practicing this method.

First, read through the passage briefly, including looking before and after the passage to get some idea of the context. Then, before you go through the passage again more slowly, read through the Observation portion in the Spiritual Reading section to refresh yourself on what to look for. Mark your observations on the text itself and then write them down under the Observation heading. Next, read the portion on Interpretation and then write down your interpretation questions and answers. Lastly, write one or two applications for your life and journal your thoughts and prayers for this application (it doesn't necessarily need to be long). Refer back to the sample study on Luke 5:1-11, if that is helpful.

For some, this method will feel pretty natural. For others, it will feel awkward at first. That's fine. Most things feel awkward when we are first learning them. You will have a chance to discuss how it went with your group, and you will have plenty of practice over the coming weeks.

Mark 1:29-39

[29]As soon as they left the synagogue, they went with James and John to the home of Simon and Andrew. [30]Simon's mother-in-law was in bed with a fever, and they told Jesus about her. [31]So he went to her, took her hand and helped her up. The fever left her and she began to wait on them.

[32]That evening after sunset the people brought to Jesus all the sick and demon-possessed. [33]The whole town gathered at the door, [34]and Jesus healed many who had various diseases. He also drove out many demons, but he would not let the demons speak because they knew who he was.

[35]Very early in the morning, while it was still dark, Jesus got up, left the house and went off to a solitary place, where he prayed. [36]Simon and his companions went to look for him, [37]and when they found him, they exclaimed: "Everyone is looking for you!"
[38]Jesus replied, "Let us go somewhere else—to the nearby villages—so I can preach there also. That is why I have come." [39]So he traveled throughout Galilee, preaching in their synagogues and driving out demons.

Observation

Interpretation

Application

This week, we look at another key aspect of our relationship with God: prayer. Prayer tends to be one of those things we think we should somehow just know how to do. The reality is that nearly all of us need help in understanding how to pray. Even Jesus' disciples, after watching him pray on one occasion, said, "Lord, teach us to pray." We're all in the same boat!

We will look at some of Jesus' teachings on prayer and some reading that together will hopefully help us clear up some misconceptions about prayer, as well as give us some practical help. There are many approaches to prayer that we will explore throughout this course, but this week we look at a good, foundational approach that we can build off of in the future.

Soaking in Scripture

The memory verse this week deals with the supplication part of prayer--our needs. Our needs often create anxiety, and it is very easy to forget to bring these needs and anxieties to God and instead to carry them ourselves. Here is our passage:

1 Peter 5:7

Cast all your anxiety on him because he cares for you.

- Read this verse several times slowly. Take a few minutes to reflect on what it means to you. Are there any key words that are meaningful to you? If so, write about them below or in your journal.

- Close your eyes and take a moment to picture yourself casting any current anxiety onto your Father. Imagine handing over your needs to him and letting him take them. Picture his concern for you and receive whatever words of care or encouragement he might want to give you.

- As in previous weeks, place this verse somewhere that you will see it at home, at work, in your car, or on your computer, if that will help remind you of this passage and help it sink into your heart.

Digging into Scripture

Matthew 6:5-15 is a key passage on prayer, and it comes from Jesus himself. Jesus discusses how we need to look at prayer, as well as some of the practical elements of prayer.

As we look at Jesus' words concerning prayer in Matthew 6:5-15, we will also continue to practice the study methods we have been learning. Read the passage through once in your Bible for an overview (as a reminder, the reason for this is to help you become familiar with using your Bible and to see what comes before and after the passage). Then walk through the steps of observation, interpretation, and application, using the text below. Again, the goal is to end up with one or two applications that you can then reflect upon and pray about, either in written form in your journal or verbally. In this case, you will be praying about prayer!

Each week a couple of questions will be included to help you get started in your thinking. Also, have someone read the passage out loud to refresh everyone's memory.

Matthew 6:5-15

5"And when you pray, do not be like the hypocrites, for they love to pray standing in the synagogues and on the street corners to be seen by others. Truly I tell you, they have received their reward in full. 6But when you pray, go into your room, close the door and pray to your Father, who is unseen. Then your Father, who sees what is done in secret, will reward you. 7And when you pray, do not keep on babbling like pagans, for they think they will be heard because of their many words. 8Do not be like them, for your Father knows what you need before you ask him.

9"This, then, is how you should pray:

"'Our Father in heaven,
hallowed be your name,
10your kingdom come,
your will be done,
    on earth as it is in heaven.
11Give us today our daily bread.
12And forgive us our debts,
    as we also have forgiven our debtors.
13And lead us not into temptation,
    but deliver us from the evil one.'

14For if you forgive other people when they sin against you, your heavenly Father will also forgive you. 15But if you do not forgive others their sins, your Father will not forgive your sins.

- What are some of the contrasts you see in vv. 5-8 between Jesus' approach to prayer and the way some others pray?

- What are some repeated words in vv. 9-13, and what do they tell us about the way Jesus prays?

Observation

Interpretation

Application

Prayer is like parenting. You're somehow just supposed to know how to do it. It just comes... naturally. Right? Riiiiight. When you don't feel really good at it, you feel embarrassed to tell anyone. That's not good, because prayer is so important to our relationship with God. It is a key way we connect with him. Through connecting with him, prayer can provide so many things we need: peace in the midst of a stressful, crazy world; much needed wisdom and direction; real change in our character; and much more.

We need to be honest and say, "I need help!" Most people need to overcome a few barriers when it comes to prayer. Here's some help with those barriers!

The Baloney Barrier

Does anyone eat baloney anymore? I don't know. But many people seem to believe you need a big helping of spiritual baloney when it comes to prayer.

"Most holy Father, we thank thee for thy most bountiful blessing that thou hast bestowed upon your creation. Receive the requests of thy most humble servants who are not worthy of thy mercy and..." Blah, blah, blah. Yada, yada, yada. That's pretty much what Jesus says in Matthew 6 about prayers like that, especially if they are done more for show in an attempt to impress others or to impress God.

Unfortunately, many people have heard prayers like that said at a church service by a pastor or priest or by Christians in other settings, and they think that's what prayer is. If so, then of course it's going to be intimidating! It's like making a little well-rehearsed speech, and people just love giving speeches! Not!

If we realize that God doesn't want all that, it can free us up to just be ourselves when we talk to him. The other day, our nine-year-old daughter said, "I like that we can talk to God like a friend, because that's what he is! TTYL, God!" (That's "talk to you later" in texting speech ☺.) Kids get it. In fact, if you want to get a good idea of genuine prayer, just listen to a child pray.

Here's an example that might replace the one above: "Father, you are so amazing. I had so much fun playing games with our kids yesterday. Family is one of your greatest gifts to us. Help me never to take that for granted and help me grow as a dad every day."

Whether you are praying on your own or with others, just be you—your words, your style, your heart. No baloney. Just you.

The "I'm Really Going to Get to That" Barrier

About a year ago, I was playing soccer and being my usual athletic stud self when I crumpled to the ground in a heap and later discovered that I had torn my ACL (the anterior cruciate ligament in the knee, if you were wondering). Now I am in the middle of physical rehab, which requires daily exercises at home and going to the gym several times a week.

Some days I do a good job, and when I go to bed at night, I think, "Wow, I did a really good job." Other days, I'm about to go to bed, and I think, "Hey, I should have done those exercises. I'm going to do a really good job...tomorrow." Ever done that? Most of us do that with a lot of things. Things that require some discipline on an ongoing basis.

I bet there are some things that you have to do on a regular, consistent basis that you do pretty well with. Like eating. For real. Okay, yes, you would die if you didn't eat, but it still requires thought and planning. What about going to work? Or showering? See how good you are?

If you are a parent with kids in various activities (soccer, dance, boy scouts, cat juggling), I bet you get your kids there on a pretty consistent basis. Or maybe you are on a sports team or a part of a book club or some other regular hobby.

You should pat yourself on the back for these many things you do on a consistent basis. But alas, for many people, prayer is not on that list. We want to do it; we know it will be a great thing, but... Why is that? Part of it is not being sure what to do when we actually do it. We have to figure that out, or it won't be very fulfilling or motivating. It can't just be something we "ought to do" and that's the end of it. More on that in a minute.

The other reason is that we don't do what we have done in all the successful examples above. What is the common denominator in those examples? Take a second and try to figure it out.

Did you try? I know. I probably wouldn't have either. In all of those examples, there is a *plan*. A plan or routine set up that can be followed regularly. It's not haphazard. Your kid's soccer practice? I'll bet it's something like Tuesdays and Thursdays from 6-7 pm. What if it was, "We're going to try to practice this week. Probably. Maybe. Not sure when or where. We'll let you know." How do you think that would go?

Similarly, we have plans and routines for work, meals, and many other things in our lives. We know when it will happen, where it will happen, and how it will happen—there's a plan.

Guess what we need for prayer? Right, a plan! A plan that will become a part of our everyday routine, like the other important routines of our lives. When we go from a random, haphazard approach to a regular routine, our prayer lives will likely begin to take off.

First, find a rhythm (frequency) that works for you. A good rhythm to start with might be 3-4 times a week for 30 minutes, which will include Bible reading as well. This is about what you need currently for completing the discipleship materials and prayer, and it is a good guide for the future. Of course, you can adjust this as you go along.

Next, choose a time that gives you the best chance of being consistent and not experiencing scheduling conflicts or distractions. Good examples: waking up in the morning before others in your household get up (remember Jesus in Mark 1?); going to a coffee shop before you go to work; using part of your lunch hour; if you work out, using the same time slot on "off" days. Poor examples: before you go to bed, unless this can be a regular, consistent time for you and is free of distractions; "hoping" you will find some time during the day.

Lastly, find a place that is quiet enough to allow you to think and pray and, if possible, is an environment you enjoy. This could be a comfortable room/chair at home or work, a coffee shop, especially if you journal your thoughts and prayers, or outdoors, walking and praying or finding a location to sit, weather permitting. Of course, sometimes you just have to go with the best you've got! Regardless, make it a regular place you go to that you can associate with prayer.

To give you one picture, here is my current routine. On weekday mornings from Monday through Thursday, I spend 30-45 minutes in prayer and reading before I go into work. To make this possible, I have to figure out when to get up each day to allow enough time. It varies a bit each day, because of taking the kids to school, so I've written it out. On Fridays, I meet early with my discipleship group. Saturdays, I try to sleep in, and Sundays, I connect with God through worship at church.

I typically go to a coffee shop, get a hot cup of coffee (I occasionally get a little crazy and order a latte), find a comfy chair, and get out my journal. Journaling, which we will discuss in a moment, helps me block out what's going on around me. Some days, especially if I want to pray silently or out loud instead of journaling, I will sit in a chair (also comfy!) in our basement, which is usually quiet at that time of the morning.

That's what works for me. What about you? It will require upfront planning, but once you get into your routine, I predict it will feel good to you, especially if you know what to do once you get there, which leads us to the last barrier...

The "What The Heck Do I Pray About" Barrier, or The "I've Prayed for Aunt Mabel 48 Times" Barrier

Now that we know we can talk like a normal person to God, and we've found a good time and place, a good routine, what do we actually say to him? We probably have some ideas, but sometimes our thinking on prayer can be pretty limited. It often needs to be expanded a bit, and this can open up a whole new conversation with him.

Slowing Down

To start with, it's helpful to find things that help us slow down a bit. Even if it's first thing in the morning, it's easy for our minds to start racing with the things we need to do. This is a challenge for most people when it comes to prayer. Here are a couple of ideas that can help.

One idea is to write your prayers down. I hesitate to use the word for it—journaling—because many people have a reflexive gagging response when they hear that word. But here's the reason to at least try writing your prayers. The mere act of writing slows you down, because it takes longer than speaking or thinking. It can also help you focus your thoughts, because it's harder to focus on other things when you are writing. The nice part is that it doesn't have to be long. God is more interested in your heart than the length of your prayer.

A second idea for slowing down, one that I picked up from a pastor and author, Bill Hybels, has been very helpful to me. It is a very simple practice that I call the "yesterday" practice. When you sit down to pray, take out your notebook, if you are writing your prayers. Begin to think about the previous day, starting with the previous morning and working through the day.

As you reflect on your previous day, write down anything that stands out to you, good or bad. These are just the highlights, so you won't be writing down everything. A good meeting at work, a hard conversation with a colleague, a fun time playing catch with your child, a realization that you were selfish with your spouse that evening.

What is the point of doing this? It slows us down and helps us begin to connect with what is going on in our lives. Most people lead very unreflective lives. We just go from one day to the next, not thinking about what is bringing us joy and disappointment or how God might want to enter into our lives in a very real way.

When we slow down and reflect, we begin thinking things like, "Wow, I really enjoy it when I stop what I'm doing and focus on my kids." Or, "That's the third time in the last week I've gotten really frustrated at work. What's going on?" This kind of reflection can lead us to make changes in our lives, and it's a perfect on-ramp into prayer. And it only takes about five minutes to do!

Branching Out

Once we've slowed down by doing the yesterday practice, we can bring these reflections into our prayer time with God. At this point, if we're still free form, we might drift off into what-do-I-need-to-get-at-the-store land, so a little structure or direction can help.

The following is a simple model for prayer called ACTS that is used by many people and utilizes many of the elements of the Lord's Prayer, which we read about in Matthew 6. It is great for expanding our prayers to go beyond simply asking for things, and it connects well with our everyday life reflections. The idea is to bring the things we have just been reflecting on into our prayer time. This helps connect prayer and God to our real, everyday lives.

The **ACTS** model also fits well with written prayers. Again, you can keep it short. Just write a brief paragraph or more on each area. Of course, you can also do this silently or out loud instead of writing your prayers.

Adoration

A great place to start is with adoration. This simply means praising God for who he is. It's a great way to start, because it lifts our eyes off of ourselves and our own needs or challenges and places them on God: how great he is and how much he loves and cares for us.

There are a number of ways to do this. You may want to praise God for something you just wrote down when reflecting on the previous day. For example, "I praise you God that you love to surprise us. The way you worked out that confusing situation at work was such a wonderful surprise that I would have never thought of!"

It may come from something you read earlier that morning in the Bible that reminded you of one of his characteristics, such as his love, forgiveness, or power. On some mornings, you may want to read a psalm from the Bible or listen to or sing a worship song. Whatever helps you focus on the greatness and goodness of God.

Worshipping God is not only what we are called to do, it will also put our problems in perspective. We can go from feeling pretty defeated to thinking, "Hey, wait a minute. My Father is an awesome God who loves me deeply! I'm not facing this stuff alone. My Father is with me!" That can change our outlook in a hurry.

Confession

Next is confession. Confession does not top the list of things people look forward to doing. As a result, it is often forgotten completely or handled in a very general way. This is unfortunate, because it is in times of specific confession that God can bring real change into our lives and draw us closer to him.

This, again, is where our daily reflections can be helpful. When we slow down and scroll through our previous day, we may remember something we did that we knew was not right. It might have been a harsh word, a judgmental attitude, or a selfish act. When we have identified something, the key is to then *honestly* and *specifically* bring this to our Father in confession.

See if this sounds honest and specific: "Sorry it didn't go so well with the kids yesterday." Are we really owning up to our part in an honest way? Are we being specific about it? When we aren't being fully honest with ourselves or God, or when we are being kind of vague about the whole thing, true confession and heart change rarely take place.

What about this approach to the same situation: "Father, I am sincerely sorry that I lost my temper with the kids yesterday and yelled at them in anger. I don't want to be like that. I want to be a father who is patient and practices self-control. Please help me and teach me to how to do this—to be more like you."

See the difference? This is where, over time, real change can begin to take place. It's humbling, but it's worth it. Surprisingly, it can bring us closer to God. This is because we are being honest and real with him in such a vulnerable way. When we are vulnerable with someone, the relationship inevitably deepens.

The key, however, is in knowing that God is our Father who loves us deeply and that he is quick to forgive. Knowing that even when he disciplines us, he does it out of his love for us. He wants us to grow into the amazing creations he intended us to be, and he is there to help us every step of the way.

Thanksgiving

Have you ever done something for a friend or a spouse or a child, and there was no verbal expression of thanks? How did that feel? It's pretty easy to be on the other side of this equation as well, forgetting to thank others, especially those closest to us. It's very easy to take them for granted.

I have to give my wife props on this one. She is very good at noticing even small, everyday things that I do and saying thank you. Taking out the trash, cooking a meal, getting crazy and changing a light bulb—she regularly makes it a point to thank me. After all these years, it still feels good and inspires me to do the same. It just feels good, doesn't it?

Guess where I'm heading with this? Yep. It is very easy to take God for granted. Like confession, it is easy to be vaguely thankful: to periodically thank God in some generic way. How do you think that feels to him?

That is why we need a *regular* practice of reflecting on how God is working in our lives and thanking him for it. Our yesterday practice is perfect for this. By slowing down, we catch the little things we might normally have glossed right over: the presentation that went well that we had been praying about, the new friend we met at school, the old friend we reconnected with, a doctor who cared well for us, a fun birthday with one of our children. There are so many things to be grateful for.

The great bonus from all of this is that, like confession, it draws you closer to God. When, day after day, you begin noticing and thanking God for so many things, it will suddenly occur to you: "Wow. God is really active in my life. He is not distant or aloof. He is so involved and interested. He really is my Father who delights in me as his child."

A regular diet of gratitude will do wonders for your relationship with God.

Supplication

Now we come to the area that comes to mind for most people when they think of prayer: supplication. Supplication is a big word that simply means praying for the needs of others and ourselves (and it starts with S, which is handy for the ACTS acronym).

When we think of prayer, we often are thinking of asking God for our needs. This isn't bad; in fact, it is important. But if that's all prayer is, you can see how it could become a bit stale, and it doesn't lead to a very robust relationship with God. If you had a friendship where all that your friend did was ask for help, you might find yourself suddenly getting very busy and not having time for coffee anymore.

That's why it is helpful to have this type of guide for prayer. By the time you get to supplication, you have related to God in a number of different ways. Remember, that is the goal of prayer: to grow in your relationship with God through talking (and listening) to him in prayer.

Having said all that, this area of prayer is still vitally important. For one thing, praying on behalf of others lifts you out of your own world and focuses your attention on something other than yourself.

It may help to pray for different groups of people on different days; for example, your family, your friends, and your coworkers. The goal isn't necessarily to pray for every person, but to pray as God is leading you at the time. Obvious needs may arise from the reflections you have been doing. A special emphasis should be on praying for those in your life who don't yet know the Father's love for them and what it means to have a relationship with Christ.

Then, of course, there are your own needs to pray for. It is important to know that your Father is genuinely interested in the concerns you have (remember our Soaking in Scripture passage this week?). There is nothing too small or too large for him—he cares about all of it, like any good Father. Bring your dreams, your desires, your frustrations, your questions—bring all of it to him. He loves it when you do this.

Putting the Pieces Together

Let's recap. No spiritual baloney: just be yourself and shoot straight with God. Create a routine that works for you: a good time, a good place, a good rhythm. And lastly, find a prayer plan that feels good to you. We've talked about the yesterday practice and the ACTS plan for prayer. This is only one approach, and you may find that you love it, that you like it but want to adapt it, or that something pretty different works for you. That's the key: find what works.

My prayer for you is that, as you take these steps and overcome these barriers, you will find richness in your relationship with God that you've never known before.

Questions for Reflection and Discussion

- How did some of the thoughts from The Baloney Barrier encourage you?

- What might be a good prayer plan/routine for you? List the days, times, and places that you think might work well for you. For example: Tuesday, Wednesday, Thursday, 7:30-8:00 am, at the coffee shop.

- What did you find helpful about the yesterday practice and ACTS approach to prayer? Any questions or concerns?

In our reading this week, one of the ideas introduced was writing your prayers down, or journaling. Often people feel that journaling does not fit who they are, or it feels foreign to them. That's fine to feel that way, but it is worth trying it out. You may find yourself being surprised at how helpful it is. One of the benefits is helping you to stay focused in prayer, which is a big challenge for many people. This reason alone makes journaling worth trying out.

Step 1: Reflecting on Your Day (The Yesterday Practice)

Find a sheet of paper, a simple notepad, or a journal. Think through your previous day (if it's evening, think back on the current day). It may help to start in the morning and work your way through the day. Write your thoughts or feelings about any events that took place, big or small, that you choose. Remember that you can keep it brief. Even brief reflections can begin to help you gain perspective and begin to understand how you are feeling about things. They give you the chance to connect with God about those thoughts and feelings, which is the next step.

Step 2: Using the ACTS Prayer Approach

Next, write your prayers to God. Write a paragraph for each of the four sections: adoration (praise), confession, thanksgiving, and supplication (praying for the needs of others and yourself). You may want to refer back to the reading to refresh your memory on these areas.

The benefit of doing the reflection (Step 1) first is that you can bring those thoughts and feelings into your prayer time. For example, something that happened the previous day may remind you of how faithful God is (adoration). Or, after reflecting on how you acted toward someone, you may realize you need to admit your wrongful attitude (confession). The two steps work very well together.

You may find later that you want to use the above process, but do it verbally or silently, rather than writing your reflections and prayers. A third option is a combination: first journal your reflections and prayers and then read your prayers silently or out loud to God. The bottom line is to find what works for you!

If knowing how to talk to God is challenging for many people, then listening to him is often even harder. We may not even be aware that God wants to speak to us, or that we have the ability to hear him. Scripture is clear that he does speak and wants to speak to us. How can someone have a relationship if one of the parties is not communicating? How can God lead us in this life if we cannot recognize his voice?

Most of us need real assistance in this area, because this relationship is a bit different from the other ones in our lives. It is a relationship with someone we cannot see and involves communication channels that are different than the ones we are used to. And yet, he actually has more channels of communication available to him if we recognize them; channels such as his Word, his creation, his people, and his ability to speak through our thoughts and ideas. All of these and more are vehicles for his voice to speak to us. He is speaking much more than most of us are aware.

We will explore some of these vehicles this week. Hopefully, through our study, reading, and prayer—and through learning from one another—we will take some steps forward in this important area.

Soaking in Scripture

In John 10:1-21, Jesus contrasts himself as the true shepherd with those who are impostors. During that teaching, he discusses the relationship of the sheep (us) with the shepherd. The following verses discuss that relationship and, in particular, how the sheep respond to the voice of the shepherd. Read the verses slowly a few times and see if there is a word or phrase that stands out to you. Reflect on that word or phrase, listening to what God might be saying to you.

John 10:2-4

2The one who enters by the gate is the shepherd of the sheep. 3The gatekeeper opens the gate for him, and the sheep listen to his voice. He calls his own sheep by name and leads them out. 4When he has brought out all his own, he goes on ahead of them, and his sheep follow him because they know his voice.

After your time of reflection, take some time to commit the following to memory (or another portion of the passage, if you feel drawn to it):

"His sheep follow him because they know his voice." (John 10:4b)

As a part of your prayer time, express your heart to Jesus, asking for his help in knowing his voice.

Digging into Scripture

Young Samuel's encounter gives us some good principles about listening to God. Use the tools of observation, interpretation, and application to help identify those principles. Try to end up with one or two applications for your life as it relates to listening to God. This application may be an active step that you want to take, some type of help you want to seek from God, an expression of confession or thanksgiving, or some combination of the above.

Read the passage in your Bible to understand the context, and then read the text below, marking your observations. You can use the next page for your observations or use your journal.

1 Samuel 3:1-10

[1]The boy Samuel ministered before the Lord under Eli. In those days the word of the Lord was rare; there were not many visions.

[2]One night Eli, whose eyes were becoming so weak that he could barely see, was lying down in his usual place. [3]The lamp of God had not yet gone out, and Samuel was lying down in the house of the Lord, where the ark of God was. [4]Then the Lord called Samuel.

Samuel answered, "Here I am." [5]And he ran to Eli and said, "Here I am; you called me."

But Eli said, "I did not call; go back and lie down." So he went and lay down.

[6]Again the Lord called, "Samuel!" And Samuel got up and went to Eli and said, "Here I am; you called me."

"My son," Eli said, "I did not call; go back and lie down."

[7]Now Samuel did not yet know the Lord: The word of the Lord had not yet been revealed to him.

[8]A third time the Lord called, "Samuel!" And Samuel got up and went to Eli and said, "Here I am; you called me."

Then Eli realized that the Lord was calling the boy. [9]So Eli told Samuel, "Go and lie down, and if he calls you, say, 'Speak, Lord, for your servant is listening.'" So Samuel went and lay down in his place.

[10]The Lord came and stood there, calling as at the other times, "Samuel! Samuel!"

Then Samuel said, "Speak, for your servant is listening."

Observation

- What is at least one way that you see each of the main characters contributing to the listening process? Include these in your observations below.

Interpretation

Application

Various Means of Communication

When you think about God speaking to you, what comes to mind? Does it seem mysterious? Dramatic? Confusing? Weird? For many people, it's one or more of the above. Talking to God can seem pretty normal, but listening can seem pretty foreign. How does it work?

To start with, we need to realize that there are a number of ways that God can communicate with us. They are ways that are often not dramatic or mysterious, as people seem to think. Communicating may be a better word than speaking, because speaking tends to make us picture only a narrow way of hearing from God.

When I used to think about listening to God, I thought it meant sitting silently, thinking about nothing, and waiting for God to somehow speak to me. Speak some message into my mind about something. That didn't happen very often, and it was pretty frustrating. Now I realize that there are many ways he can communicate to me and to all of us.

He can use something we read in the Bible, something a friend says to us, a song we hear on the radio, a quote we see on Facebook, a message we hear at a worship service, and many other avenues of communication. Typically, something we see or hear will connect with something we have been thinking about or going through. God can use these sources to communicate encouragement, conviction, or insight.

Another avenue of communication is the ups and downs of life. When you experience something that impacts you emotionally, positively or negatively, it creates an opportunity for God to use it to speak to you. Did you have a fun night out with your spouse? A cool interaction with your child? A situation at work that left you feeling discouraged or down on yourself? God can use all of it to speak into your life.

A Process for Listening

What are you saying?

How do we actually hear him? Let's break down the process a little bit. Take a look at the listening circle on the right, which was developed by 3DM Ministries. At the top, you will see something called a kairos event. The root word we usually use for time is chronos, as in chronology. This is time as we normally think of it, moving forward.

Listening Circle

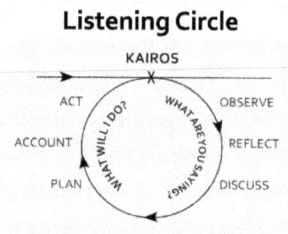

Kairos is a Greek word for an event that breaks into the timeline of our lives in a special way. It is a type of opening in which God can step into to speak to us. This would be some of the things mentioned above, such as something we see or hear and, in particular, experiences we have that cause some emotional reaction within us, positively or negatively.

When a *kairos* event happens, the first thing to do is observe it. In other words, we have to notice that it has taken place. Most of us are moving so fast that we blow right past things that may be meaningful for us. We have to recognize that the song, conversation, Scripture, or emotional situation is registering with us in some way, even though we may not realize why yet.

The second step is to reflect on what we are observing. Even fewer people do this, because it takes time and some mental energy. This, however, is where God can speak into our lives. As we begin to think about whatever the *kairos* event is, God can give us thoughts about it that bring more understanding. This usually isn't some dramatic voice in our heads, but thoughts that we have, which he can initiate. In other words, he can use our normal thinking process to speak to us. I'll give you an example in a moment.

The third step is discussing your reflections with someone else or a group. This can be very helpful, because others can add insight or bring clarity or caution to us if we seem a little off track in our thinking. We are human after all, and it is easy to bring in our own ways of thinking that may not be from God.

Taken together, these 3 steps are asking the question, "God, what are you saying to me?"

Let's look at an everyday example. Let's say the previous evening you had an argument with your eleven-year-old son—again. You were trying to finish up a few emails from work, and as you saw him walk by, you asked him to take out the trash, which escalated into a frustrating "discussion." Just another day in the life of a parent.

This time, you slow down enough to *observe* what happened, and realize that, although it was an unpleasant event, it might be an opportunity for God to speak into your life: it might be a *kairos* moment.

You invite God into your thinking process as you *reflect* on the situation. As you think more about what happened, you realize that you haven't spent much one-on-one time with your son lately, and you don't feel too connected to him relationally at the moment. It feels like many of your interactions with him lately have been stressful, like the one from the previous evening.

Later that day, you *discuss* it with your spouse (or it could be with a friend who is also a parent). As you discuss it, your spouse gently asks if your work could be part of the reason you haven't gotten to connect as much with your son. It hasn't seemed like much, but as you talk about it you realize that the "catch-up" work has become a pattern in the past few weeks.

As you can see, none of this is mysterious or dramatic, but it could prove to be very helpful in your life. Through your reflections and thoughts, and through your spouse, God is giving you simple but important insight into the situation.

<u>What am I going to do about it?</u>

If the question for the first three steps (on the right side of the listening circle) is, "What are you saying to me?" The question for the next three steps (the left side of the circle) is, "What am I going to do about it?" Getting insight from God is great, but if we don't take any action, then we won't experience any change in our lives or in ourselves, which is kind of the point!

The first step here is to develop a *plan*. In other words, what is my next step? In the above example, you might ask God what you need to do in the situation with your son. Maybe you need to apologize to him for not spending much time with him lately or not focusing on him when he's talking to you. Maybe it is initiating with him and suggesting something you could do together. Or both. When is that going to happen? What's the plan?

The next step is to give an account of your plan to someone, usually the person you shared it with earlier, in this case your spouse or friend. Knowing that you are going to circle back to share with them, and even giving them permission to ask you about it, can help give you that extra nudge to follow through.

Lastly, you need to act on that plan—actually do it. Follow through. Depending on what the next step is, it can be challenging to follow through. You may need to ask God to give you courage.

<u>Rinse and repeat</u>

For more involved situations, you may go through this same process a number of times, with God giving you the next step in the process. For these more complex situations, you usually don't want to try to do too many things at once: one step at a time.

In the scenario we have been looking at, maybe your kairos a few days later is a positive one: you've been enjoying the time in the evenings with your son. Upon reflection, you realize that it's because you have been closing down the computer, but that's also causing some stress within you. Is God speaking to you about trusting him? Maybe a next step is talking to your manager at work? Not being as concerned with your success in the eyes of other coworkers? What's the next step in this latest trip around the circle of listening?

This process can sound like a lot of steps. Once you get used to it, however, it happens pretty naturally. It's basically paying attention and asking, "God what are you saying to me through the kairos moments in my life?" and, "Okay, now what should I do about it?"

Yesterday

A spiritual practice that can be helpful in this listening process is the one we read about (and hopefully tried out) last week called the yesterday practice. Again, this is where you take five minutes at the beginning of your prayer time and write down the highs and lows of the day before.

This is a great way to identify those kairos moments as you remember the events of your day. This prevents you from overlooking the everyday events that God wants to use to speak into your life, like an argument or a fun experience with a friend.

If something stands out to you as you write or think about the previous day, then carry that into the listening process above and talk to God about it.

Next week, we will look at some extra tips for making bigger decisions in which we need God's guidance.

The Real Deal

When you get into the practice of listening to God in this way—out of your everyday experiences—and follow his leading and see real change happening, your relationship will come alive (or even more alive). This is a big part of what will make it actually feel like a relationship. It can lead you into life change and adventures you haven't dreamed of.

Questions for Reflection and Discussion

- What has been your experience of trying to listen to God in the past?

- Through what ways does God speak to you (for example, music, people, the Bible, prayer)?

- How do you think the listening circle process might be helpful to you?

Spiritual Practices
Listening Circle

We are going to give the listening circle a try. You will be working on the right side of the circle and bringing what you have to your group for discussion and next steps. As you start, invite God into this process. If it is helpful, you can write down your observations and reflections.

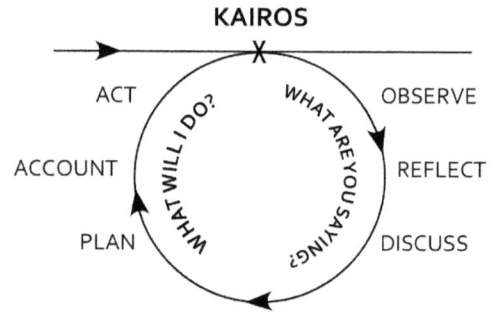

First, take a few minutes to think back over the past few days in order to observe anything going on that God may want to use to speak into your life. Did anything take place that brought joy? Perhaps a good time with friends, an enjoyable experience with your spouse or kids, something positive at work, or something that replenished you? Was there a situation that was disappointing or frustrating? Maybe a hard conversation or argument or something that didn't go well? Was it maybe something interesting that happened, like a new idea or sense of direction, something intriguing you read about, or a conversation that got you thinking?

Choose one of these observations and begin to *reflect* on it. In particular, think about *how* the situation made you feel and *why* it might have made you feel this way. What were some of the details going on in the situation? It might be helpful to look at the example given in this week's reading to give you a feel for this.

When you meet with your group, *discuss* your observation and reflections with them (this is why it may be helpful to write these down, to help you remember when sharing with the group). As a group, reflect back what you are hearing and ask any questions that might be helpful. Group members do not need to feel like they have to solve problems or figure out next steps for others; simply be a good sounding board.

After discussing your reflections with the group, try to get a sense of a *plan* (next step) God may be leading into. Share this next step with the group and a time frame for when you think you would want to do it *(account)*. Make sure it is doable. It may be one smaller step in a longer process.

During the week, *act* on your plan. Then, the following week, give an *update* to your group of what happened.

Don't feel like you have to get it all "right." Just try it out and see how it goes. If it is helpful, incorporate this into your everyday time with God.

Bonus Reading

Putting It All Together: A Plan for Our Time with God

What could your times with God look like when you combine studying Scripture and prayer? Here's a possible plan you can adapt according to what works best for you.

Finding a Routine That Works

- As we discussed last week, it is critical that you find a regular time and place that works for you. A good rhythm to start with might be 3-4 times a week for 30 minutes.
- Find a place that is quiet enough to allow you to think and pray and, if possible, is an environment you enjoy.

Spending Time in God's Word

- Next, decide what you want to read/study in Scripture. For now, that part is taken care of for you through the discipleship materials. In the future, one primary option would be going through a book of the Bible that you choose using the inductive study methods you are learning about. You would typically read and study a passage of about 8-12 verses (usually sections break out pretty naturally).
- You may want to use a notebook/journal to record your thoughts. If it is helpful, you may want to print out the passage in order to mark your observations as we have been doing in the discipleship materials (a helpful website for this is www.biblegateway.com). At the end of your study, you would then take your application(s) and carry them into your prayer time.

Of course, there are a variety of other options other than going through a book of the Bible: reflecting on one verse, as we do in our Soaking in Scripture sections, picturing events/stories in Scripture, or using Scripture-based devotionals. Reading other books is also helpful, but shouldn't replace the reading and study of Scripture; it should supplement it.

Spending Time in Reflection and Prayer

- Move into a time of reflection and prayer using the methods we have been learning about the past two weeks or another method that works for you. If using the methods we have been learning about, spend a few minutes reflecting on the events of your previous day (Yesterday practice) As you do this, see if any kairos moments come up for you. If so, spend some time using the Listening Circle process in prayer. Then continue your prayer time using the ACTS method.

- If possible, bring the application(s) from your study time into your prayer time (this application may be a kairos moment for you). Most times, your application will relate to one of the four areas of prayer: adoration, confession, thanksgiving, or supplication. For example, an application from a study of Jesus walking on the water might be to become more aware of the awesome power God has over everything, including the circumstances of your life. This could lead to praising God for his power in your adoration section or confessing your lack of trust in his power or asking boldly for him to apply his power in particular situations you are facing. By combining your applications with prayer, you bring God's truth into your everyday life.

- For now, you can do something similar using your discipleship materials. When possible, take whatever is impacting you from the various sections and utilize it in your prayer time, similar to using an application from Scripture, as described above.

Putting It All Together

- All that could sound a bit confusing, but it's really not. Here's a simple summary:

  - Find a find a good time and place (a routine that works for you)
  - Spend time reading/studying Scripture (with the goal of having an application to carry into prayer)
  - Spend time in reflection and prayer (both talking and listening to God)

  There can be great flexibility in what this looks like for you, and it will most likely change over time as you discover new expressions of study and prayer and discover what fits you best. In addition, while you will want to stretch yourself to be consistent, you will also need to have grace for yourself when you are unable to be.

- You might be thinking, "Holy cow, how long will all this take?!" It really depends on how much time you have, and how you want to use that time. If you are using a 30-minute time frame, you can use 10-15 minutes for your study time and 15 minutes or so for your reflection and prayer time. If you have more time on some days, you can expand either part.

  Some days, you may feel that you want to focus mostly or entirely on either study or prayer. Some days your focus may be on listening to God around a significant kairos moment. No problem. There's no need to be rigid about how you use your time, as long as you are able to have a mix over time of Scripture (in order to incorporate God's truth into your life) and prayer (in order to stay connected to God relationally).

Again, getting into a routine of study and prayer can be challenging, but it is vital to your relationship with God. As a result, this is a great issue to discuss as a group on an ongoing basis. Discuss what is working and what is not. Share ideas with one another. Support and challenge one another in this key aspect of your life as a disciple, more aware of the awesome power God has over everything, including the circumstances of your life. This could lead to praising God for his power in your adoration section or confessing your lack of trust in his power or asking boldly for him to apply his power in particular situations you are facing. By combining your applications with prayer, you bring God's truth into your everyday life.

Last week, we looked at listening to God. During times of decision, we are in special need of the ability to hear God—to receive guidance from him. These may be small or medium decisions related to our everyday lives, or it may be a major life decision such as whether to move, take a new job, make a significant financial investment, or marry someone.

In the past, we might have looked primarily to our own wisdom or instincts for such decisions. Now, as followers of Christ, we need to begin to look to God for his wisdom and guidance. God wants to help us during these times of decision, and he has ways of providing that help.

In our reading, we will look at the ways that God can guide us so that we have a framework for making God-directed decisions throughout our lives. In our Scripture study, we will look at how God knows us on a personal level. Some people have the mistaken view that God is too busy with more important things to know what is going on in our everyday lives, including our decisions. We will look at one passage that counters this view and clearly displays God's love and direction for our lives on a very personal level.

Soaking in Scripture

This is an excellent passage to memorize and lodge into our hearts, because we are so frequently tempted to trust in ourselves during times of need or decision.

> **Proverbs 3:5-6**
> *Trust in the LORD with all your heart and lean not on your own understanding; in all your ways acknowledge him, and he will make your paths straight.*

Note: Feel free to use the alternate ending if it is helpful to you: "and he will direct your paths."

• Read the passage a number of times and write it below in an effort to memorize it.

• Circle key words or phrases that stand out to you. Then reflect below on why they are meaningful to you.

• During your prayer time, include any of your reflections above, particularly as they relate to any decisions, large or small, that you may be facing.

Digging Into Scripture

This psalm from King David is a classic description of God's nearness to us and how he knows and cares for us on a personal level.

Psalm 139:1-16

1 O LORD, you have searched me and you know me.

2 You know when I sit and when I rise; you perceive my thoughts from afar.

3 You discern my going out and my lying down; you are familiar with all my ways.

4 Before a word is on my tongue you know it completely, O LORD.

5 You hem me in—behind and before; you have laid your hand upon me.

6 Such knowledge is too wonderful for me, too lofty for me to attain.

7 Where can I go from your Spirit? Where can I flee from your presence?

8 If I go up to the heavens, you are there; if I make my bed in the depths, you are there.

9 If I rise on the wings of the dawn, if I settle on the far side of the sea,

10 even there your hand will guide me, your right hand will hold me fast.

11 If I say, "Surely the darkness will hide me and the light become night around me,"

12 even the darkness will not be dark to you; the night will shine like the day, for darkness is as light to you.

13 For you created my inmost being; you knit me together in my mother's womb.

14 I praise you because I am fearfully and wonderfully made; your works are wonderful, I know that full well.

15 My frame was not hidden from you when I was made in the secret place. When I was woven together in the depths of the earth,

16 your eyes saw my unformed body. All the days ordained for me were written in your book before one of them came to be.

Observation

Interpretation

Application

Reading
Trusting God in Times of Decision

We all probably have decisions we wish we could do over. "If I just would have had a little more wisdom or guidance, I could have made a better decision." God loves helping us make good decisions. Decisions are a good example of one of the core beliefs of the Christian faith: the belief that God is a personal God. He's not way off, doing his own thing. He's interested in our lives and the decisions we face.

How do we trust God when we have decisions to make? How do we know if he is leading us? We're going to look at three types of God's guidance to help us follow his leading in our lives and to help us avoid the pitfalls of poor decisions. (Note: Some of the ideas below are based on a talk by Nicky Gumbel, creator of the Alpha course.)

Type #1: God's General Guidance

The first type of guidance we'll look at is God's general guidance. This is God's wisdom on an issue that is true for all people, all the time. Once we understand his wisdom on something, we don't need to wring our hands over the decision; we know what his thinking is on it. The Bible is full of God's wisdom on a variety of issues.

The challenge is that we have picked up "wisdom" from a variety of places, which is influencing our everyday decisions. This wisdom may be from friends in our lives, family members, including our parents, the media, books, government, or just what "everyone" does—the conventional wisdom of the day. Guess what? Some of this wisdom from others is wrong. Some of our own thinking is misguided.

> **Proverbs 3:5-6**
> *Trust in the LORD with all your heart and lean not on your own understanding; in all your ways acknowledge him, and he will make your paths straight.*

This is a key passage that we will return to several times in our discussion. The first part of our passage says, "Trust in the **LORD** with all your heart and lean not on your **own** understanding." This passage is saying that you shouldn't put your weight—your dependence—on your understanding, because this is what will happen: it will let you down. Instead, trust in God and his wisdom with all your heart. This gets very practical, because as you follow Christ in your lives, you are going to run up against things that will differ from what you thought made sense.

For example, our society says to buy the best, buy the newest, and buy the biggest. But Jesus says, "Do not store up for yourselves treasures on earth, where moth and rust destroy" (Matthew 6:19). Instead, he tells us to simplify our lives and find his true joy. When we get into conflict with someone at work or at church, our family patterns growing up may have taught us to avoid the situation at all costs or to become bitter at the person. God in his wisdom says, "Go and be reconciled to your brother" (Matthew 5:24).

Our friends may say, what will a little sex before marriage hurt? It's natural. You would be weird not to. God says, "I love you. I created sex for you to enjoy, but only in the context of a lifelong, committed relationship; the type of relationship where someone won't get wounded by something as deep and powerful as the bond of sexual intimacy." (See Genesis 2:24)

You will run up against God's wisdom in your finances, in your marriage, parenting, how you approach your job, your relationships—everything. The key here for us is humility, one of the core virtues of the Christian faith. It requires humility to say, "I was wrong here. I was misguided. I'm going to change my course on this." The Bible says, "He guides the humble in what is right and teaches them his way" (Psalm 25:9).

Without humility, he can't teach us his ways, his wisdom, which will bring his joy and life into our lives. Like Proverbs 3 says, it requires trust. Trust that he knows best. He knows more than our culture. He knows more than our friends or parents. At times, it will require courage on our part to go against the flow of those around us.

Particularly if you are newer in your journey with Christ, this is a good type of guidance to focus on. Ask God, "Teach me your wisdom, your ways. Show me where my own understand is misguided."

That is the first type of guidance: God's general guidance.

Type #2: God's Particular Guidance

Next we move to God's particular guidance. These are those decisions that are more specific in our lives. There's nothing in the Bible telling you whether you should take that job or move out of state or attend that college or marry that person. This is where we wrestle with God, trying to discern if he is leading us in a certain direction or not. How do we know?

Our passage goes on to say, "In **all** your ways, **acknowledge** him, and he will make your paths straight." In all of the decisions of your life, the big ones and the smaller ones, acknowledge God. In other words, come to him; seek him out. Don't try to do it on your own. He has good plans for you; he wants to make your paths straight and help you avoid unhelpful detours.

Some of us are used to doing that. For others of us, this may be a new way of thinking, to seek God when we are trying to decide about a new home, school, or job change. But God wants to be involved, and it makes sense to involve him. This is one of the ways that he becomes more central to our lives.

Let's say you had to climb out of the third story window of a building, because there was a fire, and someone said, "Hey! Here's a rope; we'll hold onto it, and you climb down the rope!" Would you feel confident if the rope looked thick and strong? Probably so. Why? Because it is made up of many smaller cords, which makes it stronger. If the person found one small, thin cord on the floor and said, "Here, use this," you'd think, "Hmm…I think I'll try the stairs." This is how God works in our decision making.

Think of one of the cords as representing one channel that God may be using to guide you in a decision. The more important or complex the decision, the more cords of God's guidance you need to be confident that he is in fact leading you in that direction. Let's briefly look at some of those different cords or channels of his guidance.

Cords

- **Holy Spirit**

  The first cord is the Holy Spirit. This is the Spirit of God within us, who may be speaking to us in some way. A common way this can happen is when we are praying about a decision and a thought comes to us—an impression or an idea concerning the decision. Often it can be when we are reading the Bible, and we get a thought about our situation. Like all the cords we will look at, here we want to say, "This may be God speaking. He may be leading in this way," as opposed to, "God is telling me to do this." That is where we can get in trouble. Because, let's face it, we are humans. We mess up. Sometimes we think we're hearing God, and we're not. He may very well be speaking, though, so we need to take note of it.

- **Wise Counsel**

  Proverbs 15:22 says, "Plans fail for lack of counsel, but with many advisers they succeed." This is one that many people, including Christ-followers, don't take advantage of. Especially in a larger decision like relocating or getting married or making a large purchase or investment, it is very wise to consult with others whose relationship with Christ you respect. They have probably followed Christ for a number of years and have sought God on decisions like the one you're facing. They are those who can ask you good questions. You want people who will be honest with you, not just tell you what you want to hear. You can find friends who will do that. You want several wise, objective people who will be honest with you. When you sense a pattern of counsel from these that also lines up with some of the other cords, then you know that God may be leading, or it may correct what you thought you were hearing from God.

- **Circumstances**

  This is one that people often put at the top of their list and make the most important. It certainly is one way God can use to guide us, but again, we don't want to put too much weight on it alone. This is the kind of situation where, one morning you're thinking or praying, and you begin thinking about, for example, a job change. That afternoon, an old boss calls about a position she thought you might be interested in. You're thinking, "Whoa." As a friend of mine used to say, "Is it odd, or is it God?" Remember our phrase: "It *may* be God." I have seen things like this happen to people, and all of a sudden they are on some wild detour that God didn't want them on. Especially if they really want something, all of a sudden circumstances seem to be pointing in that direction. If it lines up with wise counsel and other ways God may be speaking through his Spirit, then that circumstance may not just be odd; it may in fact be God guiding us.

- **God's Wisdom/Common Sense**

  This takes us back to God's general guidance or wisdom, but applied to a specific decision. For example, maybe some circumstances have seemingly lined up to buy a new car or home. However, it will require significant debt that could be challenging to you or your family. You might say, "I sense God speaking to me, and I saw this great deal!" Then you read in the Bible or hear a message at church or speak to a wise friend about what God says about debt. You read in Proverbs about debt enslaving us and hurting our lives. That wisdom—God's wisdom—sheds light on what you thought was God's guidance, or just common sense. Most of the time, God won't lead us to quit our jobs if we don't have another one or to marry someone we've only known a short while. Except for rare circumstances, God usually doesn't override common sense. When he does, the other cords will be very clear.

- **Supernatural Guidance**

  This is the last cord we'll look at. These are ways that God can guide that may be less familiar and yet are ways he has guided in the past as seen in Scripture. An example of this would be a dream: one of those vivid dreams that relate to what is happening in our lives. In the Bible, God spoke to Joseph through dreams three times. God often used dreams in the lives of people found in the Bible. He also can speak to another person on our behalf. It may be someone you know well or not so well, who may say, "I just have the strong sense I'm supposed to tell you this." In some cases in Scripture, there are pictures coming to people's minds, sometimes called visions, and even encounters with angels. Angels usually just show up for the big stuff, however. These may sound weird, but they happen, and they are biblical. God can guide however he wants. Even with this type of supernatural guidance, however, we still need the other cords of guidance.

When you are making a significant decision in your life and have several of these cords headed in the same direction, your confidence can grow. Usually what happens is that confidence leads to a deep sense of peace about the decision. Instead of feeling anxious and up and down and back and forth, you feel settled about it. If you are married, you will both have this sense of peace. If either of you don't, that is a major red flag. Don't move ahead until you have that. This is also true for a decision that involves a group of people. A group or church may not be able to have complete unanimity—complete agreement—but you do want a sense among many that God has used a number of channels to guide them in a direction and, as a result, together they are sensing his peace.

In all types of decisions requiring particular guidance, we need to acknowledge God: to seek his cords of guidance.

Type #3: "No Guidance"

But what happens when your path doesn't seem straight? You don't seem to be getting any guidance, or it seems sketchy or confusing. That can pretty quickly get frustrating or discouraging. It begins to bring up questions about God—"Are you there? Are you listening? Do you care? What is going on?"

Here are some possibilities of what may be going on:

- **Wrong motives**
  James 4:3 says, "When you ask, you do not receive, because you ask with wrong motives." In some cases, you may have already decided what you really want and are not honestly open to what God wants for you. When you let your desires go and truly open yourself up to God, you may see things start to flow.

- **Not following**
  In some cases, God has given you a small step or direction that you have not followed. Maybe you sensed that you were to make a phone call or talk to someone or research something. Perhaps a wise friend offered a suggestion you didn't follow up on. Prayerfully think back on your process and see if there were promptings you ignored. Take that step.

- **Not God's timing**
  Sometimes, it's just not God's timing. Our timing is usually...right now! But often, God's timing is not. His answer is, "No. Not now." When God's guidance does come, however, it often comes quickly. This is a pattern I've seen. Wait... wait...boom! When it's God's timing, things often move quickly.

- **A better plan**
  His timing is often tied to the last possibility, and that is that God just may have a better plan than you do. Jeremiah 29:11 says, "'For I know the plans I have for you,' declares the LORD, 'plans to prosper you and not to harm you, plans to give you hope and a future.'" God has good plans for you, but it may require waiting for them. God often has a better plan than you do. Imagine that.

In the end, it comes back to the first part of our passage: "Trust in the LORD with **all** your heart." When it comes to discovering God's wisdom and general guidance that is different from our own wisdom, or seeking him for particular guidance, or waiting patiently when no guidance seems to be coming—in all of these situations, we have to learn to trust in God's character; to truly believe that he loves us and cares about our lives. We have to believe that he will guide us in his wisdom, in his timing. Believe that he has good plans for us, if we will trust him.

Questions for Reflection and Discussion

- How confident do you feel in recognizing God's *general* guidance/wisdom?

- Which of the avenues of *particular* guidance is familiar or natural for you? Which is newer or less comfortable?

- What did you find helpful in the No Guidance section?

- During your prayer time, reflect on any current decisions you may be facing and ask God to show you any of the avenues of guidance he may be using, including general guidance/wisdom.

Spiritual Practices
Practicing with Guidance

This is a good opportunity to try out what have been reading about, and discuss the process with our group.

Take some time to think about a current decision you are facing. It may or may not be a big decision. If it is a smaller decision, that is fine. In fact, it's good for practicing! After you have something in mind, then next to the categories below, write down any type of guidance you have sensed from God. If there is nothing for that category, leave it blank. It may be helpful to refer back to the reading.

When you are done, as a part of your prayer time, take some time to pray about the situation and anything that came from your time of reflection. Then share about the process with your group when you meet.

Holy Spirit

Wise Counsel

Circumstances

God's Wisdom/Common Sense

Supernatural Guidance

We have been looking at practices that help us relate to God, such as prayer and Bible study. Now we look at what we mean when say "God," which brings us to the unique Christian doctrine of the Trinity, the belief that God is one God and yet three personal beings: God the Father, God the Son, and God the Holy Spirit. Three in one. This, of course, is beyond our full comprehension as finite human beings, but it is important to seek to understand what the Bible teaches us about this reality.

We will seek to not only understand the reality of the Trinity, but to begin to understand the role of each person of the Trinity. We will be looking more closely at the role of the Son and the Holy Spirit in the coming weeks.

Spiritual Practices
God Reminders

As a part of the session on God's guidance in our lives, we looked at how he knows us and is with us on a personal level. Sometimes, however, it is easy to forget this, especially in the midst of a busy day. In years past, church bells would chime at intervals during the day to remind townspeople of God's presence and call them to prayer. Today, a simple, updated version of this practice can be very helpful in reminding us that God is with us.

For example, if you are often in front of a computer, you can set an alarm to go off every few hours during your workday. Or, if your cell phone is always with you, you can set an alarm throughout the day, say at three- or four-hour intervals. When the alarm goes off, briefly pause and thank God for being there with you. You may want to also thank him for what you are experiencing at that moment or ask for his help. This could be as brief as thirty seconds or as long as you would like.

This simple practice can help us realize that God is with us in the midst of all kinds of daily activities: working, commuting, meals, laughter with friends, arguments with children—you name it, he is there. If you find this practice helpful, you may want to continue it on an ongoing basis. Who knew technology could be spiritual?!

Soaking in Scripture

Isaiah 44:6
"This is what the Lord says—Israel's King and Redeemer, the Lord Almighty:
I am the first and I am the last; apart from me there is no God.

Exodus 20:3
You shall have no other gods before me.

The above passages focus on the truth that the God we follow is the only true God. This may seem obvious to us, because we live in a culture that primarily believes that there is one God.

- Why do you think it would have been important to make this truth clear to the people of Israel? Why is it important that God himself is making this claim?

- What religions do you know of that believe in many gods, rather than one God?

- The passage from Exodus is not only one of the Ten Commandments; it is the very first commandment. Take a moment to read it several times in an effort to let it sink into your heart and mind.

- Reflect on what gods in your life you might be tempted to place above God. These may be things that are good when they are in their proper place (money, family, career, etc.). Write your reflections below.

- Utilize your reflections and the passages above in your prayer time as you worship and interact with God.

Digging into Scripture

For our Scripture study this week, we'll do something a little different. Instead of looking at just one passage, we will look at several short passages that give us insight into the Trinity as a whole, as well as each person of the Trinity (Father, Son, and Holy Spirit). A key question will be included with each passage, as well as an opportunity for you to share other observations or questions about the passage.

The Plurality of God

The passages below from Genesis come from the description of God's creation of the world and of human beings.

> **Genesis 1:26**
> *Then God said, "Let us make mankind in our image, in our likeness, so that they may rule over the fish in the sea and the birds in the sky, over the livestock and all the wild animals, and over all the creatures that move along the ground."*
>
> **Genesis 3:22**
> *And the LORD God said, "The man has now become like one of us, knowing good and evil. He must not be allowed to reach out his hand and take also from the tree of life and eat, and live forever."*

- Who is God referring to when he uses the term "us"? What does this tell us about the nature of God?

Observations and Questions

God the Father

2 Corinthians 1:3

Praise be to the God and Father of our Lord Jesus Christ, the Father of compassion and the God of all comfort.

- What does this passage tell us about the identity of the Father?

Observations and Questions

God the Son

John 1:1-3, 10, 14, 18

¹In the beginning was the Word, and the Word was with God, and the Word was God. ²He was with God in the beginning. ³Through him all things were made; without him nothing was made that has been made. ¹⁰He was in the world, and though the world was made through him, the world did not recognize him. ¹⁴The Word became flesh and made his dwelling among us. We have seen his glory, the glory of the one and only Son, who came from the Father, full of grace and truth. ¹⁸No one has ever seen God, but the one and only Son, who is himself God and is in closest relationship with the Father, has made him known.

John 20:27-28

²⁷Then he [Jesus] said to Thomas, "Put your finger here; see my hands. Reach out your hand and put it into my side. Stop doubting and believe." ²⁸Thomas said to him, "My Lord and my God!"

- Who is the Word in John 1:1? What do we learn about Jesus from John 1 and John 20?

Observations and Questions

God the Holy Spirit

Acts 5:1-4

¹*Now a man named Ananias, together with his wife Sapphira, also sold a piece of property.* ²*With his wife's full knowledge he kept back part of the money for himself, but brought the rest and put it at the apostles' feet.*

³*Then Peter said, "Ananias, how is it that Satan has so filled your heart that you have lied to the Holy Spirit and have kept for yourself some of the money you received for the land?* ⁴*Didn't it belong to you before it was sold? And after it was sold, wasn't the money at your disposal? What made you think of doing such a thing? You have not lied just to human beings but to God."*

- What does this passage tell us about the Holy Spirit?

Observations and Questions

God the Father, God the Son, God the Holy Spirit

John 14:25-26

²⁵*"All this I [Jesus] have spoken while still with you.* ²⁶*But the Advocate, the Holy Spirit, whom the Father will send in my name, will teach you all things and will remind you of everything I have said to you.*

- What does this passage reveal about God as three persons (the Trinity)?

Observations and Questions

Utterly Unique

The doctrine of the Trinity teaches that God is one being who exists eternally in three persons: Father, Son, and Holy Spirit. This view of God is unique among world religions. All three share the same essence—the same divine DNA, you might say. All three persons are distinct, and yet make up one being. Is your head spinning yet?

Analogies have been attempted to get at the nature of the trinity, but all fall short. One that at least begins to give us the idea was offered by the Christian author, C.S. Lewis. Lewis uses physical dimensions to help us.

In the physical world, a line forms one dimension. A square forms two dimensions, and includes the first (the line). A cube forms three dimensions, and includes the first (the line) and the second (squares). Each dimension is distinct, but is found within the one object (the cube).

Similarly, God is one being, but made up of distinct persons. In the same way that it would not be possible for a two-dimensional square to "conceive" of a higher, three-dimensional cube, human beings cannot fully conceive of a higher, "three-dimensional" God.

The Dance of God

Beyond attempting to understand the technical nature of God, it may be more beneficial to consider what this all means to our understanding of what God is like and what that means for us.

In his book, *The Reason for God: Belief in an Age of Skepticism*, Tim Keller writes beautifully about the "divine dance." Keller writes that what we see in Scripture is a picture of each person within the Trinity glorifying the other. We see the Spirit glorifying the Son (John 16:14), the Son glorifying the Father (John 17:4), and the Father glorifying the Son (John 17:5). Each desires to honor, serve, and love the other.

When someone is *self*-centered, they are static, still, asking others to orbit around *them*, serving and glorifying them. When someone is *other*-centered, they are moving, orbiting around the other person.

Within the Trinity, you find each person acting other-centered. Each is orbiting around the other in a kind of beautiful dance. We begin to see that the very essence of God is self-giving love. A love lived out in community for all of eternity.

The Dance and Us

God did not create humans because he was lonely. He created them so they could get caught up in the divine dance. When we begin to believe in and experience God's unconditional, self-giving love for us, we are getting caught up in the dance. When we begin to love others and desire to lift them up—serve them and honor them, orbit around them—we are getting caught up in the dance. When we begin to love God and long to glorify him—praise him, reflect his goodness, and point others to his love—we are getting caught up in the dance.

Our God is amazing. Beyond our comprehension. Father, Son, and Holy Spirit. Three in One. Love personified. He invites us to get caught up in the dance.

Questions for Reflection and Discussion

- What do you like about the picture of God as a dance?

- Who is someone you know that is a good example of one who is "caught up in the dance"?

- During your time of prayer, praise God in your own way for who he is, as revealed in the dance of Father, Son, and Holy Spirit.

This week, we begin looking more closely at Jesus. In the upcoming weeks, we will look at Jesus as our Savior and Lord, but this week, we will look at who he is as a person. What was Jesus like when he was on earth? Sometimes we focus so much on Jesus as the Son of God (which, of course, is crucial) that we forget to focus on him as the Son of Man—as human. Because of this, Jesus can seem somewhat removed or unreal.

It is interesting that the people of Nazareth (the town Jesus grew up in) were shocked when he began to preach—and preach with authority. It tells us that Jesus was most likely seen as a regular person as he grew up, not as someone who was so "religious" that people could not relate to him. What does this mean for us? If we are called to be like Jesus, we need to understand what he is really like. If we are to follow him as Lord and friend, as he called his disciples, we need to know the person we are following. It is difficult, if not impossible, to feel close to someone you don't really know.

Group leaders: *Please look at the Spiritual Practice section early in the week to have time to order necessary resources.*

Soaking in Scripture

One way we can feel closer to Jesus in our relationship with him is to think more deeply about the things we have in common with him. He chose to live as a human being. We may not have given as much thought to the human challenges he faced while on earth; those challenges can give us confidence that he understands and sympathizes with our struggles. The following passage speaks especially to the challenge of temptation that Jesus faced, but it can also help us reflect on the broader human challenges he would have encountered as well.

> **Hebrews 4:15**
> *For we do not have a high priest who is unable to empathize with our weaknesses, but we have one who has been tempted in every way, just as we are—yet he did not sin.*

- Read over the passage slowly several times in an effort to allow it to sink in.
- What are some of the weaknesses or challenges Jesus would have had to experience as a human being (physical, emotional, relational, and spiritual)?

- How might the awareness of Jesus' human challenges affect your relationship with him?

- During your time of prayer, talk to Jesus about some of your reflections above. Share any struggles you are facing (physical, emotional, relational, or spiritual) with him and ask him to share any feelings of empathy he might have as someone who has experienced similar challenges.

Digging into Scripture

One of the challenges of the writings about Jesus in the Bible is that they focus primarily on his teachings, his miracles, and his death and resurrection. This makes sense, of course, but it also means that we need to look a little more closely to get a sense of Jesus' humanity.

This week's passage is a good example. This account once again displays the miraculous abilities of Jesus. It also, however, demonstrates his humanity through the relationship he has with his disciples.

As always, read the passage in your Bible first to understand the context. As you read this passage, consider the questions below when making your observations and interpretations, but don't feel limited to these questions. After studying this passage, you may want to imagine the scene in your mind as we have done before, in order to get an even better feel of this encounter—and of Jesus' humanity.

Questions to consider for observation or interpretation:

- What do Jesus' actions and words tell you about what he is like and his relationship with the disciples?
- What do the disciples' actions tell you about their feelings for Jesus?

John 21:1-14

[1]Afterward Jesus appeared again to his disciples, by the Sea of Galilee. It happened this way: [2]Simon Peter, Thomas (also known as Didymus), Nathanael from Cana in Galilee, the sons of Zebedee, and two other disciples were together. [3]"I'm going out to fish," Simon Peter told them, and they said, "We'll go with you." So they went out and got into the boat, but that night they caught nothing.

[4]Early in the morning, Jesus stood on the shore, but the disciples did not realize that it was Jesus.

[5]He called out to them, "Friends, haven't you any fish?" "No," they answered.

[6]He said, "Throw your net on the right side of the boat and you will find some." When they did, they were unable to haul the net in because of the large number of fish.

[7]Then the disciple whom Jesus loved said to Peter, "It is the Lord!" As soon as Simon Peter heard him say, "It is the Lord," he wrapped his outer garment around him (for he had taken it off) and jumped into the water. [8]The other disciples followed in the boat, towing the net full of fish, for they were not far from shore, about a hundred yards. [9]When they landed, they saw a fire of burning coals there with fish on it, and some bread.

¹⁰Jesus said to them, "Bring some of the fish you have just caught." ¹¹So Simon Peter climbed back into the boat and dragged the net ashore. It was full of large fish, 153, but even with so many the net was not torn. ¹²Jesus said to them, "Come and have breakfast." None of the disciples dared ask him, "Who are you?" They knew it was the Lord. ¹³Jesus came, took the bread and gave it to them, and did the same with the fish. ¹⁴This was now the third time Jesus appeared to his disciples after he was raised from the dead.

Observation

Interpretation

Application

Jesus once said that if you've seen him, you've seen his Father (John 14:7). This is a very important statement, because it tells us that we can know what God the Father is like by looking at Jesus. The reality is that many people have a distorted picture of what God the Father is like. We pick these pictures up from wrong teachings, our own fears, or the culture around us—all kinds of places. We may feel that God is relationally distant, lacking in joy, usually angry, mostly focused on our mistakes—and on and on. These distortions have a huge impact on how we relate to him.

This is why our understanding of Jesus is so critical. Because God's Son became human, we can understand him in a special way through our shared humanity. We can relate. If we can have a better understanding of Jesus, it can open up a whole new way of relating to him, as well as to the Father, since they share the same nature. We can relate to God on a deeper, more personal level, because we begin to understand his heart—who he really is.

What Jesus was Really Like

With all of that in mind, what was (and is) Jesus really like? Can we get a good idea from looking at the Bible? One of the challenges when looking at the descriptions from the gospels (Matthew, Mark, Luke, and John) is that we often just get the facts. There's not a lot of "color" commentary. We need to look closely and think about what the facts tell us. When we do look closely, we find that even brief encounters tell us a lot about Jesus.

An example of this is Jesus calling Levi, the tax collector, to be one of his followers.

> **Mark 2:13-17 (NLT)**
>
> [13]*Then Jesus went out to the lakeshore again and taught the crowds that were coming to him.* [14]*As he walked along, he saw Levi son of Alphaeus sitting at his tax collector's booth. "Follow me and be my disciple," Jesus said to him. So Levi got up and followed him.*
>
> [15]*Later, Levi invited Jesus and his disciples to his home as dinner guests, along with many tax collectors and other disreputable sinners. (There were many people of this kind among Jesus' followers.)* [16]*But when the teachers of religious law who were Pharisees saw him eating with tax collectors and other sinners, they asked his disciples, "Why does he eat with such scum?"*
>
> [17]*When Jesus heard this, he told them, "Healthy people don't need a doctor—sick people do. I have come to call not those who think they are righteous, but those who know they are sinners."*

First of all, we discover that crowds of people were coming to hear Jesus. People were drawn to Jesus because his teaching offered real life, meaning, and hope. The interesting thing is that it wasn't just those who were already religiously inclined that came to hear him. We find out later in this account that "*many* tax collectors and sinners...were among his followers" (v. 15). What does this tell us about Jesus?

Maybe a better question is: what does it *not* tell us about Jesus? It tells us that Jesus wasn't so religious and spiritually aloof that the non-religious felt uncomfortable with him. Instead, he must have been down-to-earth and approachable. They seemed to enjoy him, and vice versa.

We can learn a lot from the contrast between how Jesus felt about the less religious and how the Pharisees (a highly religious group) felt. While Jesus enjoyed them, the Pharisees were shocked that he was spending time with them. And not just teaching them, but having a good time with them! In fact, one of the smear tactics of the Pharisees was to say that Jesus was a drunkard and a glutton. In other words, this guy was having way too much fun! Something must be wrong with him!

In his book *The Jesus I Never Knew*, Philip Yancey writes,

> He would accept almost anybody's invitation to dinner, and as a result no public figure had a more diverse list of friends, ranging from rich people, Roman centurions, and Pharisees to tax collectors, prostitutes, and leprosy victims. People liked *being with Jesus; where he was, joy was.*

One gift Jesus often offered to this range of people was availability. Many times, he and his followers would be stopped while they were journeying somewhere. Typically, it was because of someone in need or someone with a question. Often his disciples would try to brush off the person, presumably because they thought they were getting in the way of the day's agenda, but Jesus would stop and give them undivided attention—children, lepers, the wealthy—whomever.

Jesus also showed a full range of emotions: frustration, deep sadness, and great joy. He was not feelings-averse, or, as Yancey put it, he was no "Prozac Jesus."

What This Means for Us

Think about the implications for our relationship with Jesus and with the Father. This means that Jesus isn't standing at a distance if we haven't been "religious" enough or if we have made significant mistakes. He is approachable and calls us to come to him and figure out things with him. We do not need to wait until we get things all figured out; we don't need to get ourselves all polished up and shiny.

He loves it when we are just real with him: when we come to him with our stumbles, our questions, our frustrations, and our pain. Because he is real, honest, and experiences pain.

In *Blue Like Jazz*, Donald Miller writes about how a friend named Penny came to follow Jesus in her life. She had had a negative view of Christianity because of some less-than-stellar Christians she had met. But then she met Nadine, someone who really seemed to know God, and who, amazingly to Penny, believed that God really liked her.

Nadine asked Penny if she would like to read through the book of Matthew in the Bible to learn more about Jesus. Penny said she would, and she made an amazing discovery.

> *We started reading through Matthew, and I thought it was all very interesting, you know. And I found Jesus very disturbing, very straightforward. He wasn't diplomatic, and yet I felt like if I met Him, He would really like me. Don, I can't explain how freeing that was, to realize that if I met Jesus, He would like me. I never felt like that about some of the Christians on the radio. I always thought if I met those people they would yell at me. But it wasn't like that with Jesus. There were people He loved and people He got really mad at, and I kept identifying with the people He loved, which was really good, because they were all of the broken people, you know, the kind of people who are tired of life and want to be done with it, or they are desperate people, people who are outcasts or pagans.*
> (Donald Miller, *Blue Like Jazz*)

Did you know that he likes you? He doesn't just love you in some vague, abstract way—he likes you. He enjoys you. He loves it when he sees you laughing, enjoying others, and enjoying life because *he* enjoys the life and people he created. Most of all, he enjoys you and loves seeing you enjoying the gifts he has created for you.

He loves seeing you express your personality—the personality he created within you. Reserved, extroverted, organized, spontaneous, a dreamer, a planner—whatever it looks like; he enjoys seeing you be you.

He loves seeing you using the gifts and talents he has given you. Listening to others and giving them helpful counsel; working with your hands; analyzing data or working with technology; leading others; creating with words or art or music; serving those in need. Whatever shape it takes, he loves watching you and helping you use all he has given you. As we will learn in the weeks ahead, he loves to use who you are in the adventures he has planned—adventures that impact the world and bring his kingdom.

How It Impacts Our Relationship with Jesus

How does it feel to know and follow this kind of person, this kind of God? You can approach Jesus and the Father with great confidence, knowing that they love you deeply and aren't afraid of your messiness. Yes, Jesus will challenge you and stretch you and call you to put him first in your life, because he is Lord. But he is a Lord you can be real with: a Lord who loves you; who likes you.

I love the scene from this week's Digging into Scripture study. During the uncertain days after Jesus' death and resurrection, some of the disciples decided to do what they knew best, fishing. It was probably kind of like eating comfort food.

Jesus tracked them down; he wanted to be with them. He called out to them while they were out on the water. Notice what he called them: "Hey, friends!" Not just followers or disciples or believers, but friends. Then he did what friends do; he gave them a hard time. "What, no fish?" What would get under a fisherman friend's skin faster than that! And Jesus knew it!

Then he told them to do something he had done years before when they had first met him. He told them to throw their nets on the other side of the boat, and all of sudden, they could barely haul all the fish. Did he have to do that? No. It just sounds like something you might do for a friend if you could.

Immediately, they knew it was Jesus. What was their reaction? John began yelling, "It is the Lord!" He was thrilled to see Jesus. Peter was so excited that he grabbed his clothes and, in true Peter style, jumped off the boat and swam to Jesus on shore. Why? If they had some kind of dry, distant relationship with a stoic teacher and leader, why would they stumble over themselves with joy when they realized their Lord was on shore? Because he wasn't just their Lord; he was also their friend.

Look at what he was doing. Preparing a teaching to give to them? No, preparing fish for breakfast. The Lord of the universe was making breakfast for his friends. He had shared countless moments like these with them over the years. Out of the spotlight, just he and them, eating, laughing, learning, and growing. Yes, he was their Lord and teacher, but he was also their friend.

The same is true for us. Because he is both Lord and friend, we can share anything with Jesus. We can know that he cares about the big events and the little moments of our lives. The spiritual highs and the spiritual blahs. The victories and the failures. All of it. He wants us to come to him often because he genuinely cares. He is sincerely interested. He cares enough to challenge us, convict us, and lead us into new territory in our lives, like a good friend—and Lord—would.

He loves you. He likes you. Live your life with him, knowing that. The Lord of the universe wants to lead your life—and have breakfast with you.

Questions for Reflection and Discussion

- What in the reading was new for you or made you think differently about Jesus?

- What did you find interesting about how Jesus sees you or wants to relate to you?

- How does this impact how you relate to Jesus? The Father?

- In your prayer time, talk to Jesus about what you are learning about him and what that might mean to your relationship with him.

Spiritual Practices
Grab some popcorn!

That's right, it's movie time. This week's practice will be watching a movie about Jesus together as a group. Watching a movie about Jesus and the times he lived in can help to bring Jesus and the Bible alive in new ways for us.

The one challenge with movies about Jesus is that a lot of them are not that good. They often depict him as less-than-human, what Philip Yancey calls the Prozac Jesus, sort of floating above the rest of the world.

One of the better movies in terms of depicting Jesus' humanity is a TV miniseries, *Jesus,* made in 2000 and re-released in 2010. The movie does a good job of bringing Jesus to life for us and helping us see how others might have reacted to him. While the movie overall is consistent with Scripture, the creators do utilize imagination in some scenes, depicting events not included in the Bible. Examples would be the death of Jesus' father, Joseph, and Jesus' reaction; the romantic interest of a woman toward Jesus; a miracle performed by Jesus as a child; and the depiction of Satan during his temptation of Jesus. Try not to be distracted by Hollywood's use of creative license!

Here's how it will work. The group will spend this week's group time discussing what they have learned about Jesus from the Scripture study and reading. The group leader will need to rent or order the movie (see below for ordering information). The following week, the group will meet somewhere that they can watch the movie. When the movie is over, the group will take some time to discuss what stood out to them in the movie as it relates to Jesus. It might help to take some brief notes as you watch, in order to jog your memory for discussion.

Note: *You will need to plan a longer group time in order to watch and discuss the movie or watch it in two parts. The movie is about 2 hours and 45 minutes long.*

Here are some questions to consider as you watch and discuss:

- What do you notice about Jesus that may be different than how you have perceived him in the past?

- What do you notice about the reaction of others to Jesus?

- Were any scenes from the Bible brought to life for you in a new way?

Jesus can be purchased at: http://tinyurl.com/PurchaseJesusMovieHERE
(Directed by Roger Young and produced by Sony Pictures)

If you have watched many football games, you have probably witnessed the following scene: the quarterback drops back for a pass and looks toward one side of the field. Meanwhile, from the other side, you notice a defender barreling toward the quarterback at full speed, and you realize that the quarterback has no idea that the defender is about to crush him from behind. It's called being blindsided, and it's painful to watch.

This is what can happen to us as followers of Christ if we are not aware of and familiar with our enemy, the Devil. If we are not aware of how the Devil and those in his army (called demons or evil spirits) operate, we can easily be blindsided and see our relationship with God derailed and our relationships with those we love torn apart. In other words, knowing the enemy is serious business.

At this point in your journey, you may have little knowledge in this area, and you may even be a bit skeptical about it. The goal of this session is to help you see what the Bible says about whom the Devil is, how he operates in the lives of believers and non-believers, and how we can resist him. The Devil and his forces are cunning and powerful, but as we have seen in the previous session and in our lives, we serve a God who loves us and is *all*-powerful.

Note: Due to the nature of the exercise for the Spiritual Practice section this week, it will be helpful to look at it early in the week.

Spiritual Practices
Taking Thoughts Captive

One of the key strategies of the enemy is to use our thoughts against us. As we learn in our Digging into Scripture section this week, the Devil is a liar, and one of the key ways he deceives us is through our own thoughts. In particular, he will speak lies to us about ourselves, others, and God.

When we begin having thoughts such as, "I won't be ever be successful; I'm not worthy of being loved; I've made too many mistakes for God to truly accept me; I'll never be beautiful/handsome," we can be assured that the father of lies is somehow in the mix. When we take in these thoughts without analyzing them, they can be very destructive.

In 2 Corinthians 10:5, Paul says, "We take captive every thought to make it obedient to Christ." In Romans 12:2, he says to "be transformed by the renewing of your mind." We need to step back and look at those thoughts coming in and see which ones line up with God's truth and which ones do not.

To help us in this, we will try a reflection exercise this week to become more aware of those thoughts coming in—thoughts that we might normally not even be aware of. For three days this week, keep a "thoughts journal" (this might be a small notebook you keep with you). Each time you notice a negative thought about yourself, another person, or God, write it down. You may end up with a handful of thoughts written down, or dozens.

At the end of the three days, look over your journal and see if you notice any patterns. Are there repeated thoughts about how you see yourself? How you see or think about God? Do you have negative thoughts or feelings toward someone else?

If you notice any patterns, use the lists of truths from God's Word on the following pages to counter those lies. What is the truth about God? About your identity in Christ? Thinking about our Soaking in Scripture passage from Ephesians 6, how might God want us to address negative thinking toward others, knowing that they are not our enemy?

In the future, when these unhealthy, negative thoughts come to your mind, bring God's truth to mind. In fact, speaking his truth out loud can be very powerful. Lie: "I messed up again. God can't truly love me." Truth (spoken out loud): "'No. I am a child of God. He loves and delights in me regardless of what I do."

Simply beginning to recognize these negative thinking patterns and countering them with God's truth may play a significant role in furthering God's healing in your life, in your relationship with him, or with another person.

ACKNOWLEDGING THE TRUTH ABOUT YOUR FATHER GOD

I renounce the lie that my Father God is...	I choose to believe the truth that my Father God is...
Distant and disinterested	Intimate and involved [see Psalm 139:1-8]
Insensitive and uncaring	Kind and compassionate [see Psalm 103:8-14]
Stern and demanding	Accepting and filled with joy & love [see Zephaniah 3:17, Romans 15:7]
Passive and cold	Warm and affectionate [see Isaiah 40:11, Hosea 11:3-4]
Absent or too busy for me	Always with me and eager to be with me [see Jeremiah 31:20, Ezekiel 34:11-16, Hebrews 13:5]
Impatient, angry and rejecting	Patient and slow to anger [see Exodus 34:6, 2 Peter 3:9]

From *Steps to Freedom in Christ* by Neil T. Anderson.

Soaking in Scripture

The following passage from Ephesians tells us a lot about the reality of the spiritual battle we are engaged in. This awareness can be very helpful in the various challenges we may face.

Ephesians 6:10-13

[10]Finally, be strong in the Lord and in his mighty power. [11]Put on the full armor of God, so that you can take your stand against the devil's schemes. [12]For our struggle is not against flesh and blood, but against the rulers, against the authorities, against the powers of this dark world and against the spiritual forces of evil in the heavenly realms. [13]Therefore put on the full armor of God, so that when the day of evil comes, you may be able to stand your ground, and after you have done everything, to stand.

Note: For more about the armor of God, see Ephesians 6:14-18.

- According to this passage, who is our struggle with? Who is it not with?

- What might the implications of this be for your life, particularly when it comes to relational struggles?

- In light of this reality, what are we encouraged to do (vv. 10-11)? Put this in your own words.

- Memorize this phrase: "Our struggle is not against flesh and blood."

- During your prayer time, ask God to work "in his mighty power" against the schemes of the Devil in situations you may be facing, especially ones that are relational in nature.

🏗️ Digging into Scripture

This week, we will do something a little different for our Scripture study. We will look at a number of brief verses that discuss the Devil. For each passage, mark any characteristics you observe about the Devil or how he operates. Where applicable, also note what we are instructed to do. Write down these observations below the passage. At the end, write down an application you want to act on, reflect upon, or pray about further.

Observation

1 Peter 5:8-9
8Be alert and of sober mind. Your enemy the devil prowls around like a roaring lion looking for someone to devour. 9Resist him, standing firm in the faith, because you know that the family of believers throughout the world is undergoing the same kind of sufferings.

Ephesians 4:26-27 (NLT)
26And "don't sin by letting anger control you." Don't let the sun go down while you are still angry, 27for anger gives a foothold to the devil.

2 Corinthians 4:4 (NLT)
Satan, who is the god of this world, has blinded the minds of those who don't believe. They are unable to see the glorious light of the Good News. They don't understand this message about the glory of Christ, who is the exact likeness of God.

John 8:44
You belong to your father, the devil, and you want to carry out your father's desires. He was a murderer from the beginning, not holding to the truth, for there is no truth in him. When he lies, he speaks his native language, for he is a liar and the father of lies.

Luke 4:13
When the devil had finished all this tempting, he left him [Jesus] until an opportune time.

John 13:2
The evening meal was in progress, and the devil had already prompted Judas, the son of Simon Iscariot, to betray Jesus.

Application

Spiritual Reading
Understanding How Our Enemy Operates

Jesus called Satan, "the father of lies." This is his main tactic: deception. If we can learn how to detect his lies, it will go a long way in protecting us from his schemes. We can reduce the number of times he is able to blindside us in our lives.

We will look at three ways Satan tries to deceive us: **1)** Deceiving us about God, **2)** Deceiving us about others, and **3)** Deceiving us about ourselves.

Deceiving Us about God

One of Satan's chief tactics is trying to make us doubt God's goodness. Right from the very beginning, he deceived Eve into doubting God's motives. When she told him that God had commanded them to not eat or touch the tree, Satan responded, "You will not surely die. For God knows that when you eat of it your eyes will be opened, and you will be like God, knowing good and evil" (Genesis 3:4-5, ESV).

In essence, Satan was telling Eve that God was lying to her, that God was really trying to keep them from being like him. That they couldn't fully trust God and his concern for them. The truth, of course, is that God was trying to protect them and wanted only the best for them.

Satan has been doing this ever since. When we look at Adam and Eve, it may seem so obvious that they were being tricked. But isn't this exactly what happens to us? It's simply that we don't realize it when it's happening.

When things in life become uncertain and we become anxious, subconscious feelings and questions begin to bounce around in our minds and hearts: "Has he forgotten us? Does he really care about me? Maybe I've messed up and he's angry with me." When a tragedy hits, these kinds of questions can strike with great force. Who might want us to question God's goodness and care for us?

One of the most difficult things for us to continually believe in is God's grace and love for us. When we fail in some way, Satan is quick to raise more questions and thoughts: "You've blown it—again. How can he forgive me—again? He is probably so disappointed in me. Why would he love me? I can't measure up. Why even try?"

Satan loves to bog down our relationship with God with ongoing feelings of guilt, disappointment, and shame. The truth, as we have looked at, is that the Father loves us deeply as his children, and he is quick to forgive us when we sin.

In these situations, it is imperative that we identify these lies and their source and that we counter them with the truth—and do it quickly. Reading and speaking the truth of Scripture (for example, using the passages found in our Spiritual Practice this week) can be very powerful in refuting these lies and squelching Satan's voice.

Deceiving Us about Others

In our Soaking in Scripture passage this week, Paul tells us that our struggle is not against flesh and blood, but against Satan and his forces. This is a very important truth to understand and remember, because it impacts our relationships on a regular basis.

What Paul is saying is that often it seems we are struggling with others in our lives. We are frustrated with a co-worker or a neighbor. We have a long-term problem with a family member. We can't seem to find peace in our marriage. We have been hurt by someone in our church. Relational struggles are all over the place.

What we may be completely unaware of, however, is that this is one of Satan's favorite playgrounds. He loves to frustrate and destroy relationships—the more important they are, the better. He knows this brings great pain and stops the ministry of God in our lives from moving forward. When we approach these relational challenges on a purely human level, we are fighting blind. In fact, we are fighting the wrong person!

We have to learn how to respond in the most effective ways, which means learning how to resist Satan and how to humble ourselves. When we humble ourselves and begin to ask God to show us what our part is in the situation or what his perspective is, it greatly reduces the damage the enemy can do.

People will make mistakes. It's inevitable. The problem is that Satan will take these mistakes and often twist our thinking on them. He will cause us to question people's motives and their characters, often making the situation much worse than it actually is. When this begins happening, it should alert us to his activity.

The following questions are from Dennis McCallum's book, *Satan and His Kingdom: What the Bible Says and How It Matters to You*, and they are very helpful to ask when we begin to have thoughts of accusation toward others.

1. Is my suspicion based on objective, factual knowledge, or is it based on hearsay, my own imagination, or circumstantial evidence?

2. Have I taken the time to suspend judgment until I hear the other side of the story from the one I suspect?

3. Even if the wrongdoing I suspect is real, is it significant? Or is this a common failing and not important enough to make a big deal out of?

4. Am I being self-righteous? Am I upset about sin that's no different from what I do all the time? Can I recall times when I struggled with a similar problem? Should I show more grace?

5. Am I judging motives? Is it the deed or the suspected motivation that upsets me?

6. If the problem is real and serious, am I prepared to help the person? Am I an armchair critic, or am I an engaged believer prepared to extend loving discipline or advice?

In addition to asking questions like these, we need to respond through prayer. Pray for the other person, that God would bless them and that he would show you his love for them. Pray that he would show you his perspective on the situation and anything about the person that would be helpful.

Pray for yourself that God would reveal anything in your own heart that is not right. Then pray for reconciliation and any steps he might have you take. We will look at the reconciliation process more closely in session 16: Becoming a Peacemaker.

Do not let the sun go down while you are still angry, and do not give the devil a foothold (Ephesians 4:26-27).

Deal with anger and relational challenges quickly and humbly. The main thing to remember is that these are not just human struggles, so you cannot just approach them from a human standpoint.

Deceiving Us about Ourselves

Then we come to one of Satan's deadliest deceptions: deceiving us about ourselves. The way that Satan will use us to hurt or destroy ourselves is insidious, but that's exactly what he does. He takes our own tendencies toward self-injury and accelerates them. He loves to attack our sense of self worth.

There are many opportunities to get down on ourselves. When we fail at anything—something at work, parenting, marriage, giving in to temptation, not meeting a goal we set for ourselves, struggling financially—we are ripe for his lies about who we are. We tell ourselves that we are failures, and he is only too happy to add fuel to the fire.

When we compare ourselves to others who seem more successful, happier, or more attractive, we open ourselves up to his lies. Comparison is a major trap. Others become our reference point instead of God's truth about who we are. How God sees us must be our reference. We need to know the truth about how he sees us and then constantly return to it.

For example, here's what **Psalm 139:13-14 (NIRV)** tells us about how God made us:

> [13]You created the deepest parts of my being.
>   You put me together inside my mother's body.
> [14]How you made me is amazing and wonderful.
>   I praise you for that.
> What you have done is wonderful.
>   I know that very well.

He has created us inside and out. And the way he has made us—our personality, our gifts, our bodies—is amazing. He is the master artist. This is the truth we need to believe.

We have made mistakes, and we will make mistakes. But 2 Corinthians 5:17 tells us, "If anyone is in Christ, the new creation has come: The old has gone, the new is here!" We are new creations through Jesus. This means that we see life and see ourselves through Jesus and what he has done for us.

When we feel that we have failed at something, we don't see ourselves as failures; instead, we know that he will help us move forward and will help us. When this includes sin, we know that he is quick to forgive us and help us change.

For example, if I lose control and get overly angry with my kids, I can think, "I've blown it again. I'm a failure as a parent, and God is probably disappointed in me." Satan loves to drum this kind of thinking into our heads. The truth, however, goes something like this: "I didn't control my tongue and my anger. I made a mistake and sinned against my kids and God. Father, please forgive me. I know you want to help in this area and that you are for me. I know you love me deeply."

This kind of thinking, based in the truth of how God sees us, can short-circuit the schemes of Satan.

Our spiritual practice this week should be helpful in this regard. It is critical that we catch ourselves when we begin listening to the enemy's lies. It is subtle, so we have to be paying attention, and then we need to counter it with the truth.

Awareness, Not Fear

We don't need to be afraid of Satan, but we do need to be aware of his schemes. We need to know how he operates. His primary strategy is deception, about God, others, and ourselves. Stay on your toes!

Questions for Reflection and Discussion

- What are some of the key lies you think Satan has tried to tell you about God in the past?

- What examples from the reading did you recognize when it comes to the ways Satan tries to damage relationships between people?

- What are some lies about yourself that you feel Satan has tried to tell you?

- Take some time in prayer to focus on at least one of the areas above (God, others, or yourself) in which you may have believed Satan's lies. Ask God to show you more about this and ask for his help in countering these lies. You may want to use the truths about God listed in the Spiritual Practices section and speak them aloud to counter the lies you have believed.

By now, you have most likely made the decision to follow Jesus—to become a Christian. There can sometimes be misconceptions or confusion that lingers when it comes to understanding salvation. We will look at Scripture and readings that will hopefully ensure that we have a clear understanding for ourselves and for others that we may try to help in the future.

A key point of clarity is the understanding that salvation is a gift from God: what the Bible calls "grace." It is not something we earn or achieve, but something we receive as a gift. This must be clear in our minds and hearts in order to experience what God has for us and so that we don't get off on the wrong track. As we look at this issue and others, we will again be looking more closely at who Jesus is and the role he plays in bringing us into relationship with God.

Note: If, after completing this session, you are unsure of whether you have taken the step to accept Christ as your Savior, discuss this with your leader or your group and pray to accept Christ, if you are ready to do so.

Soaking in Scripture

Our passage for reflection and memory is a key one, because it clarifies the difference between God's grace and our efforts when it comes to the salvation found through Jesus. Read this passage slowly several times before responding to the questions below.

Ephesians 2:8-10 (NLT)
⁸God saved you by his grace when you believed. And you can't take credit for this; it is a gift from God. ⁹Salvation is not a reward for the good things we have done, so none of us can boast about it. ¹⁰For we are God's masterpiece. He has created us anew in Christ Jesus, so we can do the good things he planned for us long ago.

- According to v. 8, what is our part when it comes to salvation?

- In your own words, what does v. 9 tell us the relationship of our salvation to the "good things we have done" is not?

- According to v. 10, what is the right relationship between salvation and the good things we can do?

- Write v. 8 below. Read it several times slowly in order to let it sink into your heart and mind.

- During your prayer time, take the opportunity to thank God again for this gift he has given you and what it means to your life.

Digging into Scripture

Two weeks ago, we looked at Jesus' humanity. In this passage, we learn more about the amazing, divine nature of Jesus and how he has made relationship with God possible. Because some of the terminology of this passage can be challenging, *The Message* translation has been used.

Colossians 1:13-23 (MSG)

13-14God rescued us from dead-end alleys and dark dungeons. He's set us up in the kingdom of the Son he loves so much, the Son who got us out of the pit we were in, got rid of the sins we were doomed to keep repeating.

15-18We look at this Son and see the God who cannot be seen. We look at this Son and see God's original purpose in everything created. For everything, absolutely everything, above and below, visible and invisible, rank after rank after rank of angels—everything got started in him and finds its purpose in him. He was there before any of it came into existence and holds it all together right up to this moment. And when it comes to the church, he organizes and holds it together, like a head does a body.

18-20He was supreme in the beginning and—leading the resurrection parade—he is supreme in the end. From beginning to end he's there, towering far above everything, everyone. So spacious is he, so roomy, that everything of God finds its proper place in him without crowding. Not only that, but all the broken and dislocated pieces of the universe—people and things, animals and atoms—get properly fixed and fit together in vibrant harmonies, all because of his death, his blood that poured down from the cross.

21-23You yourselves are a case study of what he does. At one time you all had your backs turned to God, thinking rebellious thoughts of him, giving him trouble every chance you got. But now, by giving himself completely at the Cross, actually dying for you, Christ brought you over to God's side and put your lives together, whole and holy in his presence. You don't walk away from a gift like that! You stay grounded and steady in that bond of trust, constantly tuned in to the Message, careful not to be distracted or diverted. There is no other Message—just this one. Every creature under heaven gets this same Message. I, Paul, am a messenger of this Message.

Here are some questions to consider as a part of your observations and interpretations:

- Which of the statements about Christ in vv. 13-20 strike you the most?

- How do vv. 13-14 and vv. 21-23 make you feel on a personal level?

Observation

Interpretation

Application

Spiritual Reading
Salvation and the Father's Heart

Coming Home

You may know about the famous evangelist, Billy Graham. You probably don't know, however, about his daughter, Ruth. You might think that the daughter of someone so used by God would have a pretty smooth path in life, but this was not to be the case. As she writes in her book, *In Every Pew Sits a Broken Heart: Hope for the Hurting*, Ruth struggled with depression, suffered through a disastrous marriage that ended in divorce, and wrestled with a number of issues in her children's lives, including teen pregnancy, drug abuse, and eating disorders.

One day after her marriage—her second marriage—had ended, she went home to see her parents, Billy and Ruth Bell Graham.

> *I had made a terrible choice and went into a disastrous second marriage. I realized the mistake, and I was going home. These fears multiplied and my adrenalin kept my feet on the gas. Questions rolled in my mind. What will my life be like? What will they say to me? What will I say to them? As I rounded the last bend in my parent's driveway and saw my father standing there, I got out of the car and he wrapped his arms around me and said, 'Welcome home.' It was a wonderful picture of a father's love for a broken child.*

Welcome home. That's all our heavenly Father has ever wanted: for us to come home so he can wrap his arms around us. If you wanted to boil down the story of God and mankind, that would be it. He simply wants us all, no matter who we are or what we have done, to come home to him.

God created human beings not because he was lonely (he has lived in community as Father, Son, and Holy Spirit for all eternity), but because he wanted to share his love with created beings. His very essence is love (1 John 4:8-10). His desire is to have close, intimate, joyful relationship with all of those he has created, both during our lifetime on this earth and throughout eternity.

Here is where many people have a key point of confusion. Many believe that God's *primary* interest is that we become "better" people. More giving, more pure, more—you get the picture. Although these things are important to him, they are *not* his highest priority or desire.

His greatest desire is *you*. Relationship with you. Does Billy Graham want his daughter to be a person of character who is loving and giving? Of course. What if she was all of these things, but didn't have any interest in having a relationship with him? How would he feel? He would be crushed. He loves her and wants to share his love with her—that is his highest desire. Then, *out of his love for her*, he wants to see her be the person God has created her to be. That flows out of their relationship.

It's the same with our heavenly Father. He doesn't just want people who are running around trying to be good without having a true relationship with him. He wants to be our

Father first, and out of that deep, loving bond with him, we can become the people he created us to be.

Barriers and Bridges

Tragically, God's dream of relationship was shattered when human beings, beginning with Adam and Eve, chose to live life according to their own desires and wisdom rather than God's. This became known as "sin." This formed a fundamental barrier between us and God: a barrier that made intimate relationship impossible.

The barrier is the fact that we have a different nature from God. God is holy—pure and completely free of sin. His *nature* is holy. We, however, have a sin nature. This means that even the best among us, the Billy Grahams of the world, still have an innate or natural propensity to sin.

Here's the kicker: because of his nature, it is not possible for God to have close relationship with creatures who have a sinful nature. It is like oil and water: they don't mix. They *can't* mix. But here's the other kicker: God *desperately desires* to have that type of close, intimate relationship with us.

That's why he took the huge step of sending his Son into the world to not only show us what God is like by becoming human, but by dying on our behalf, becoming a bridge between us and God. Jesus took our sin nature and the consequence of that nature (separation from God) on himself and crucified it on the cross. When we recognize our need for his death and ask to receive that gift, God the Father sees us *through* Jesus' perfect, sin-free nature. Although it is hard (impossible?) to fully comprehend, Jesus' death on our behalf and our acceptance of it makes it possible to experience what the Father has always wanted—relationship with us.

With all of this in mind, look at one of the better-known passages in the Bible.

> ### John 3:16-17
> [16]*For God so loved the world that he gave his one and only Son, that whoever believes in him shall not perish but have eternal life.* [17]*For God did not send his Son into the world to condemn the world,* but to save the world through him.

This isn't just anyone saying this; it is Jesus himself saying it. He should know! This passage tells us two things:
1. God really loves us and really wants relationship with us.
2. He has made that possible through Jesus, not through our efforts. Jesus can save us; we can't save ourselves.

Common Confusion

This leads us to some common confusion around what can save us or bring us into relationship with God. Many people, in one way or another, think *they* can save themselves. That it is through *their* efforts. This actually is a quite natural or intuitive thing to think. It's what we think about most things. Is there is a problem? We fix it. A boss' approval or a high grade or an athletic accomplishment? We earn it. But we are not talking here about a problem to be fixed or something to be won through effort. We are talking about a Father who loves us and has made a way home for us—a way that we can't do on our own.

Here are some of the common ways that we might try to save ourselves:

- **Being good**

  This is what we've been discussing: the idea that through our goodness, we are trying to earn God's acceptance or approval. He wants to accept us into relationship with him, but it comes through Jesus, not through our efforts.

- **Being religious**

  This one can be even trickier for some. Again, it might seem intuitive that through religious activity like going to church, we would please God. It is relationship, not religious activity, however, that he is looking for. Once his love for us through Jesus has captured our hearts and minds, we will desire to be with his people (the Church) and join them in serving the world.

- **Being American**

  This one may sound funny, but it is simply the idea that, especially if you live in an area where the Church and Christianity are a large part of the culture, it can feel like you are a Christian, because that's simply what everyone does. Not so much.

- **Being from a Christian family**

  Clearly, growing up in a family environment that emphasizes belief in the type of relationship with the Father through Jesus we have been talking about often makes a significant difference in our desire to have this type of relationship. It still needs to be our own decision, not simply that of our parents or siblings. If we have grown up in a family or church environment that emphasizes religious activity rather than relationship, we will need to make sure that we understand this important difference and step into that relationship. For many people, this is an "aha" moment in their spiritual journey.

- **Being in intellectual agreement**

  Some may intellectually agree that Jesus is the Son of God, and even that his death provides the pathway to relationship with the Father. But at the risk of sounding like a broken record, God is not interested in intellectual agreement or beliefs alone. He is interested in having a true relationship with us. It is not only believing, but also saying to God that we want this relationship and understand that we need what Jesus has done for us.

Starting the Relationship

If you or someone you know desires to begin this type of relationship with God, it simply requires sharing your heart with him. There are no magic words, but a simple guide such as the following can sometimes be helpful. The following prayer is adapted from materials used in the *The Alpha Course: A Practical Introduction to the Christian Faith.*

Sorry

Express anything you feel sorry for from the past. This may be specific sins, as well as generally living apart from God in your life.

Please

In your own words, ask God to please forgive you through Jesus' death for you and share your desire to live life in relationship with him.

Thank You

Thank him for his forgiveness and his promise to come and live within you through the Holy Spirit and guide you. Thank him for anything else you would like to thank him for.

If you have taken this step, congratulations! Of course, this discipleship process is all about looking at what living in relationship with God is like in our everyday lives, so you are in the right place! For many of you, the above reading and prayer affirms the decision you have made or possibly clarifies some misunderstandings.

It's all about coming home. When that happens, nothing could thrill the Father's heart more.

Questions for Reflection and Discussion

- If you were explaining it to someone else, what would you say the essence of salvation is?

- What did you find helpful in gaining a clearer understanding of salvation?

- Did any of the descriptions in the Common Confusion section of what does not result in salvation clear up any misunderstandings for you?

(continued on next page)

- Are there any questions that the reading brought up or that you still have?

- During your time of prayer, take time to reflect on and thank God for how he brought you to a saving relationship with him. If you feel that you now have a clearer understanding of salvation and desire this for your life, follow the steps under *Starting the Relationship* and share your heart with God.

  If you take this step, make sure to share it with your group!

Spiritual Practices
Communion

Because we are discussing salvation and the role of Jesus in our salvation, it seems appropriate to discuss the practice of communion. Communion is one of two practices commanded by Jesus to be observed by all of his followers. The other is baptism. Having a deeper understanding of communion can deepen our experience of this practice.

To begin with, various terms are used for this practice:
> *Communion* (1 Corinthians 10:16)
> *The Lord's Supper* (1 Corinthians 11:20)
> *The Eucharist* (Luke 22:17; from the Greek word that means "giving thanks")
> *The Lord's Table* (1 Corinthians 10:21)
> *The Breaking of Bread* (Acts 2:42)

Regardless of the terminology, the practice refers to Jesus' last meal with his disciples before his death. Jesus and the disciples were sharing the Passover meal together, because it was the time of Passover. This has significance for Jesus' words and actions during this meal. The Passover feast and festival was a time to remember and celebrate God's deliverance of the Israelites from the Egyptians hundreds of years before. As recorded in Exodus 12, God instructed the Jewish people to kill an unblemished lamb and spread its blood on the sides and top of the doorposts of their homes. Later that night, God would come to strike down the firstborn sons of the Egyptians in judgment. When he saw the blood on the doorposts of the Jewish families, he would "pass over" their homes, which meant life instead of death and judgment to their homes and families.

He also instructed them to not put yeast in their bread, because his deliverance of them from Egypt and the Pharaoh would be so swift that the bread wouldn't even have time to rise. Every year, the Jewish people were to remember what God had done. They did this and still do this through the drinking of wine, which represented the blood of the lamb that God used to protect them from death and judgment, and eating unleavened bread, which represented the freedom from bondage and slavery that God miraculously provided.

Imagine, then, at this Passover meal that Jesus is sharing with his disciples, the thoughts going through the disciples' minds as Jesus picks up the cup of wine representing the blood of the Passover lamb and says, "This cup is the new covenant in my blood, which is poured out for you" (Luke 22:20). He is saying, "*I* am the Lamb who will bring escape from judgment," the judgment for our sin. "It is *my* blood on the cross that will bring this escape."

Then he takes the unleavened bread and says, "This is *my* body given for you; do this in remembrance of me" (Luke 22:19). The bread that represented God's freedom from the slavery and bondage of the Egyptians now represents the body of Jesus that will be broken on the cross to give us freedom from the slavery of our sin. From the bondage that sin brings to our lives. This must have all been way beyond what his disciples could comprehend at that time, but one day soon they would understand.

Jesus' main request in instituting communion seemed to be simple but profound: Remember me. Remember who I am in your life, and remember what I have done for you on the cross. Remember the love that motivated this supreme sacrifice on your behalf. Remember what it will mean for eternity: relationship with me, and the Father, and the Holy Spirit, and my people.

One way of remembering Jesus is to follow some simple steps of reflection and prayer. Try these steps the next time you receive communion.

First, look back and remember. Remember afresh what Jesus did on the cross for you and why: because he loves you and desires relationship with you. Thank him for this supreme display of his sacrificial love.

Next, think about the present. Reflect on any current sin that has taken place in your life and ask for his forgiveness and help in changing any patterns of sin. Receive his love afresh for you and think about how that love impacts the situations you may be facing in your life. If you have been feeling distant, this is a great opportunity to reconnect with Jesus.

Lastly, think about the future. Think about the fact that one day, because of what Jesus has done for you, you will share this meal with him and a multitude of others. During the last meal with his disciples, Jesus said, "I tell you, I will not drink of this fruit of the vine from now on until that day when I drink it anew with you in my Father's kingdom" (Matthew 26:29). Regardless of what is going on in your life, rejoice in the fact that one day you will be with your King.

Past, present, future. As you can see, this requires reflection. Often people rush through communion, and it can easily become an empty ritual. Taking time to prayerfully reflect can help us to do what Jesus asked of us: *Remember.*

- Give it a try. Even though you are not receiving communion, use part of your prayer time today to try out the reflection exercise above, reflecting on the past, present, and future love of Jesus.

Accepting the incredible gift of salvation that the Father has offered us through the death of his Son is a wonderful beginning—but it's only the beginning. When he was on earth, Jesus called those who were beginning to believe in him to something more than belief. He called them to follow him—to become his disciples.

When we begin to understand more about Jesus' picture of what it means to be one of his disciples, it might begin to look a little extreme: complete devotion to him, costly sacrifices, and significant changes in our priorities. But being a disciple of Jesus can also offer something else: adventure. When we begin to deeply trust in the One we follow and to pursue his mission in this world, we can find ourselves on the adventure of a lifetime.

Soaking in Scripture

The passage below is a very challenging statement from Jesus to his disciples. Here he clearly lays out his expectations for those who want to follow him.

Matthew 10:37-39
37 Anyone who loves their father or mother more than me is not worthy of me; anyone who loves their son or daughter more than me is not worthy of me. 38 Whoever does not take up their cross and follow me is not worthy of me. 39 Whoever finds their life will lose it, and whoever loses their life for my sake will find it.

- Read the passage several times slowly. What strikes you about Jesus' words?

- What feelings does it raise in you?

- Read the last sentence a number of times to let it begin to soak in. Write in your own words what it means to you.

- During your prayer time, express your feelings to God related to living out this passage.

Digging into Scripture

What would it have been like to be one of Jesus' disciples? Not just one of the casual listeners in the crowd, but one who *followed* him? One who was willing to hear Jesus' instructions and attempt to carry them out?

In this passage, we get a chance to see what this would have been like. Jesus sends out seventy-two of his followers into the towns to carry out his instructions. What costs would they have had to make, and what challenges would they have encountered? At the same time, what adventures would they have experienced?

This is another good passage to try to imagine. This can help bring out the feelings and experiences the disciples may have had. With this in mind, read over the passage in your Bible and then take a few moments to picture it in your mind, imagining what it might have been like. Read it again below and write your observations down.

Luke 10:1-12, 17-20 (NLT)

1The Lord now chose seventy-two other disciples and sent them ahead in pairs to all the towns and places he planned to visit. 2These were his instructions to them: "The harvest is great, but the workers are few. So pray to the Lord who is in charge of the harvest; ask him to send more workers into his fields. 3Now go, and remember that I am sending you out as lambs among wolves. 4Don't take any money with you, nor a traveler's bag, nor an extra pair of sandals. And don't stop to greet anyone on the road.

5"Whenever you enter someone's home, first say, 'May God's peace be on this house.' 6If those who live there are peaceful, the blessing will stand; if they are not, the blessing will return to you. 7Don't move around from home to home. Stay in one place, eating and drinking what they provide. Don't hesitate to accept hospitality, because those who work deserve their pay.

8"If you enter a town and it welcomes you, eat whatever is set before you. 9Heal the sick, and tell them, 'The Kingdom of God is near you now.' 10But if a town refuses to welcome you, go out into its streets and say, 11'We wipe even the dust of your town from our feet to show that we have abandoned you to your fate. And know this—the Kingdom of God is near!' 12I assure you, even wicked Sodom will be better off than such a town on judgment day."

17When the seventy-two disciples returned, they joyfully reported to him, "Lord, even the demons obey us when we use your name!"

18"Yes," he told them, "I saw Satan fall from heaven like lightning! 19Look, I have given you authority over all the power of the enemy, and you can walk among snakes and scorpions and crush them. Nothing will injure you. 20But don't rejoice because evil spirits obey you; rejoice because your names are registered in heaven."

Observation

- Include any examples of costs these disciples would have endured, as well as any examples of adventure they would have experienced.

Interpretation

Application

Jesus' Love for Pies

Forrest Gump famously compared life to a box of chocolates. When it comes to being a disciple of Jesus, life is like a box of chocolate pie. Think of the different parts of your life as pieces of a pie. The slices might be your work, your marriage, your finances and possessions, your friendships, your hobbies, and so on. Based on the Scripture passages we've looked at this session, which slice do you think Jesus wants to impact in your life? One slice? A section? Maybe you've guessed it: he doesn't want to impact a slice of your life at all. He wants to influence the whole thing!

Here's another way of thinking of it. Jesus wants to be at the center of the pie—the center of your life. He wants to deeply influence *every* area of your life. He wants to shape the kind of heart you have toward your wife or husband, the priorities you have in using your (his?) money and possessions, the career choices you make with the talents he has given to you. On it goes. He wants to lead you in all areas of your life.

For many people, this is a game changer. Maybe Jesus has been on the edge of the pie of your life. Who has been at the center of the pie? Yep—you. It's true for all of us: natural human instinct is to look to our own wisdom, priorities, and desires when it comes to how we manage the slices of life. As a result of our "wisdom," some of us have experienced some pretty messed-up pies!

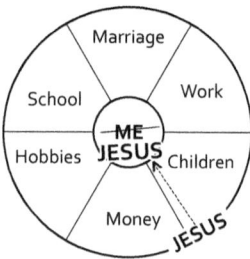

Out of his love for us, Jesus asks to take his rightful role in our lives: the very center. The biblical title for this is "Lord." He wants to be Lord over our lives. Why? Because he is a controlling micromanager? Thankfully, no! Besides deserving our worship as the Son of God and Lord of the universe, he is the one who actually knows best how to lead us—better than we know how to ourselves. This requires significant trust: trust in his goodness and his deep love for us and trust in his incredible wisdom. It also requires humility: humbly realizing that it's time to look to him instead of to our own intelligence.

How does this putting-Jesus-in-the-center thing work in real life? It simply means starting to turn to him and asking for his direction, his wisdom—his leadership—as you face the different questions of everyday life. "Jesus, I'm frustrated with my husband again! How do *you* think I should respond?" "Jesus, it's about the time I normally look to buy a new car; what do you think I should do this time? How should I use *your* resources?" "Which team should I bet on this week, Jesus?" Oh wait, that's not right. Well, you get the idea.

How do we begin to hear him and receive his wisdom? The main way is by placing ourselves in settings that he typically uses to teach us. The mentoring relationship/group you are in right now is an excellent example. Regularly listening to trusted teachers at church, learning from others in small group settings, reading the Bible and other helpful books, and learning to listen to God in prayer as we discussed in earlier sessions—all of these give us opportunities for Jesus to teach us and speak to us. Over time, you will notice your "wisdom bank" grow and grow. You will begin to notice that many decisions become second nature, because you have learned his wisdom. This, of course, is a process, but some people begin to learn and grow quite quickly, because they are hungry for his insight to pour into all areas of their lives.

In some cases, things that seem good have become such large pieces of our life that they have moved into that center place. For example, our children may have become such a focus that they have determined how we spend our time and what our priorities will be. The same thing can happen with our work, which is intended to be positive, meeting our needs and providing fulfillment. If it moves toward the center, replacing the role of Christ in our lives, then things begin to be thrown out of whack.

This is part of the reason that Jesus said, "Anyone who loves their father or mother more than me is not worthy of me; anyone who loves their son or daughter more than me is not worthy of me" (Matthew 10:37). When even the most important relationships in our lives begin to move into the center, things will not go well. Jesus is worthy of this place in our lives and, as a bonus, the rest of our lives will go much better when he is in his rightful place!

As his disciples, Jesus wants to be at the center of our lives. But he also wants to lead us on an adventure...

Jesus as an Adventure Guide

In 1912, Ernest Shackelton reportedly placed this ad in a London newspaper, recruiting men for a first-ever journey across the entire continent of Antarctica, passing through the South Pole:

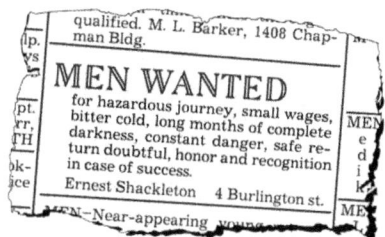

Would *anyone* respond to such an ad? Well, it's claimed that over *five thousand* did exactly that. Why? Why would anyone be that crazy? Because there's something deep within us that wants to do something significant, something noble. Something that makes a difference. There is something about an adventure, the sense of the unknown, that draws us. Yes, there is risk, but that's what makes it an adventure.

There was something else key about this risky, costly adventure: the leader. Over time, Ernest Shackelton became *Sir* Ernest Shackelton because of his famous exploration exploits. Beyond this, he became one of the most respected leaders in modern history: a leader who not only cared for the goals of the expedition, but a leader who also cared well for his men.

Does any of this sound familiar? In our *Digging Into Scripture* passage this week, Jesus sends out a group of seventy-two disciples to the surrounding villages ahead of him and gives these encouraging words, "Now go, and remember that I am sending you out as lambs among wolves. Don't take any money with you, nor a traveler's bag, nor an extra pair of sandals. And don't stop to greet anyone on the road" (Luke 10:3-4, NLT).

"Ummm...Jesus? It's kind of hard to hear back here, but it sounded like you said something about wolves? Did you actually say, 'You will be like a lamb with plenty of wool?' Like there's nothing to worry about? Everything will be cool, that sort of thing? Oh, you did say wolves. Okay, got it. Right. No, I'm good with wolves. In fact, I was hoping you said wolves. I always say, 'When do we get to go hang with some wolves?' This is so awesome."

The crazy thing is, they do it. They go! Why? Why would they do this crazy thing? Maybe they had this same deep desire to do something meaningful with their lives, even if it meant risk and sacrifice. But they had developed something else: trust in their leader. They trusted the One who was sending them out. Because of that trust and their willingness to risk, they came back high-fiving each other, racing to tell Jesus about what they had experienced. That is the reward for following Jesus into new terrain, new adventures—you feel like you are truly alive.

Unfortunately, even some of those followers who put him at the center of their lives are not willing to follow Jesus into the unknown. In fact, many are not even aware he wants to call them into these kinds of adventurous missions. They begin to see the changes that putting him at the center of their lives brings. Greater peace, better relationships, happier family life, increased stability. "This is great!" they think to themselves. "Having Jesus in my life helps so much!" And it does.

A happier, more stable life is not all he is calling you into. He is calling you into his risky, costly, exciting, fulfilling mission to change the world. *His* adventure. This can take many forms, but the common marks are that it will make you feel a little (or a lot) nervous and excited. It will nearly always somehow result in Jesus working through you to impact someone's life in some way, directly or indirectly.

This can start in small but significant ways. You may feel Jesus nudging you during a conversation to tell a friend that God is playing a bigger role in your life now or that you have started to go to church, but it's a little scary... An idea begins to germinate in your mind about hosting a barbecue so that your neighbors can meet one another and community can begin to grow; will people come...? You meet a teenager who is great, but has a really tough home life; could you be a big sister to her? What would the first step be?

Over time, as we step out and take risks and learn that Jesus can be trusted and find that even our stumbles aren't so terrible after all, we are willing to take on even greater adventures. We use the cords of guidance we learned about a few weeks ago to help us discern when Jesus is leading us into these new, exciting territories. We move from security to adventure.

Some good friends of mine, I'll call them Mark and Anne, because that's their names, are a great example of how saying yes to Jesus' crazy adventures can lead to real life.

After hearing some teaching and being in a group that was discussing God's heart of compassion for those in our world who are often forgotten, Mark and Anne began feeling a tug toward being foster parents. Deciding that they were open to this, the tug moved in the direction of adopting.

Anne then began to remember how her heart had been stirred nine years before as a college student on a mission trip to Zambia, ministering in an orphanage there. They began to get a strong sense that they were supposed to adopt a child from Zambia—not an easy thing to do. To adopt there, you must remain in the country a minimum of eight weeks after being approved and receiving your child. But again, they said "yes" to Jesus. It would mean spending the good part of a summer in Zambia.

After arriving, it became quickly apparent that, because of a bureaucratic system resembling the line for a ride at Disney World, the days they expected it to take for approval would turn into weeks of riding an emotional roller coaster, not knowing what the outcome would be.

Here is a blog post Anne writes after they finally discovered that they would indeed be approved for adoption and be able to take their new treasure home to the U.S. (after many more weeks). It captures the costs, challenges, and incredible reward of following this risk-taking leader we call Jesus.

Victoria Falls - one of the seven natural wonders of the world. It's massive, powerful, and breathtaking. It's hard for pictures to capture the true nature and beauty of the falls. I was looking through pictures we took during our visit this week thinking about the water of the Zambezi flowing serenely along, oblivious of the 360 foot drop just ahead. Then the thought struck me that this waterfall, river, and its surroundings were analogous to our life recently.

Water in the Zambezi before the falls is smooth and calm with a few dips and bumps...like my life until a year and a half ago.

As my little boat gets closer to the falls, I can start to hear them, very softly at first, just enough to catch my attention. Then I start to realize what I hear; the volume grows louder. I start to float faster, and I start to panic. The boat ride doesn't seem so comfortable and relaxing anymore. Then I look over at the shore not so far away and contemplate paddling with all my might over to the bank. It certainly looks safe and comfortable. But if I look closer, despite being along the edge of a great river, it's dry, dusty, brown, and parched. I could certainly survive at the edge of the river with water and food that would undoubtedly be available by such a water source. But would I thrive?

The falls are roaring, and I know that I'm supposed to see what's on the other side, but the intensity is almost overwhelming. What if I don't make it, what if the boat isn't made for this, what if the boat is damaged, I can't afford to replace it, what if...

With my heart racing, I decide to surrender to the now rushing water and speed past the safe shore.

*I'm falling,
tumbling,
can't see which way is up. The roar is almost deafening, it's all a confusing blur...I've lost control, and I wonder what on earth I was thinking deciding to take the plunge!*

*I reach the bottom which is
still bubbling and tumultuous, but I know that I'm alive
- in fact maybe more alive than I was before!*

*Then I look out and see calm waters ahead and to either side, lush green, almost tropical beauty
that surrounds me.*

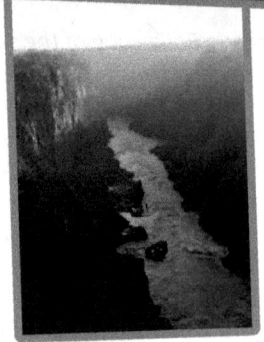

Now I can see a little ways down the river before the next bend. It's smooth with just a few dips and bumps...

Oh the things I'd miss if I went for the safe but dry, dusty existence!

The sound of the approaching waterfalls God puts in my life are scary! But I can't imagine life if I had paddled over to the shore (like I wanted to!) We wouldn't have sweet Elijah!

What a precious gift we have thanks to that waterfall!

The truth of the matter is that, for many people looking in, the Christian faith may look kind of boring—and they are right. If we are not following our untamed, living-on-the-edge Leader, then things get pretty domesticated and dull. It doesn't have to be that way. We can put him at the center of our lives and then begin to venture out into new, unknown territories, following his lead.

What's it going to be? Will you live on the shore, or head toward the waterfall?

Questions for Reflection and Discussion

- How do you feel about trying to put Jesus at the center of your life?

- What (or who) is most tempting to put at the center of your pie?

- What energizes you about the thought of following Jesus as being an adventure? What, if anything, about it scares you?

- During your prayer time, ask God to show you any area of your life he wants to influence more deeply. Is there any type of adventure he is calling you to step into?

Spiritual Practices
Baptism

Along with communion, baptism is the other practice commanded by Jesus, which tells us how vitally important it is. You may or may not have experienced baptism at this point. Hopefully this description can help in your understanding, if you have not been baptized, or be a reminder of what your baptism meant to you, if you have.

Baptism is a public, symbolic expression of the commitment you have made to be a disciple of Jesus. A great analogy for baptism is a wedding. Most grooms (and sometimes brides!) propose to their prospective spouses in private. This is a major step of commitment that is usually shared in an intimate moment. The wedding, by contrast, is often very public. Here you declare your love and life-long commitment to your bride or groom before your family and friends. You want everyone to know about and celebrate this relationship!

Similarly, it is often in a private moment that you share with the Father your belief and acceptance of what Jesus has done for you on the cross and your desire to live as a disciple of Jesus. Through baptism, you have the opportunity to publicly declare before your family—both your biological and church family—that you want to commit your life to Jesus. Just as with a wedding, this is a big step in your life.

The act of baptism actually enacts what Jesus has done for us on the cross and the new life we want to live with him. It is the physical picture of what we are discussing this week: the decision to become an extreme follower of Jesus. Read this description of baptism:

Romans 6:1-11 (MSG)

1-3So what do we do? Keep on sinning so God can keep on forgiving? I should hope not! If we've left the country where sin is sovereign, how can we still live in our old house there? Or didn't you realize we packed up and left there for good? That is what happened in baptism. When we went under the water, we left the old country of sin behind; when we came up out of the water, we entered into the new country of grace—a new life in a new land!

4-5That's what baptism into the life of Jesus means. When we are lowered into the water, it is like the burial of Jesus; when we are raised up out of the water, it is like the resurrection of Jesus. Each of us is raised into a light-filled world by our Father so that we can see where we're going in our new grace-sovereign country.

6-11Could it be any clearer? Our old way of life was nailed to the cross with Christ, a decisive end to that sin-miserable life—no longer at sin's every beck and call! What we believe is this: If we get included in Christ's sin-conquering death, we also get included in his life-saving resurrection. We know that when Jesus was raised from the dead it was a signal of the end of death-as-the-end. Never again will death have the last word. When Jesus died, he took sin down with him, but alive he brings God down to us. From now on, think of it this way: Sin speaks a dead language that means nothing to you; God speaks your mother tongue, and you hang on every word. You are dead to sin and alive to God. That's what Jesus did.

Baptism symbolizes our desire to die to our old self (symbolized by being lowered into the water) and be raised to a new self, a new way of living life under the leadership of Jesus in our lives (symbolized by being raised out of the water). Unfortunately, the act of baptism doesn't automatically make us new in our actions and thinking—wouldn't that be nice!—any more than a wedding automatically makes us good husbands or wives. But, just like our vows of commitment at our weddings, baptism does express our desire—our vow—to follow and obey Jesus.

The Holy Spirit may be the least understood Person of the Trinity. What is he like? What does he do? How do we recognize when he is at work in our lives?

These are important questions, because if we are going to live this adventure of following Jesus, we need to be able to recognize the Spirit's voice and activity in our lives. Similarly, if we are going to be changed more and more into the likeness of Jesus, to be transformed, we need to understand how the Holy Spirit brings that about.

In a later study, we will look more closely at the power of the Holy Spirit and how this power was expressed in the early Church and is still being expressed today. Also, it might be helpful to look back at Session 6, which focused on listening to God in prayer, to refresh your memory on how the Holy Spirit speaks to us in practical ways.

Soaking in Scripture

In our passage this week, Paul talks about the relationship between the Holy Spirit and our minds—our thinking. This is a key place in which the Holy Spirit has influence in our lives. Note the significant contrast between those influenced by the Spirit and those who are not.

Romans 8:5-6

⁵Those who live according to the sinful nature have their minds set on what that nature desires; but those who live in accordance with the Spirit have their minds set on what the Spirit desires. ⁶The mind of sinful man is death, but the mind controlled by the Spirit is life and peace.

- Read the last sentence several times slowly in an effort to let it begin to sink in.

- What do you think it means to have a mind that is controlled by the Spirit?

- On a practical level, how do you think the Spirit speaks through our thoughts to help us?

- During your prayer time today, ask for God's help in recognizing the Spirit's influence on your thinking and in experiencing the life and peace that this brings.

Digging into Scripture

Not surprisingly, Jesus gives us some of the most important teachings about the Holy Spirit: who he is and what he does in our lives. Although these passages are brief, if we look closely, they will tell us a good bit about the Holy Spirit.

The context of this passage is important. These are some of Jesus' last words to his disciples before his death, resurrection, and return to heaven. In other words, he is providing them with key information before he has to leave them.

John 14:15-17, 25-26

15"If you love me, you will obey what I command. 16And I will ask the Father, and he will give you another Counselor to be with you forever—17the Spirit of truth. The world cannot accept him, because it neither sees him nor knows him. But you know him, for he lives with you and will be in you. 25 All this I have spoken while still with you. 26But the Counselor, the Holy Spirit, whom the Father will send in my name, will teach you all things and will remind you of everything I have said to you."

Observation
- Note the things you have learned about the Holy Spirit. What would it look like to apply one of these observations to your life this week?

Interpretation

Application

Spiritual Reading
Who is the Holy Spirit?

Easily Forgotten

Have you ever felt invisible? Forgotten. Left out. Well, when it comes to God—Father, Son, and Holy Spirit—the Holy Spirit couldn't be faulted for feeling that way.

When we think of God, most people think of God the Father: the One who is invisible to us, who sits on the throne; the One who acts throughout Scripture. In the Old Testament, he is creating, warning, and leading his people. In the New Testament, he is sending his Son and leading him during his time on earth.

We can relate to God the Son, Jesus, because he has taken on human flesh. We can read about what he taught, how he treated others, the miracles he did, and the sacrifice he made for us. We can picture him sitting at the right hand of the Father.
What about the Holy Spirit? Who is he? What is he like? What does he do? Is it important that we know? Many people simply don't have much understanding around these questions and, as a result, the Holy Spirit can seem foreign to us. It is easy to ignore him and to be ignorant of how he works. When we do this, however, we miss out on one of the key ways God wants to help us in our lives.

What We Know

What do we know about the Holy Spirit from the Bible? There's a lot we can tell even just from the passage we looked at in John 14.

First, we see that the Holy Spirit is a "he," not an "it." Many people think the Spirit is some type of ghost or impersonal force, but Jesus refers to the Spirit as "he." A personal being who interacts with us in a personal way. This makes even more sense as we look at some of the other characteristics and roles of the Holy Spirit.

Jesus says that the Father will send the Spirit. Similar to the way that the Father sent his Son into the world, he sends the Spirit once Jesus returns to heaven.

Along with this, Jesus says that the Spirit will be *another* Counselor. In other words, the Spirit will counsel and guide the disciples (and us), much as Jesus had done.

Even more specifically, the Spirit will remind them of everything Jesus had said to them. The Spirit will teach them new things. He will teach them what is true. He will be with them and in them at all times.

In essence, this is similar to having Jesus with us at all times. If you read the book of Acts, you will see that the apostles really understood this. Many times they referred to the Spirit guiding them, sending them out, and warning them.

Other passages describe the Spirit empowering the disciples to do miracles, praise God in supernatural ways, and recognize the Spirit's voice in ways that are less familiar to many of us. We will look at this more closely in one of our later sessions.

How Does the Spirit Work in Our Lives?

How does the Spirit work in our everyday lives? How does he counsel or teach or remind us of God's truth?

The Holy Spirit is talking to us, teaching us, correcting us, and reminding us way more than we probably realize. One way he does this is through our thoughts, when we are paying attention. Let's look at an everyday situation between a married couple, Joe and Mary. You will notice that this sounds similar to examples from our session on listening to God.

Let's say Joe is beginning to realize that he often uses words to hurt others, especially his wife. He says sarcastic comments or critical jabs that he thinks are innocent, but which in reality are causing ever-deepening wounds.

One evening, Joe walks into the kitchen and sees a sink full of dishes, and he's about to say something clever to Mary like, "I guess the bridge party went long, huh?" But in the next moment, he has another thought, "Maybe *I* should do the dishes. It actually sounds like she's had a long day." Weird; where did that thought come from? Could it be, oh I don't know...the Holy Spirit?

The Spirit isn't as mysterious as he might seem. He is speaking to us through our thoughts, prompting and reminding us in the moment.

It might happen during times of prayer. Let's say Joe chooses to go with his previously planned witticism about the dishes, and it results in a fifteen-minute argument. The next morning, as he reflects on the previous day during his prayer time, Joe remembers the argument. As he now slows down, he remembers his initial comment that got the ball rolling (he had forgotten all about it after getting so frustrated during the argument). He starts to think about how that could have gone differently had he chosen to say nothing or, better yet, to help out.

Joe can choose to rationalize that he had had a long day too, or that he was "just joking." Or he can humble himself and say, "Father, you are right. I know you have spoken to me through the Spirit. I was sarcastic and selfish. I should have held my tongue and been sensitive to the tough day Mary had. Please help me choose to respond differently next time." He can also take the next step of apologizing to Mary.

In the days and weeks to come, sometimes Joe makes a good choice, and sometimes he forgets or chooses what feels good to him. But over time, Joe begins to change in this area.

Other Ways He Speaks

The Spirit will also speak through the Bible, others, things we read, music, teachings, serving experiences, and many other avenues.

For example, we may be feeling discouraged, and he uses the words of a song or a Scripture passage or of a friend to remind us of God's love and promise to walk with us.

It may be a prompting, an idea that comes to us, to reach out to someone and encourage him/her or see how he/she is doing.

Most of the time, these reminders, conviction, encouragement, or promptings aren't dramatic. That's why we need to be paying attention in the moment and having times of prayer and reflection as we have discussed. We can't dismiss those thoughts when they come, because they are often the Spirit speaking to us.

A Caution

In our passage from John 14, Jesus refers to the Spirit as the "Spirit of truth." It is important that what we sense the Spirit saying to us lines up with God's truth. We discussed this in the session on God's guidance. Much of the time, it will be clear that it is in fact the Spirit speaking, because it is clearly true.

The story above about Joe and his response is a good example. This is how we would expect the Spirit to guide someone: to a place of humility and love toward one's spouse.

There are other times when it may be less clear. Particularly if you are a newer follower of Jesus, it can be a bit confusing as to whether you are hearing from the Spirit or simply yourself. If you think back to our discussion on listening to God and the circle, this is where discussing with others comes in.

You may have a situation where you feel bad about something, for example, but in reality you don't need to. It's misplaced guilt. Or you feel like the Spirit is leading you to do something you normally would have done in the past, like moving in with someone or being sexually active as an unmarried person, but in talking to a more mature believer, you realize that this is not God's best for you and is actually a sin.

Having this type of check-in with a more seasoned follower is important throughout our lives, because we are all human, and we can all make mistakes.

A Gift

The Spirit loves us and wants to help us. He is always with us, teaching us, correcting us, encouraging us, guiding us, and helping us become the people God created us to be. He is a gift—a gift not to be ignored.

Questions for Reflection and Discussion

- What is something new about the Holy Spirit that you learned from this reading?

- What is still unclear to you about the Holy Spirit?

- How have you seen the Holy Spirit work in your life?

- During your prayer time, ask the Holy Spirit to reveal more about himself to you in the future.

Spiritual Practice
Lectio Divina

One of the ways that the Spirit uses to speak to us is through God's Word. We usually think of this in the way we learned about in Session 4: studying Scripture and finding applications that connect with our lives. While this may be the most common approach we use, there is another approach we may want to utilize at times that it is less study oriented and a little more personal—meaning that the Spirit uses it to speak to us in a personal way.

This approach is called lectio divina, which is Latin for "sacred" or "divine" reading. It is a practice that has been used for hundreds of years in the Church. It is a simple approach that combines prayer and the reading of Scripture. Below is a simple outline.

Read

Take a short section of Scripture, six to ten verses, sometimes even less. Take a moment to pray and ask God to help you slow down and relax in order to hear from him.

Read the passage slowly two or three times. Take your time.

Reflect

As you read, see if any word, phrase, or sentence stands out to you. If there is something that stands out, take time to just think about that word, phrase, or sentence. Ask God to show you why that may be connecting with you and your life right now. Express your heart to him. Is there anything he wants to tell you or any way he wants to encourage you?

Respond

Be aware of anything God is inviting you to do in response. There may be a practical step he is encouraging you to take or simply an encouragement to receive his love.

Rest

Finish your time by simply resting in God's presence and experiencing his love for you as his son or daughter.

Trying It Out

Give it a try now using the passage below, spoken by Jesus. The steps are listed again for your convenience.

Note: The word "yoke" was an agricultural term used for two farm animals harnessed together to do work. Jesus is referring to his way of doing things when someone chooses to be connected to him or follow him.

> **Matthew 11:28-30**
>
> [28]"Come to me, all you who are weary and burdened, and I will give you rest. [29]Take my yoke upon you and learn from me, for I am gentle and humble in heart, and you will find rest for your souls. [30]For my yoke is easy and my burden is light."

- **Read**
- **Reflect**
- **Respond**
- **Rest**

Other passages you may want to use in the future: Psalm 23:1-6; 2 Samuel 22:29-37; Isaiah 40:28-31; Matthew 14:25-33; 1 Corinthians 13:1-8; Ephesians 3:14-21.

You most likely have a belief in both heaven and hell. Both, however, tend to be confusing for many people. Heaven may seem like a place that we can't relate to. As a result, if we are honest, it may seem a little strange or even boring. We need a deeper understanding that more accurately reflects the amazing reality of what life will be like in our true home.

Hell, of course, is a very challenging topic. What is it like? Does it fit with our understanding of a just and loving God? Even though it is not a pleasant issue to reflect on, we need to wrestle with it.

In our Spiritual Practice section, we will look at how eternity impacts our day-to-day lives. Do we have an eternal perspective? Do we live with the awareness that this life is not the end? Are we focused on things that will go on into eternity? Hopefully, this unique exercise will help us reflect on these important questions.

Soaking in Scripture

This passage from Revelation offers us many insights into heaven. As a reminder, Revelation is a vision given to the apostle John of future things to come, including heaven.

The implications of this passage are significant and will be explored further in the Spiritual Reading section. We can begin to see the wonders of heaven as we reflect on this passage.

Revelation 21:1-5

[1]Then I saw "a new heaven and a new earth," for the first heaven and the first earth had passed away, and there was no longer any sea. [2]I saw the Holy City, the new Jerusalem, coming down out of heaven from God, prepared as a bride beautifully dressed for her husband. [3]And I heard a loud voice from the throne saying, "Look! God's dwelling place is now among the people, and he will dwell with them. They will be his people, and God himself will be with them and be their God. [4]'He will wipe every tear from their eyes. There will be no more death' or mourning or crying or pain, for the old order of things has passed away."

[5]He who was seated on the throne said, "I am making everything new!" Then he said, "Write this down, for these words are trustworthy and true."

- How does the idea of a new earth impact your view of heaven?

Continued

- What excites you about what is described in vv. 3-4?

- How might v. 4 impact how you view the challenges you face in life?

- During your prayer time, share with God whatever feelings of excitement and praise you have concerning heaven.

Digging into Scripture

In his parable about the kingdom of heaven, Jesus teaches the crowd and his disciples about what will take place at the end of the age. Jesus' words may evoke a variety of feelings and may be disturbing. He is describing a reality that is a cause for celebration for some and a sober warning for others. One thing is for certain: his message is very clear.

Matthew 13:24-30, 36-43

24Jesus told them another parable: "The kingdom of heaven is like a man who sowed good seed in his field. 25But while everyone was sleeping, his enemy came and sowed weeds among the wheat, and went away. 26When the wheat sprouted and formed heads, then the weeds also appeared.

27"The owner's servants came to him and said, 'Sir, didn't you sow good seed in your field? Where then did the weeds come from?'

28"'An enemy did this,' he replied.

"The servants asked him, 'Do you want us to go and pull them up?'

29"'No,' he answered, 'because while you are pulling the weeds, you may uproot the wheat with them. 30Let both grow together until the harvest. At that time I will tell the harvesters: First collect the weeds and tie them in bundles to be burned; then gather the wheat and bring it into my barn.'"

36Then he left the crowd and went into the house. His disciples came to him and said, "Explain to us the parable of the weeds in the field."

37He answered, "The one who sowed the good seed is the Son of Man. 38The field is the world, and the good seed stands for the people of the kingdom. The weeds are the people of the evil one, [39]and the enemy who sows them is the devil. The harvest is the end of the age, and the harvesters are angels.

[40]"As the weeds are pulled up and burned in the fire, so it will be at the end of the age. [41]The Son of Man will send out his angels, and they will weed out of his kingdom everything that causes sin and all who do evil. [42]They will throw them into the blazing furnace, where there will be weeping and gnashing of teeth. [43]Then the righteous will shine like the sun in the kingdom of their Father. Whoever has ears, let them hear."

Observation

- What are the various roles in the explanation of the parable, according to Jesus?

Interpretation

- Why do you think a separation must take place (v. 41)?

Application

Spiritual Practices
Reflecting on Your Funeral

Doesn't that sound exciting? In 2 Corinthians 4:18, Paul says, "We **fix our eyes** not on what is seen, but on what is unseen. For what is seen is temporary, but what is unseen is eternal." What are those things in our lives that are truly important, those things that will go on into eternity? This exercise may sound a little strange, but it can help us get a picture of what it might mean to live our lives with eternity in mind.

After reading the directions below, take a moment to quiet yourself. Take a number of slow, deep breaths to help you focus. Pray and invite God to lead this time of reflection. When you are ready, follow the instructions below. Be sure to take your time.

You have lived a long and fulfilled life. Imagine that your funeral is taking place. Picture where it is happening. Picture the people walking into the church or the location of the funeral. Who are they? Look at their faces. Imagine them being seated.

People are given the opportunity to share about you and your life. Friends and family members have the chance to come up one by one to share about what you and your life have meant to them. This could be adults, youths, or children. Picture specific people sharing the things that they love and appreciate about you—your qualities—as well as how you have impacted their lives. Take your time. How do you feel as you hear what they share?

Now imagine the service coming to a close. Picture the people leaving. When you are ready, open your eyes.

Take some time now to reflect on the exercise.

- What strikes you as you reflect on what people said about you?

- In light of this exercise, what about your life seems more important? Less important?

- Take some time to pray about what you have experienced.

Almost Heaven

One summer during college, I worked at a Christian camp in east Texas. It was a beautiful area filled with tall pine trees and a sparkling lake. I got to know a great team of other college students and wonderful people who oversaw the camp, people who were full of God's love and joy. My newfound friends and I had a blast as counselors for elementary-aged kids coming to camp to have fun and learn more about God.

One morning, I was sitting there among the trees having some time with God, and it hit me: this place is like heaven. At first, I was just thinking of it in the sense of, "this is a really great place." As I thought about it more, I realized that it probably really was a taste of what heaven will actually be like.

Who Will Be in Heaven?

For starters, all of the people who worked at the camp really loved God. They were excited to know him better and to serve him by loving others. Because of this, there was wonderful community among the people there. There was a lot of joy and laughter, and when there were challenges, they were quickly addressed.

Heaven will be filled with people who love God. People who are excited to be with him and to be with those who love him. The more we get to know God and realize just how amazing he is, the more we want to be with him. This is why the apostle Paul was so torn. He writes, "Yet what shall I choose? I do not know! I am torn between the two: I desire to depart and be with Christ, *which is better by far*; but it is more necessary for you that I remain in the body" (Philippians 1:22-24).

The clearest descriptions in Scripture of those who will be in heaven are those who love God and, as a result, have accepted what Jesus has done for them through his death. This love for God doesn't stop at accepting this gift, but instead propels them into a life of following him and living for him, what Jesus calls the sons and daughters of the Kingdom. After a life lived this way, their greatest joy is getting to live with Jesus in his Kingdom, along with the Father, the Spirit and all those who love God.

Many have questions, of course, about people in various situations: those who have not heard about Jesus, those in countries practicing other religions, young children, and those who do not have the capacity to understand the fullness of a decision to follow Christ. With these questions, and others like them, the key is understanding the character of God. God's nature and character is far above ours. This means he is far more just, loving, caring, and wise than we are. He will know what to do, and he will do the right thing: the just, and even merciful, choice. We can be confident of this and entrust people to him.

What Will Heaven Be Like?

Many depictions of heaven reveal how limited people's imaginations are when it comes to this topic and how small their understanding of God is. Some picture heaven as white clouds and harps, with not much to do but sit around and sing. Really?! Look out the window or take a tour of the world via the internet. Do we really think the God who created our world—the God of imagination, creativity, and endless variety—has created a boring, lifeless Kingdom for *himself*? I don't think so.

What seems to get people off track is that they think heaven will be so different and less real than what they experience right now, but the Bible seems to say something different.

In the Soaking in Scripture passage from Revelation 21:1-5, it tells us that in the vision John saw "a new heaven and a new earth, for the first heaven and the first earth had passed away." He writes that he saw the "Holy City, the new Jerusalem, coming down out of heaven from God, prepared as a bride beautifully dressed for her husband."

It is a picture of heaven joining earth—a new earth. The idea of a new earth has many implications. A new earth would seem to indicate that it will be a world we are familiar with, but new and even better, even more real and vivid and amazing. A world that will be filled with the elements we are used to, landscapes and mountains and waterfalls, but without any of the corruption that has come with the sin and brokenness of our current world.

It has a heavenly city, the capital, you might say, in the center of it. This city is later described in amazing ways with incredible dimensions; it has a square that, in each direction, is *1,400 miles*—now that's a city—and is created out of fantastically beautiful elements.

Some people seem to think we will have no purpose, just kind of lying around like one long retirement, but this doesn't sound like the God I know. The God of the Bible is always on the move, always moving toward something. He always seems to want to use people in his plans. This new world will be full of purpose and adventure, and his people will be at the center of it all.

This world will be lacking one thing, however—fear. That's one of my favorite parts: no fear. "There will be no more death or mourning or crying or pain, *for the old order of things has passed away*" (Revelation 21:4). That has to be one of the most exciting passages in all of Scripture. The old order, with all of its sin, pain, fear, shame, death, and on and on, *will pass away*. It will be over. Done.

A new day will dawn. "He who was seated on the throne said, 'I am making everything new'" (Revelation 21:5). I don't know about you, but living in a new world free of pain and fear and death sounds pretty good to me. I'm ready for a new order of things.

What Will We Be Like?

Here's a passage from Philippians 3:20-21 that should be very exciting.

20But our citizenship is in heaven. And we eagerly await a Savior from there, the Lord Jesus Christ, 21who, by the power that enables him to bring everything under his control, will transform our lowly bodies so that they will be like his glorious body.

That's awesome! First of all, it tells us that we will have bodies in this heaven on earth. We won't be floating spirits. God has made us human, and humans have bodies.

The good news is that those bodies will be transformed so that they are similar to Jesus' glorified body. It is kind of like the new world being familiar, but better—glorified. Our bodies will be free of the effects of a broken world, sickness and aging, and most likely will have abilities we don't have now. We see this in Jesus' resurrected body; it is still a body, but has abilities such as walking through doors, appearing, and disappearing. We may not have precisely the same abilities as Jesus, but it gives us an idea of new things to come.

This, of course, is tremendous news for those who have suffered with physical challenges in this life. Everything—and every body—will be made new!

What about Hell?

This is a big question. It brings up the same question that we looked at above about whether we can trust the character of God. In the end, we must trust that if God knows what he is doing when it comes to heaven, what it will be like, who is going to be there, then we must trust him when it comes to hell.

There are different understandings of what the Bible means when it describes hell. For example, is the fiery furnace that Jesus refers to in our Digging into Scripture passage a literal description for hell, or is it metaphorical?

Does someone's existence in hell go on and on, or is there an end, when someone ceases to exist? Revelation 20:14, for example, says that those whose names are not written in the book of life at the time of judgment will be thrown in the lake of fire, which is called "the second death."

What is most clear from Jesus' description of events in the passage we studied this week is that there will definitely be some kind of separation. There will be those who will go to be with God in his Kingdom and those who will be forever separated from him. It is a popular idea that everyone will be in heaven, but there is simply nothing to support that idea in the Bible. We can trust that God will know and do precisely the right thing out of his infinite wisdom and goodness.

The Best Thing about Heaven

Often when people talk about heaven or it is depicted in movies or elsewhere, the main focus is on what it is like, who is there, and how we will relate. These are natural, human things to think about. For those who have come to know and love God, the thing that is anticipated the most is God himself.

When you have come to see that this God is the father described in the parable of the prodigal son, waiting to welcome his children home with hugs and kisses, you will want to meet him face to face. You will want to meet the One who has guided you, provided for you, and transformed you. You will want to experience the embrace of your Father.

In Revelation 21:3, it says, "Look! God's dwelling place is now among the people, and he will dwell with them. They will be his people, and God himself will be with them and be their God."

At last, we will be home with our Father.

Questions for Reflection and Discussion

- What were some new things you discovered about heaven from the reading?

- How do these discoveries impact your feelings about heaven?

- During your prayer time, ask God to help you let your imagination run free as you picture life in heaven. Picture what you see, what you're doing, and whom you are doing it with. Take time to praise God and talk to him about your eternal home.

We have now looked at a number of key beliefs, and we have explored some key practices in helping us in our relationship with God. What if we stopped here? Would it be enough? The answer is no. Beliefs and practices are good, but a key part of our life with God is that we are experiencing ongoing transformation: that we are changing more and more into his likeness. Here's another way of saying it: belief without transformation equals spiritual deadness.

One picture of this change is referred to in Scripture as the fruit of the Spirit. This is the good fruit that begins to form in our lives when we follow the leading of the Holy Spirit. This is good news in itself: we do not have to carry out this change process on our own; the Holy Spirit is very much involved in the process. He is guiding the process of helping us change.

This week, we will look more closely at the different fruit or characteristics the Holy Spirit wants to develop in our lives. We will do some self-assessment around these characteristics to help us zero in on areas to work on.

Spiritual Practice
Examining the Fruit

Typically, at any given time, God will be developing one or more types of spiritual fruit in our lives. This is a nice way of saying that there are areas he is working on in our lives that need changing. When we are more familiar with what these various fruit are, we can cooperate more fully with the Holy Spirit to develop them in our lives.

Below you will find the fruit of the Spirit, listed in our Digging into Scripture passage from Galatians. Each has a brief definition (these are based on *The Christian Life Profile Assessment Tool*, Workbook by Randy Frazee), followed by examples. After reviewing the definitions, choose one or two areas you believe that God is working on in your life. In addition, think about the areas of your life where this comes up most frequently, such as in your marriage, in workplace relationships/decisions, with your children, or in your friendships.

During this week, pay attention to when this area comes up. In particular, see if you sense the Holy Spirit prompting you to do or say something (or *not* say something) and follow his lead. Share any of the steps you take with your group this week. This is an ongoing process, but this will give you a feel for how the process works. Keep in mind that you will never perfectly reflect each fruit as it is described; you are trying to take on these characteristics more and more in your life.

Here is an example. Someone might identify that they struggle with the area of patience and, in particular, getting angry quickly with their children. In the moment, or when thinking back on a situation during prayer, they may sense the Spirit encouraging them to pause before responding next time or asking their child a question to gain more information. Maybe they feel prompted to use a more respectful tone. These are small steps, but over time, this is how the Spirit guides us and how change happens.

FRUIT OF THE SPIRIT

Love: Choosing to love others *sacrificially* and *unconditionally*.

Examples: Seeking to love difficult people, striving to forgive others, giving up what you want for the sake of others, loving others regardless of race or economic status.

Joy: Experiencing contentment on a regular basis, including when things are not going as planned.

Examples: Often expressing gratitude for God's blessings in life, being content with the amount of money and possessions you now have, your moods not following the up-and-down nature of circumstances in life, laughing and expressing joy frequently.

Peace: Feeling free from anxiety, because things are right between God, yourself, and others.

Examples: Not experiencing excessive worry during challenging or uncertain times, consistently experiencing God's love and forgiveness for you as his child, forgiving people who hurt you.

Patience: Taking a long time to "overheat" and patiently enduring the unavoidable pressures of life.

Examples: Keeping your composure, even when people or circumstances irritate you; not getting angry with God, but trusting him when having to endure confusing or challenging circumstances.

Kindness: Regularly expressing words or actions that tangibly demonstrate God's love to others.

Examples: Intentionally speaking words of kindness to others, especially those in need of encouragement; serving others in small or large ways without expecting anything in return; giving to others in financial or material need; seeing material goods as opportunities to share with others, rather than use them only for yourself.

Goodness: Doing the right things in relationships, resulting in the trust of others.

Examples: Being a person of honesty and integrity even in the small things, in what you say or do in the different areas of your life, such as at home, work, and in friendships; genuinely caring for others in such a way that allows them to feel safe sharing their needs with you.

Faithfulness: Faithfully fulfilling commitments made to God and others.

Examples: Following God faithfully, even when it is difficult to do so; following through on commitments made to God and to others, being faithful to your spouse, being a loyal and trusted friend, finishing well when transitioning out of career or volunteer roles.

Gentleness: Relating to others in a thoughtful, non-judgmental, and calm manner.

Examples: Being sensitive to the feelings of others, being respectful of the opinions of others, considering your own shortcomings when faced with the failures of others, not raising your voice and treating others respectfully when handling relational challenges.

Note: Gentleness is not a type of personality or temperament, such as a reserved, quiet, or shy person. Any personality type can exhibit gentleness in dealing with others.

Self-control: Controlling, with the help and power of Christ, your unhealthy or sinful urges.

Examples: Changing any ongoing *pattern* of sin in a particular area; becoming free from any addictive substance or activity, such as food, alcohol, drugs, sex, tobacco, or materialism; restraining from sexual activity that is contrary to biblical teaching; controlling the tongue, particularly in the areas of gossip or angry outbursts.

Humility: Choosing to see yourself in a healthy manner and esteeming others above yourself.

Examples: Viewing yourself as a deeply loved child of God, without a need for excessive pride or proving yourself to others, and no need to hold an unhealthy, low view of yourself either; intentionally opening yourself up to God's loving discipline and change in your life; not being overly concerned with hiding weaknesses or faults from others, because you are secure in being a child of God; not getting upset when achievements are not recognized, but also able to receive appreciation when it is given.

Note: Humility is not listed in the Galatians passage, but is found in other passages describing the Spirit's work in our life. Humility tends to be the characteristic that "unlocks" the other fruit, because we are humble and open to God's change in our lives.

- Below, write the one or two areas from above that you believe God wants to work on in your life right now.

- As you sensed the Spirit leading you during the week to take steps in this area, write down what you felt he was leading you to do and how you responded. Share this with your group.

Soaking in Scripture

Psalm 92:12-15

[12]*The righteous will flourish like a palm tree,*
   they will grow like a cedar of Lebanon;
[13]*planted in the house of the Lord,*
   they will flourish in the courts of our God.
[14]*They will still bear fruit in old age,*
   they will stay fresh and green,
[15]*proclaiming, "The Lord is upright;*
   he is my Rock, and there is no wickedness in him."

- What would it look like to flourish in your life?

- Describe someone you know who "still bears fruit in old age" and who is also still "fresh and green" spiritually. Note: "Old age" can be flexible here. The idea is someone who has walked with God for a long time.

- How do you think they have stayed that way?

- During your prayer time, express your desire to God to flourish and grow in your life with him and to bear fruit throughout your life.

⛏ Digging into Scripture

This passage from the apostle Paul describes the struggle that goes on within each one of us between the desires of our sinful nature, and the person the Spirit is trying to lead us to become. It is helpful that Paul gets specific in the description of what the "fruit" of the sinful nature looks like and what the specific fruit of the Spirit looks like. We can begin to look at what some of the specific changes are that need to happen in our lives as the Spirit leads us and helps us in that process.

Galatians 5:13-26 (NLT)

13For you have been called to live in freedom, my brothers and sisters. But don't use your freedom to satisfy your sinful nature. Instead, use your freedom to serve one another in love. 14For the whole law can be summed up in this one command: "Love your neighbor as yourself." 15But if you are always biting and devouring one another, watch out! Beware of destroying one another.

16So I say, let the Holy Spirit guide your lives. Then you won't be doing what your sinful nature craves. 17The sinful nature wants to do evil, which is just the opposite of what the Spirit wants. And the Spirit gives us desires that are the opposite of what the sinful nature desires. These two forces are constantly fighting each other, so you are not free to carry out your good intentions. 18But when you are directed by the Spirit, you are not under obligation to the law of Moses.

19When you follow the desires of your sinful nature, the results are very clear: sexual immorality, impurity, lustful pleasures, 20idolatry, sorcery, hostility, quarreling, jealousy, outbursts of anger, selfish ambition, dissension, division, 21envy, drunkenness, wild parties, and other sins like these. Let me tell you again, as I have before, that anyone living that sort of life will not inherit the Kingdom of God.

22But the Holy Spirit produces this kind of fruit in our lives: love, joy, peace, patience, kindness, goodness, faithfulness, 23gentleness, and self-control. There is no law against these things!

24Those who belong to Christ Jesus have nailed the passions and desires of their sinful nature to his cross and crucified them there. 25Since we are living by the Spirit, let us follow the Spirit's leading in every part of our lives. 26Let us not become conceited, or provoke one another, or be jealous of one another.

Observation

- How does the Spirit help us in this process?

- How do some of the characteristics of the sinful nature contrast with some of the fruit of the Spirit (for example, quarreling and peace)?

Interpretation

Application

We are fascinated by transformation. Why? Because it is super cool.

It's why reality shows went from being a passing fad (didn't you think it would be a fad?) to being all over the place: many of them are about transformation. A person who has struggled with weight much of her life now looks like a different person. I don't know how many times I have seen a picture in a magazine or someone on TV and thought, "That can't be the same person!" It's incredible.

Sometimes, it's a home that has been dramatically altered. There's some outdated '70s ranch home that is somehow transformed into this super cool place you would take in a second. You're thinking, "NO WAY is that the same house! It can't be!" It has been transformed into something completely new.

It's almost like God wired us to love and appreciate transformation. Like it's natural to the world he created.

The coolest transformation is not of homes or bodies—it's the transformation of people. This is something to behold. To watch someone over time go from being selfish, proud, easily angered, controlled by unhealthy desires, or wracked with worry or bitterness into someone who is humble, giving, patient, filled with joy and peace and forgiveness. What could be more amazing? How God must love watching—and helping—this unfold in the lives of those who truly love him.

This is what can happen, what should happen, within everyone who follows Jesus. When this ongoing transformation is not happening, something is wrong. Those who don't follow Jesus intuitively know this. "Shouldn't there be something different about this person if he is following Jesus?" As a matter of fact, there should be.

What can we do in order to see change happen within us now and throughout our lives? How can we be like those whom the writer describes in Psalm 92? Those that will flourish and grow and still bear fruit in old age, staying "fresh and green" spiritually throughout their lives. How can we experience transformation until we take our last breath?

The Importance of Humility

There are several factors that are important to be aware of if we want to experience the greatest degree of transformation. Understanding these and acting upon them can be the difference between minimal and major change in our lives.

A good place to start is humility. A humble attitude is the gateway to real change. Psalm 25:9 says that God "guides the humble in what is right and teaches them his way." Someone who is humble is like a soft piece of clay that can be shaped by the master artist. They are malleable, shapeable.

When we are initially confronted with the reality that we may need to change in some area, the natural instinct is to resist or deny this reality. Who really wants to say, "Yep, that's me, Mr. Selfish!"? Who wants to admit that they struggle with their temper or wrestle with laziness or have unforgiveness lurking within them? We want to push these thoughts away if we even are aware of them at all.

The humble do something really weird: they welcome the truth. After the initial, human response of wanting to deny that something like this might be true of them, they say, "Okay, Father. It's true. I know it. I don't want to admit it, but it's true. Start the re-shaping process. I trust you. Teach me *your* way."

I have a friend who is malleable. She has been walking with God for many years. She has a strong personality: an independent straight-shooter. But within that Annie Oakley-style personality lies a gentle, kind spirit that has been cultivated over years of being completely open to God. Every time she has become aware of something that needs to change or grow in her, she has been humble and has opened herself up to God's loving handiwork. A humble heart is a beautiful thing.

If we want to see significant growth and transformation, we need to stop the denials, lay down our pride, and courageously open ourselves up to God's shaping work in our lives.

The Importance of the Holy Spirit

With a humble attitude in place, we then need to know how the Holy Spirit works in our lives to bring change and what steps we can take to respond. In our passage this week from Galatians 5, we looked at the fruit of the Spirit. These are the traits that the Holy Spirit is developing within us when we respond to and cooperate with his activity in our lives.

As you remember from our reading about the Holy Spirit a couple of weeks ago, Jesus taught about the role of the Spirit as a teacher and counselor. The Holy Spirit is talking to us, teaching us, correcting us, and reminding us much more then we probably realize.

During certain seasons, the Spirit will zero in on one of these areas or fruits. Let's say patience, for example. He may begin to speak to us through situations in our lives where we are not showing patience (with our kids, for example), through Scripture we are studying, through messages we hear, or through books we are reading.

If we are humble and aware of how the Spirit is working, we can begin to see real change as he drills down into these areas of character in our lives. It is not always fun, but it is very rewarding as we see real change happening.

The Importance of Knowing Ourselves

In addition to being humble and aware of the Spirit's work in our lives, the more we know ourselves, the more we will be able to cooperate with the Spirit.

What does it mean to know yourself? It means being aware of your personality, your past experiences, the significant hurts you may have encountered—all of the things that might impact who you are as a person and how you see the world. Understanding these things can help you be aware of where change may need to take place and reduce the number of blind spots in your life.

I'll use myself as an example, even though I might regret it...If I look at my personality, I think I'm a laid-back, easygoing kind of guy by nature. This typically makes me pretty easy to be around, and I naturally lean toward joy and peace in my life. However, the flipside of that is that, if I'm not careful, one of my blind spots can be laziness (I hate that ugly word!) disguised as being "laid back."

I'm also aware that, because I essentially grew up as an only child (my siblings were a lot older), my wonderful, loving mom kind of spoiled me, which at the time was awesome! I loved it! Cook, clean, and do laundry? Whaaaat?

Guess what one of the things is that I have to be very aware of? Right, making sure I have a wife who will do all of those things. Wait, that doesn't seem right.

Okay, for real, when situations at home or work come up that can tempt me toward laziness or its close cousins, lack of self-control and unfaithfulness, something often goes off in my head, "Warning! Warning! Laziness: dead ahead!" Of course, I can choose whether or not to respond to that warning, but at least I'm not usually blindsided by it the way I would be if I weren't aware that this is something I am susceptible to.

This relates to a later session we will do on being emotionally healthy. The more we are aware of how patterns of hurt from the past can result in struggles with anger and anxiety, among others, the more we can cooperate with both the Spirit's healing work in our lives and the way he wants to bring transformation to our characters around these things.

This is significant. Otherwise, we can be trying to grow and change, but be confused as to why we struggle with, say, anger. If we don't know how our past hurt plays into that, we are fighting blind.

Over time, as you get to know yourself better through reflection, you will be that much more aware of the areas the Spirit will likely be working on, and you'll be less susceptible to getting blindsided.

The Importance of Knowing the Father's Love

The last important factor we will look at in the transformation process is the importance of knowing the Father's love. You may have noticed that we keep coming back to this theme! That's because it impacts so many things in our lives, including experiencing deep transformation.

In particular, having a deep awareness of the Father's love for us is essential if we want to experience the first three fruit of the Spirit: love, joy, and peace. Even if they don't know it, these are the deeper things in life that people are searching for. How do we get to a place of loving people deeply, sacrificially, and unconditionally? How do we experience ongoing joy and peace in the midst of a very up-and-down life and world? These can seem elusive.

When I was attending seminary in the early '90s, I lived in a community house made up of six or seven students and a faculty couple, Rob and Julie Banks, who started the house. Living in that house was one of the highlights of my life, because of the friendships that were fostered there, but also because of how much I learned from Rob and Julie. I had a front row seat to a couple whose lives were filled with the big three: love, joy, and peace.

I can remember hearing about a young woman who took an unusual route to seminary. She sold all the drugs she had in her possession in order to pay for her first semester's tuition. She came to seminary to seek God. Not too long after I had heard this story, there she was at one of our evening dinners. Rob, a highly respected scholar and professor at the seminary, had invited her. Rob and Julie would go on to mentor her in the months and years to come, showing her—and me—what the love of God looks like in action.

Because of Rob and Julie, our student home was filled with joy and laughter. They were filled with a love for life that was contagious. There was an easy freedom about them. You just wanted to be around them. They loved things as varied as theology, gardening, and movies. In fact, Rob had a secret desire to be a movie director, resulting in regular movie nights that would attract large groups of students.

Where did this come from? Looking back, I realized that it came from years of living in the love of their Father. They had a deep sense of his love for them as his children that flowed out in tangible love for others. They had a trust in him and his love for them that resulted in wonderful joy and freedom.

Pray that God would continue to reveal his deep love for you. Living out of his love will change you in ways beyond what you thought possible.

Seeking Transformation

There are a few things you can actively pursue that will lead you toward real transformation in your life: seek to grow in humility, ask God to show you more about yourself and any blind spots you may need to be aware of, and ask him to reveal his amazing love for you.

The best part in all of this is that we have the promise that the Holy Spirit, who lives within us, will be guiding us in all of this. It's not all on our shoulders, which is good news! He will lead, remind, convict—he is a good teacher and counselor. It is the fruit *of the Spirit*, which he is developing within us as we follow his lead. We just need to say, "Here I am! I'm open! Lead me and change me. I will cooperate!" Be patient; this is an ongoing, lifelong process.

You are in your own reality show: a program that's all about really cool changes. Except it's not a show, it's your life. And your Father is the director—and your greatest fan.

Questions for Reflection and Discussion

- How do you feel when you see different examples of transformation, such as on TV or in other people?

- Which important key to transformation—humility, the Holy Spirit, knowing ourselves, or knowing the Father's love—connected with you the most, and why?

- During your prayer time, ask God to show you a step you could take in the area you connected with the most.

When we examine the fruit of the Spirit, we realize that most take place in the context of relationships: love, peace, patience, gentleness. Looking at the negative side, much of what the sinful nature produces also happens within relationships: hostility, quarreling, divisions. Much of our growth in becoming more like Jesus through the help of the Holy Spirit will happen in our relationships with others. This could be in our friendships, marriages, or relationships with co-workers, neighbors, extended family, or with our children.

There is one key area we will encounter in every type of relationship: conflict. If the fruit of the Spirit is going to grow in our lives, we must learn how to handle conflict well and become people who know how to bring peace. These could be situations that range from an annoying encounter with a stranger to a significant rift within a relationship.

Without the heart and skills to deal with conflict effectively, we will experience damaged relationships in our lives. Conflict is one of the enemy's most frequently used tools in tearing people apart, whether that be in friendships, marriages, or churches.

With this in mind, we will look at Scripture and readings to help us gain wisdom and God's heart in this important area.

Soaking in Scripture

The book of Proverbs in the Bible provides a wealth of wisdom when it comes to relationships, including the issue of conflict. The passage below is a good example of this wisdom.

Note: the encouragement to overlook an offense in the passage below could be confusing, sounding as if we should avoid dealing with any conflict. This is not the case, as we will see in the rest of this week's materials. Some offenses, however, don't need to rise to the point of conflict when we are walking in God's wisdom and patience.

> **Proverbs 19:11**
> *A person's wisdom yields patience; it is to one's glory to overlook an offense.*

- What types of offenses do you think this passage is encouraging us to overlook?

- How easy or difficult is it for you to overlook an offense? If it is difficult, why do you think this is?

- Why do you think someone's wisdom gives him or her patience and the ability to overlook offenses?

- This is an excellent verse to memorize, because it is a situation we often face. Write the verse in the space below, and repeat it until memorized. Then, when faced with a situation in which you feel offended, try to bring this verse to mind.

- During your prayer time, express your feelings to God related to carrying out this passage.

Note: Here are other passages from Proverbs on this subject that may be helpful: Proverbs 12:16, 15:18, 20:3, 17:14.

Digging into Scripture

This is a short passage that focuses on judging others, but it contains some important principles that can be applied to resolving conflicts. Take your time while reading, in order to closely observe Jesus' teaching.

Matthew 7:1-5

[1]*"Do not judge, or you too will be judged.* [2]*For in the same way you judge others, you will be judged, and with the measure you use, it will be measured to you.*

[3]*"Why do you look at the speck of sawdust in your brother's eye and pay no attention to the plank in your own eye?* [4]*How can you say to your brother, 'Let me take the speck out of your eye,' when all the time there is a plank in your own eye?* [5]*You hypocrite, first take the plank out of your own eye, and then you will see clearly to remove the speck from your brother's eye."*

Observation
- How could you see Jesus' teaching applying to conflict in your life? Is there a specific situation it would apply to at this time? What kind of attitude would it require?

Interpretation

Application

Spiritual Reading
Practical Help for Pursuing Peace

In Ephesians 6:15, Paul says to stand firm "with your feet fitted with the readiness that comes from the gospel of peace." The gospel of peace will help us to be ready to stand strong in our lives, and to stand strong against the schemes of the Devil.

I used to just read this as "the gospel," but Paul specifically says the gospel "of peace." I believe that Paul is saying that the gospel brings peace first in our relationship with God. But Paul is saying more; he is saying that this gospel brings peace between us and others. In several places earlier in Ephesians, he describes the peace that the gospel of Christ can bring between groups, such as the Jews and Gentiles, and between individuals, such as brothers and sisters in the Church.

I believe with Paul that our ability to bring God's peace into our relationships will have a direct effect on our ability to stand strong against the Devil in our lives. We're going to look at three steps to take in bringing the gospel of peace into our relationships, in order to help us stand strong against the Devil.

Step 1: Recognize the Seriousness of Unresolved Conflict

The first step we need to take is to recognize the seriousness of unresolved conflict.

Gives the Devil a Foothold

It's strange to me that an issue as common as conflict seems to rarely be addressed in sermons. I haven't heard very many messages on conflict. My experience has been that many Christ-followers haven't been equipped or challenged to handle conflict properly, and this is very unfortunate, because the Devil uses unresolved conflict to ravage people's lives. It can easily be another blind spot that the Devil can take advantage of.

Earlier in Paul's letter, he had this to say about anger and conflict:

> "In your anger do not sin: Do not let the sun go down while you are still angry, and *do not give the devil a foothold*" (**Ephesians 4:26-27**).

Think about that word, "foothold".

Foothold: 1. A place or thing that will support the foot of a climber, especially a crack, hollow, or ledge in a rock face. 2. A secure starting position from which further advances can be made.

Paul says that unresolved conflict and ongoing anger give the Devil a great place to just burrow into our lives and then launch new attacks that ripple out from that conflict.

When my wife and I chose the neighborhood we now live in, part of the reason we chose it was because the houses were more colorful than the average Minnesota neighborhood. We loved the variety of colors and architecture styles. We chose a color that we loved and thought went well with the style of architecture for our house, which comes from beach homes on the East Coast. Many people loved our color, periwinkle, but one neighbor... well, he didn't quite appreciate it like we did.

When we started hearing what this neighbor was saying to other neighbors, we were not really happy. We began to grumble to ourselves, venting our anger and growing bitterness. Then we began to vent a little to other neighbors. We called it venting, but I think the technical term might have been gossip. We certainly felt awkward around the neighbor himself. Do you see the foothold effect at work? The Devil gets a hold, a secure starting position, and then launches further advances of bitterness, gossip, and distance between people.

A few weeks later, Jacki, my wife, did a very strange thing: she talked to the neighbor we were having the problem with about the situation. We were at the pool, and I looked over and she was talking to him. I was thinking, "I think she's talking to him about it." I started getting very nervous, and I wasn't even the one talking to him, which shows you who the spiritual one in our family is. Jacki just explained that we were trying to be sensitive to him and others in regards to our house, that we did try to modify the color a bit, and they discussed their different color preferences. In the end, they agreed to disagree, but in a very cordial manner. That has pretty much ended that. There has been no more talk about it, no more weird or angry feelings. The foothold has been destroyed. The Devil doesn't have a place from which to launch future advances in that situation.

A Foothold in the Church

I want to get a little more specific here. Unresolved conflict not only gives the Devil a foothold in our individual lives, it gives him a foothold in the Church. Without a doubt, this has been one of his primary schemes to harm and, at times, destroy churches. This probably comes as no surprise to you. We may forget that it is not just a coincidence that so many churches experience conflict either among members or between members and pastors; the enemy is ready to gain a foothold and take advantage of our weaknesses.

In Ephesians 4:3, Paul writes, "Make *every* effort to keep the unity of the Spirit through the bond of peace." Even 2,000 years ago, Paul was saying, "Be vigilant. The unity of the Church is of the highest importance. You must stay bonded together in peace."

When the dynamic I described above happens in the Church, it's like a virus. A person hangs onto their anger and then often spreads it to others. Sides are taken, and before you know it, the virus has taken hold. It can be over a personal matter or some decision made or a million other things. Any time you have a community of people, there is going to be conflict of some kind. In some ways, it can actually indicate that relationships have gotten deep enough for someone to be honest. Like a healthy marriage, we will probably experience disagreements in a church family or a small group or between friends within the Church. It's what we do with those disagreements that is important. That is what we're going to discuss now—what to do with conflict.

The first step in standing against the Devil through peace is to recognize just how serious unresolved conflict is to our lives and to the life of the Church.

Step 2: Examine Yourself First

Let's say that you have a conflict with someone at work or in your family or in your church. You think, "I do not want to give the Devil a foothold with this thing. I am motivated to do something about it." What do you do?

The first thing to do seems simple, but is actually pretty counterintuitive. In Ephesians 4:26, Paul says, "in your anger do not sin." It's a human response to feel emotions of anger at times, but the sin is when we remain in that place of anger. We hold onto that anger. In fact, if we're honest, sometimes we even enjoy being angry. It can feel kind of good.

When we remain in our anger, who are we usually focused on? The person who has wronged us, right? We're thinking about what was said or done to us. We're often thinking about what kind of person could do or say such a thing. We replay a conversation in our head, over and over and over. We get angrier and angrier and angrier.

What usually doesn't occur to us is to examine ourselves. To ask the difficult questions: What role have I played in the conflict? What have I said or done that was not helpful or even hurtful? What attitude have I been holding on to that has played into this problem?

Matthew 7:3-5

3"Why do you look at the speck of sawdust in your brother's eye and pay no attention to the plank in your own eye? 4How can you say to your brother, 'Let me take the speck out of your eye,' when all the time there is a plank in your own eye? 5You hypocrite, first take the plank out of your own eye, and then you will see clearly to remove the speck from your brother's eye."

First take the plank out of your eye. Examine yourself first, and then you'll have a clearer picture of the problem and the other person's role in it. This is where prayer can really help—asking God to lovingly but firmly remove the plank and show you your part. This is not easy. It is humbling. It doesn't feel as gratifying as anger and bitterness, at least not at first. This is what we had to do in our conflict with our neighbor. We examined our own wrongful attitudes and tried to see his perspective, and this changed how we approached the situation.

This is a very important step in all relational conflicts, but especially in marriage. Often when I'm counseling couples, I'll hear the complaints of one of the spouses. Sometimes they'll come alone at first and voice their frustrations. I validate their frustrations, but pretty quickly I'll ask the question, "So what do you see as your contribution to some of these problems?" Sometimes when I ask this question, the person will look at me with sort of a blank look. It becomes clear to me—and them—that this particular question has never crossed their minds.

When you do ask this question of yourself and pray about it, and then approach your spouse with a humble attitude, admitting your part in the conflict, you will often find that your spouse will be much less defensive and willing to admit his/her own part of the problem. This is true in other relationships as well.

Sign of Maturity

We can be encouraged that the righteousness of Christ is being formed in us when we find ourselves regularly and quickly asking ourselves that tough question, "What is my part in this problem?" I believe this is one important benchmark of maturity for Christ-followers. Being humble enough to admit that we may have been at fault in some way shows that we have shed some of the pride that so easily fills the human heart.

Unfortunately, many Christ-followers still struggle with this issue of pride. We may have grown in many ways into the character of Jesus, but when conflict comes, it's easy to slip into patterns of pride and the feeling that we are in the right. It's a hard change to make. That's why it's so significant when this aspect of humility begins to grow in our lives. We're taking up the breastplate of righteousness in a significant way.

You've taken the step of recognizing the seriousness of unresolved conflict and how it gives the Devil a foothold in your life, and you've taken the step to examine your own heart in the situation. Now we come to the big step: take the initiative.

Step 3: Take the Initiative

Listen to the advice of Jesus in **Matthew 5:23-24**:

> [23]"Therefore, if you are offering your gift at the altar and there remember that your brother or sister has something against you, [24]leave your gift there in front of the altar. First go and be reconciled to them; then come and offer your gift.

First go... This should be our motto when it comes to conflict with others. Sometimes our instinct is to say, "Oh, I'll just let it go. Let it fade away." But usually, it doesn't. If the memory of the situation keeps returning to you, or the feelings of hurt or anger linger, then it has not faded away. You know when it is still affecting you.

Or our instinct is to say, "Hey, let them come to me and apologize." But Jesus says, "No. Don't hope it fades away. Don't wait until they come to you. You go to them. You examine your own heart and then take the initiative and go to them. Be a peacemaker. Go and make peace."

Our instinct is to do everything except go to the person. Often our instinct is to talk to others about the situation, explaining our perspective, how we've been wronged. Or to talk to ourselves about it and play out in our minds what happened or what we would like to say to them. None of these really help. The only thing that helps is to talk to God about it and then to go and talk to the person and, as Jesus says, "be reconciled" with them.

Sometimes it's the case that the person doesn't even know that they've hurt us. Until we go to them and express this in a gentle way, we will carry around this hurt. Sometimes we've done more of the hurting, and sometimes it's mutual. Regardless, we need to go.

Jesus and Paul both say to do this quickly. Jesus says, "Leave your gift at the altar and go." Don't waste any time. Reconciliation should be a high priority. Jesus makes it clear that our moving quickly toward reconciliation is important to him. Notice that he chooses a very spiritual act—placing your offerings to God—and says, "Making things right with your Christian brother or sister or colleague or spouse is a spiritual act and is just as important. In fact, go do that first and then come back to give your offering."

Paul says, "Do not let the sun go down while you are still angry." Take care of it as soon as possible. Some conflicts drag on for days, weeks, months, years. Paul and Jesus say, "Drop everything and go. Nip it in the bud. Don't give the Devil a foothold in your life."

Conclusion

A friend who has walked with Christ for a good while was telling me about a recent breakfast he had with a couple of guys who were also from his church. He said that he got pretty opinionated about the situation they were all discussing, and it got a little personal, particularly with one of his friends. Throughout the morning after he had left, he said that he just didn't feel good about what he had said; he didn't feel at peace with himself or his friend.

That afternoon, he called his friend and said, "I've called to tell you that I've broken my leg." His friend was surprised and exclaimed, "Broken your leg?!" He said, "Yeah, I've been kicking myself so many times that I broke my leg." He went on to apologize and then ended by saying, "I want you to know that you are a dear friend and brother in Christ, and your friendship means a lot to me."

Here is a follower of Christ who understood the seriousness of unresolved conflict. He examined his own heart and actions and quickly went to his friend to make things right. He put on his shoes of peace, and the Devil never had a chance.

Spiritual Reading – Part 2
Destructive Conflict

The second reading is a brief article called *Destructive Conflict: Recognize it. Stop it.*, written by Mary Yerkes. In it, she discusses what to do in serious situations where the other person is unwilling to change, and the conflict is destructive as a result.

> "Danger. Pesticides. Keep people, especially children and pets away from the area being treated," read the signs posted along the path. I swung wide to the left, being careful to lead my dog away from the toxic environment as we continued our afternoon walk. For the remainder of the walk, I found myself thinking, "Wouldn't it be great if people came with warning signs, too? 'Danger: Toxic Person.' 'Warning: Destructive Conflict Ahead."
>
> In a sense, they do. Destructive conflict flows from unhealthy people and relationships. Where there is destructive conflict, you will often find a pattern of cruelty, neglect, deception, control, indifference and even abuse in the relationship. What differentiates destructive conflict form healthy disagreement is that it involves a pattern of unhealthy communication. Destructive conflict flows from individuals who consistently fail to admit their weakness, lie, rationalize, deny, apologize instead of changing their behavior, blame others instead of "owning" their part of the problem and who are defensive instead of open to feedback. Similar to ingesting poison, a steady diet of destructive conflict can kill you – emotionally, spiritually and even physically. Just ask David.
>
> **Destructive Conflict**
>
> He is still working to overcome the damage caused by destructive conflict. Raised in a home where conflict deteriorated into emotional, verbal and even physical abuse, he grew up thinking the way he was treated was "normal". "While in college I accepted Christ," says David. "He helped me to forgive my abusers and brought healthy relationships into my life. Unfortunately, my abusers didn't change; and for years I could not deal with the emotional fallout." To overcome the damage caused by years of unhealthy conflict, David attended anger management classes at a local church, worked with a mentor, and continues to see a Christian psychologist, who is helping him apply biblical truth to his sense of self and his relationships. "My abusive family members haven't changed," says David. "I have."

How to Deal with Destructive Conflict

Leslie Vernick, licensed clinical social worker and author of The Emotionally Destructive Relationship: Seeing It, Stopping It, Surviving It, works with individuals like David. She identifies three steps, based on Matthew 18:15-17, we should take when dealing with destructive conflict:

Speak up. "*If your brother sins against you, go and show him his fault, just between the two of you*" (Matthew 18:15 NIV). "God calls us to be peacemakers, not peacekeepers," points out Vernick. She says pursuing peace might mean risking conflict in order to bring about a genuine peace (Psalm 42:14; Hebrews 12:14 NIV). Speaking up is very different from venting, which can have negative consequences. We should speak the truth to someone in love after we have spent time praying and preparing for our time together. Approach that person in gentleness and with humility. (Galatians 6:1 NIV).

Stand up. "But if he will not listen, take one or two others along, so that 'every matter may be established by the testimony of two or three witnesses" (Matthew 18:16 NIV). God calls us to stand against sin, evil, deception, abuse and wickedness. When others are blind to their sing, God calls us to enlist the help of others. With supportive person or church by your side, say, "I will not continue to live in fear," "be lied to" or "be degraded."

Step back. "If he refuses to listen even to the church, treat him as you would a pagan or a tax collector (Matthew 18:17 NIV)," says Jesus. In biblical culture, Jews did not have close, personal relationships with pagans and tax collectors. Vernick says when someone refuses to respond to our concerns, the relationship changes. "You cannot have fellowship with someone who refuses to respect your feelings, doesn't' care about you, won't respect you and who isn't honest. When we step back from the relationship, it helps minimize the damage and gives the other person time to reflect on his behavior and the relationship. It sends a message that a pattern of sinful, destructive behaviors is unacceptable to us and to God.

She points out that even when we find it necessary to step back from a situation, God calls us to love. The apostle Paul says, "*We bless those who curse us. We are patient with those who abuse us,*" (1 Corinthians 4:12 NIV). And in Romans 13:10, "*Love does no harm* (NIV)."

As we learn to identify destructive conflict and apply God's Word to our situations, we can minimize its damage in our lives. What's more, we move from victim to victor, honoring God in even the most difficult of circumstances.

For more resources on resolving conflict, go to www.peacemaker.net.

Questions for Reflection and Discussion

- What makes it difficult to examine your own role in a conflict?

- Have you used any of the principles mentioned in either reading and found them helpful? If so, in what ways?

- During your prayer time, ask for God's help in whatever aspect of resolving conflict that is most challenging for you.

Spiritual Practices
Reading Proverbs

As mentioned in the Soaking in Scripture section, Proverbs is loaded with wisdom and practical help. A regular "diet" of reading Proverbs can be very helpful. A good practice to consider for the future is reading through one chapter of Proverbs a day. There are thirty-one chapters, making it perfect for reading through the entire book in a month. This is the practice that Billy Graham has followed for many years (and things have worked out pretty well for him!).

To get a taste of this, look at today's date. Then take that number and read the corresponding chapter of Proverbs. If it is December 17th, for example, then you would read Proverbs, Chapter 17.

After reading through the chapter, go back and see if there are one or two verses that caught your attention. Because each chapter contains so much information, it is usually best to focus in on one or two truths for your life. Reflect on these truths and what they might mean for your life. Try to be as specific as possible. Take some time to talk to God or journal about what this might look like in your life. See how he might speak to you about it.

As we seek to be transformed by God, growing in the fruit of the Spirit, we need to be aware of particular challenges within our culture that can trip us up and keep us from experiencing everything God wants for us.

Every culture or society has particular patterns of sin embedded in that culture because of its history and development over the years. The Devil uses these societal patterns of sin (sometimes referred to as strongholds) to damage the lives of individuals, including Christ-followers. This can even happen on a regional level. For example, a region of a country may have had a deep pattern of racism that continues to impact people.

Because these patterns of sin are so embedded in our culture, we may not recognize that they are a part of our lives and thinking and that they are not what God wants for our lives. Without realizing it, we can be choosing the ways of our culture over God's ways. We need to first identify these cultural patterns of sin and then seek to understand and live out God's perspective on these issues.

In our American society, two of the strongest patterns of cultural sin are materialism and a distorted understanding of sexuality. These probably don't come as a surprise, but many of us, even as followers of Christ, probably don't recognize the depth to which they impact us. Our culture is so saturated with messages about these two areas, which are counter to the truth and wisdom of God, that it is difficult to identify the difference.

In our future session on God's perspective on money, we will look at the challenge of materialism and how it affects us and keeps us from living out God's mission in our lives. This week, we will look at the area of sexual wholeness. Because this issue often affects men and women in different ways, some of the materials will be designed for men and some for women.

For men, one of the biggest challenges tends to be lust. For women, a common challenge is having a healthy self-image due to our society's distorted views on beauty and physical appearance. To address these issues, the *Digging into Scripture* and *Spiritual Reading* sections will each have a men's version and women's version.

This is another important area to support one another in as we share from our personal lives each week in our groups. This kind of support will bring the type of life change that is challenging, but makes a real difference in our lives.

Note: The spiritual practice we will try out this week is fasting. Because this will require planning, it will be helpful to look at this section early in the week.

Spiritual Practice
Fasting

This week, we are going to "kick it up a notch" and explore the spiritual practice of fasting. Many Christians are not aware of the broad use of fasting in the Bible, as well as the spiritual and physical benefits of fasting. Fasting is particularly beneficial when you have a focus or question going into your time of fasting. This could be a significant decision you are trying to make, a new season of your life (new living location, new job, or new life stage), or a crisis you or someone you know is going through.

If the area of sexuality is a challenge for you in one form or another (through temptation, self-image issues, or other ways), this would be a good focus for your time of fasting, in order to see what God might show you. If not, you may want to choose another area of focus. You will find thoughts and instructions for fasting below.

The general premise or benefit of fasting is that the lack of food and the accompanying hunger that comes with it is a great method for reminding us of God and focusing us on God throughout the day. In addition, if at all possible, take the time you normally would spend eating and use it to pray and spend time in God's Word. If you simply don't eat, not much will be accomplished besides being hungry!

Read over the information below. Choose the type of fast you would like to do this week and choose the day(s) you will do the fast. I would suggest the partial, 24-hour fast described below (please note that it is a good idea to drink juice as well as water; a water-only fast is more challenging). If you have fasted from food before, you may want to try a "normal" fast or a longer fast (36-hours or longer). Fasting from something other than food is also described below so that you can utilize this type of fast in the future. A food fast, however, is recommended for this week's experience. Make sure to write down your reflections from your time of fasting either in a journal or in this workbook to share later with your group.

Why Should We Fast?

- Jesus, along with many other biblical leaders, fasted. It is clear that those who have walked closely with God have utilized fasting as one way to draw closer to him and to be led by him in challenging times or times of decision.

- Particularly when we have an area of focus during the fast, God can speak to us more clearly, because we are intentionally trying to be tuned in to him during the fasting period.

- Fasting, when combined with prayer, helps us realize our dependence on God. When we are denied our usual physical sustenance through food, we realize that God is truly the Bread of Life and provides what we need. When we feel pangs of hunger and use them to draw us to God in prayer, it deepens our connection and reliance upon him.

- Fasting can also reveal things that are controlling us, such as pride, anger, and bitterness. We are more attuned to God and also more attuned to what is going on within us.

- Fasting can reveal things that have become a barrier between us and God. In these cases, it could be helpful to fast from some activity that we suspect has become a place we run to instead of running to God. Some examples would be watching TV, spending time on the internet or computer, or shopping. Fasting from one or more of these activities for a period of time and using that time to be with God instead may reveal a good deal about what is going on within us, as well as practically freeing up time to be with God.

Different Types of Fasting

- Normal Fast: Fasting from all foods and drinks other than water for a specified period of time. This is the most stringent type of fast and should normally be tried only after some experience with a partial fast.

- Partial Fast: Similar to a normal fast, but with some exceptions. This type typically includes drinking juice along with water. This is a good way to start for those learning to fast.

- 24-Hour Fast: Skipping two meals during a 24-hour period. For example, eating dinner, fasting from breakfast and lunch the following day, and breaking the fast by eating dinner. A partial 24-hour fast—skipping two meals and drinking only juice and water—is the recommended way to begin fasting.

- 36-Hour Fast: Skipping three meals. This is recommended after several experiences with a 24-hour fast. Longer fasts of several days can be beneficial if one has experienced shorter fasts.

- Non-Food Fasts: Other activities can be abstained from for a period of time. Typically, a minimum period of several weeks is needed to begin experiencing some of the benefits of this type of fast.

Special Considerations

- Fasting is intended to be a private discipline between you and God and should be discussed with others only when you feel it will encourage them. In addition, *all types of fasting should be accompanied by prayer to be effective.* In particular, utilize what would be your normal meal times to pray.

- There are normal physical challenges that often accompany fasting from food: hunger pains, headaches, less energy, and even bad breath! These are normal and will not harm the body. In fact, fasting is helpful in that it releases unhealthy toxins that have been stored in the body.

- Individuals should not fast if they are expectant mothers, sick, traveling, under undue stress, or suffering from a debilitating physical condition.

Soaking in Scripture

This is an excellent passage to lodge in our hearts and minds. It concisely captures the essence of what we discussed in the introduction concerning the patterns of our culture.

Romans 12:2

Do not conform to the pattern of this world, but be transformed by the renewing of your mind. *Then you will be able to test and approve what God's will is—his good, pleasing and perfect will.*

- Read the portion in bold several times slowly in an effort to let it soak into your heart and mind. Circle any key words and reflect on them.

- Read the entire passage. Write your own paraphrase of the passage.

- The Message version of this passage is a very helpful paraphrase. Read the paraphrase below, and then write down what stands out to you.

Romans 12:2 (MSG)

Don't become so well-adjusted to your culture that you fit into it without even thinking. Instead, fix your attention on God. You'll be changed from the inside out. Readily recognize what he wants from you, and quickly respond to it. Unlike the culture around you, always dragging you down to its level of immaturity, God brings the best out of you, develops well-formed maturity in you.

- During your prayer time, share with God any sinful cultural patterns you believe are affecting you. Ask for his help and listen for any direction or ideas he may provide. If no patterns are apparent, ask him to show you any that may be impacting you.

Digging into Scripture (For Women)

One of the lies that women can pick up from our society is that they are not beautiful enough. This lie can lead to a distorted self-image, harm to relationships with other women, and challenges to sexual intimacy in marriage. This is a good passage, because it counters those lies with God's truth.

A few weeks ago, we learned about the spiritual practice called lectio divina, where God may use one phrase or word to speak to us in a personal way. This is a good practice for this passage. Read the passage slowly and see if any word or phrase stands out to you. Ask God to show you what he may be saying to you in a personal way through that word or phrase. If it helps, you may want to look back over the lectio divina directions (Session 13, Spiritual Practice) before reading the passage.

Allow God to speak to you personally through this passage concerning the truth about how *he* sees you. About how *he* created you.

Psalm 139:13-16 (MSG)

Oh yes, you shaped me first inside, then out;
*   you formed me in my mother's womb.*
I thank you, High God—you're breathtaking!
*   Body and soul, I am marvelously made!*
*   I worship in adoration—what a creation!*
You know me inside and out,
*   you know every bone in my body;*
You know exactly how I was made, bit by bit,
*   how I was sculpted from nothing into something.*
Like an open book, you watched me grow from conception to birth;
*   all the stages of my life were spread out before you,*
The days of my life all prepared
*   before I'd even lived one day.*

- **Read**
- **Reflect**
- **Respond**
- **Rest**

Digging into Scripture (For Men)

This passage is an account of King David's temptation and fall to sexual sin. It is a longer passage, but it is helpful in seeing how the process of temptation often works, as well as the consequences of sin in general and sexual sin in particular. Because this is a longer passage, you will find questions below to provide some guidance. The rest of the story is continued in Chapter 12. Although it may be too much to study, it would be helpful to read in order to get the full picture.

2 Samuel 11:1-27

[1]*In the spring, at the time when kings go off to war, David sent Joab out with the king's men and the whole Israelite army. They destroyed the Ammonites and besieged Rabbah. But David remained in Jerusalem.*

[2]*One evening David got up from his bed and walked around on the roof of the palace. From the roof he saw a woman bathing. The woman was very beautiful,* [3]*and David sent someone to find out about her. The man said, "She is Bathsheba, the daughter of Eliam and the wife of Uriah the Hittite."* [4]*Then David sent messengers to get her. She came to him, and he slept with her. (Now she was purifying herself from her monthly uncleanness.) Then she went back home.* [5]*The woman conceived and sent word to David, saying, "I am pregnant."*

[6]*So David sent this word to Joab: "Send me Uriah the Hittite." And Joab sent him to David.* [7]*When Uriah came to him, David asked him how Joab was, how the soldiers were and how the war was going.* [8]*Then David said to Uriah, "Go down to your house and wash your feet." So Uriah left the palace, and a gift from the king was sent after him.* [9]*But Uriah slept at the entrance to the palace with all his master's servants and did not go down to his house.*

[10]*David was told, "Uriah did not go home." So he asked Uriah, "Haven't you just come from a military campaign? Why didn't you go home?"*

[11]*Uriah said to David, "The ark and Israel and Judah are staying in tents,[a] and my commander Joab and my lord's men are camped in the open country. How could I go to my house to eat and drink and make love to my wife? As surely as you live, I will not do such a thing!"*

[12]*Then David said to him, "Stay here one more day, and tomorrow I will send you back." So Uriah remained in Jerusalem that day and the next.* [13]*At David's invitation, he ate and drank with him, and David made him drunk. But in the evening Uriah went out to sleep on his mat among his master's servants; he did not go home.*

[14]*In the morning David wrote a letter to Joab and sent it with Uriah.* [15]*In it he wrote, "Put Uriah out in front where the fighting is fiercest. Then withdraw from him so he will be struck down and die."*

[16]*So while Joab had the city under siege, he put Uriah at a place where he knew the strongest defenders were.* [17]*When the men of the city came out and fought against*

Joab, some of the men in David's army fell; moreover, Uriah the Hittite died.

[18]Joab sent David a full account of the battle. [19]He instructed the messenger: "When you have finished giving the king this account of the battle, [20]the king's anger may flare up, and he may ask you, 'Why did you get so close to the city to fight? Didn't you know they would shoot arrows from the wall? [21]Who killed Abimelek son of Jerub-Besheth? Didn't a woman drop an upper millstone on him from the wall, so that he died in Thebez? Why did you get so close to the wall?' If he asks you this, then say to him, 'Moreover, your servant Uriah the Hittite is dead.'"

[22]The messenger set out, and when he arrived he told David everything Joab had sent him to say. [23]The messenger said to David, "The men overpowered us and came out against us in the open, but we drove them back to the entrance of the city gate. [24]Then the archers shot arrows at your servants from the wall, and some of the king's men died. Moreover, your servant Uriah the Hittite is dead."

[25]David told the messenger, "Say this to Joab: 'Don't let this upset you; the sword devours one as well as another. Press the attack against the city and destroy it.' Say this to encourage Joab."

[26]When Uriah's wife heard that her husband was dead, she mourned for him. [27]After the time of mourning was over, David had her brought to his house, and she became his wife and bore him a son. But the thing David had done displeased the LORD.

Observation

- What do you see as the steps of temptation, which led to David's initial sin?

- What consequences or further sin do you see coming from that initial sin?

Interpretation

Application

📖 Spiritual Reading (For Women)

Our reading this week comes from a book and program called *Unveil: Beginning the Process of Lust Free Living*. This eight-week course is the women's counterpart to the men's program called *Dangerous Men: the Process of Lust Free Living*. Both programs attempt to address the deeper issues surrounding this issue for men and women, as well as some practical issues, which may or may not be more obvious.

Portions from several chapters have been selected to provide some beginning help and to spark conversation. The themes covered include the following: understanding the critical importance of where we find our identity, celebrating God's gift of sexuality, and having a deeper understanding of how temptation works in the area of sexuality. One of the biggest helps for some may be in realizing that challenges surrounding sexuality is an issue in their lives. By broadening our understanding, we may come to realize that this is an area in which God wants to begin showing us some things for our lives.

Obviously, this topic is personal in nature. Hopefully by now you have developed some trust in your group and would feel comfortable sharing some of your feelings and experiences in this area. By bringing things into the light, we can begin to break the power of the enemy, of sin, and of our culture in our lives.

If you or others in the group find this material helpful, you may want to consider going through the full course in the future. If you would like more information, go to www.LustFreeLiving.org.

Identity Theft – Taking Your Life Back

And that's the way it was with us before Christ came. We were slaves to the spiritual powers of this world. But when the right time came, God sent his Son, born of a woman, subject to the law. God sent him to buy freedom for us who were his slaves of the law, so that he could adopt us as his very own children. And because you Gentiles have become his children, God has sent the Spirit of his Son into your hearts, and now you can call God your dear Father. Now you are no longer a slave but God's own child. And since you are his child, everything he has belongs to you. (**Galatians 4:3-7 NLT**)

Yet to all who received him, to those who believed in his name, he gave the right to become children of God. (**John 1:12**)

Concept

"Understanding your identity in Christ is absolutely essential for your success at living a victorious Christian life. No person can consistently behave in a way that's inconsistent with the way he perceives himself."[1]Dr. Neil T. Anderson

Who we are and how we see ourselves determines now we act and live, so this question of identity is of extreme importance to us. Often this seems to be the missing chapter in our thinking.

In this chapter I will give you an outline view of the concepts, but I think you should do more reading on the subject later. One of the best books and teaching on this subject is *Victory Over Darkness* by Dr. Neil T. Anderson. I highly recommend you read it. I also recommend Donald Miller's book *Searching for God Knows What*.

Fighting

Read the following statements from a bookmark from *Freedom In Christ Ministries*. See if you can tell which statements are God's truth and which ones are lies from the evil one. Where do you really get your identity from?

- You are a sinner because you sin.
- You are a saint (one declared righteous by God) who sins.

- Your identity comes from what you have done.
- Your identity comes from what God has done for you.

- Your identity comes from what people say about you.
- Your identity comes from what God says about you.

- Your behavior tells you what to believe about yourself.
- Your belief about yourself determines your behavior.

Yes, the first lines are all lies. But the sad fact is that most of us believe or at least live by them. When we gave our lives to Jesus and started following Him there wasn't a "reset" button that we could push to make all our old habits (or what the Bible calls our flesh) go away. *We have to learn how to renew our minds.*

> *Do not conform any longer to the pattern of this world, but be transformed by the renewing of your mind. Then you will be able to test and approve what God's will is – is good, pleasing and perfect will* (**Romans 12:2**).

We have to choose to believe the promises of God about us. We have to get God's truth into our minds. Not only do we need to think as we should about who we are, we must also let these truths filter into our hearts (easier said than done).

God's Girl

Sometimes familiarity is a problem with those of us who have grown up in the Christian church. We hear about a concept or truth so many times that it fails to become a reality to us.

The reality is that we really are God's children, adopted into His family. Our identity in Jesus Christ is one of the most basic principles in the Bible. We seem to intellectually know it, but it does not permeate our lives like it should. We need our hearts to soak in this truth.

Here is the truth (read these out loud):

> *His unchanging plan has always been to adopt us into his own family by bringing us to himself through Jesus Christ. And this gave him great pleasure* (Ephesians 1:5 NLT).

I love that last part "...*this gave him great pleasure."*

But to all who believed him and accepted him, he gave the right to become children of God. They are reborn! This is not a physical birth resulting from human passion or plan – this rebirth comes from God (John 1:12 – 13 NLT).

But the person who is joined to the Lord is one spirit with him (I Corinthians 6:17 NLT).

It is difficult to sink this truth into our hearts. We have all heard it said that we are a child of God, but somehow we still don't get it. Identity is a concept that we have to get from the head to the heart in order to live it out every day. If we change one word it can become new to us. It can start to mean something again. Let's change the word "children" to "girl." Say it out loud, "We are God's girls, I am God's girl. I am His daughter, adopted into His family, He is my daddy, and I am His girl." No matter our age, we are our daddy's little girl. Now doesn't that somehow resonate with all of us? What girl hasn't at one time wanted to associate herself as her daddy's little girl? Even if our relationship with our earthly father didn't fit this idea, if we are honest, we all have that desire somewhere in us. And this is just what we are to our Father and our Creator – *his girl*!

I heard a saying once and I adapted it to this: *Be a woman to women, a warrior to demons, and always a child of God.* You are God's girl! He is your Father!

The more you say that out loud, the more it becomes believable for you. However, it is not true because you say it to yourself many times; it is true because the Bible says it is true, and you make the choice to believe the truth. It is also spoken to your heart by the Holy Spirit, and it becomes real in your soul.

We often seem to go to lesser gods to satisfy our wants, needs and desires. Somehow they never satisfy our deep longings. We turn to rebellion, cynicism, alcohol, lust and other gods for comfort. We have trouble learning how to go to the true Comforter as our only source of comfort.

Jesus talks to us about how to abide in His love.

I am the vine; you are the branches. Those who remain in me, and I in them, will produce much fruit. For apart from me you can do nothing. Anyone who does not remain in me is thrown away like a useless branch and withers. Such branches are gathered into a pile to be burned. But if you remain in me and my words remain in you, you may ask for anything you want, and it will be granted! When you produce much fruit, you are my true disciples. This brings great glory to my Father. I have loved you even as the Father has loved me. Remain in my love (**John 15:5-9 NLT**).

We seem to wander from His love so easily and without much of a fight. Hopefully as you go through the rest of the study you will learn how to fight and how to remain in your true identity. You are truly God's girl! Satan is always opposed to God's truth and will always try to trick us into thinking and believing that we are unacceptable, unworthy and will never be seen by God as important. We need to abide in who we are in Christ; abide in Him, who is in us.

Sexuality: Celebrating It!

So God created human beings in his own image. In the image of God he created them; male and female he created them. (**Genesis 1:27 NLT**)

Concept

Celebrate our sexuality? How in the world do you do that and remain pure before God and pure in relationships?

For many of us, we have grown up not clearly understanding our sexuality and God's intentions for it. Maybe we tried to stuff, stifle or ignore it because we thought it was a negative thing. That could not be more false. In order to celebrate this amazing part of who God created us to be, we must first uncover some lies so we can clearly see the truth given to us in God's word.

What is true?
- We are created in God's image.
- God created sex.
- God created us sexual people.
- God created us male and female.
- God wants us to have great sex (after all He invented it).
- God intended sexual intercourse to be one of the greatest expressions of marital intimacy.

Of course, Satan will try to mess up something that is this positive and good for humans. Satan twists our sexuality from something wonderful, as God intended it to be, into something shameful, lustful, strictly physical and/or something to control to use as a source of power. *We need to rethink how we think about our sexuality.*

We are sexual. We have physical desires. Our bodies were made by God to do certain things to produce stimulation and to respond physically in ways that are amazing. We need to celebrate and enjoy that. Our mind, our emotions and our spirit were all created to desire certain things sexually and to respond in a way that is very natural and positive. With this in mind, the question that follows is often, "Then what are we to do with this part of us?" The answer is simple: *Enjoy being sexual! Celebrate it!* That doesn't mean take advantage of it, tempt with it, manipulate it or enhance it. *Just enjoy being a sexual person.* This might not make sense to man of us at first, so let's look at it through a different example:

Most of us love to eat. We have this craving and desire for food. We eat to nourish our bodies. So let's say we have just had a meal and our stomach is satisfied. We go for a walk and pass a bakery that has been baking fresh goods all day. The aroma is amazing and our mouths are watering even though we aren't hungry.

It is so cool that our bodies respond in this way. It is so natural and good. Part of why God created us to respond this way is so we might enjoy nourishing our body when it is time to eat. We should celebrate and enjoy the way our intricate bodies work in times like this.

That doesn't mean we should bolt into the bakery and indulge in everything they have to offer us. A healthy response would be to pause and notice how our body is responding to our senses, celebrate how cool it is and move on.

So *enjoy* and *celebrate* your sexuality! Be aware of all that it is, how it all works and how enjoyable that part of you is. It is natural, good and God-given.

Here is the hard part: Our surroundings (the world) mess with our minds from the time we are little. We are told the beautiful, erotic and sexual parts of us are something to use for power and self-fulfillment. We receive the message we are no longer simply beautiful just as we are, but we are to become a "temptress" to draw the attention of men.

Then as Christians we are taught we are to live pure and "save ourselves" until we are married. Most people have interpreted that to mean we are to stuff or hide the sexual aspects of who we are and not recognize then until we are married. When those two worlds collide there is confusion, shame, fear, self-destruction, manipulation, etc. It is hard to understand God made us sexual – married or unmarried, man or woman – and He wants us to celebrate that part of us.

Funny how the enemy switches sides so quickly. One minute he's whispering in our ear, "It's okay to fantasize about that guy. It's not going to hurt anything." So we go ahead and indulge in lustful thinking. Then the enemy shows up again, but this time he's shooting accusations at us, "You really screwed up. You are so stupid – you did it again! See, I knew you weren't good enough to be a Christian." Lies, lies and more lies, always accusing us: One of Satan's greatest desires is to keep us away from God and the enjoyment and freedom that come from living within God's boundaries for us.

Along with enjoying how we were created, God also wants us to be free. In fact this is the key to truly enjoying our sexuality. He wants us to be:

- Free from all the stereotypes the world puts on us as to what is beautiful and sexy.
- Free from the desperate need for acceptance from a man.
- Free from the desire to gain power and control by using our bodies to manipulate men (that "temptress" role).
- Free from any addictions we have.
- Free from lust.
- Free from romance novels, women's magazines, TV shows and Internet sites that keep us thinking lustfully.
- Free from pornography and pornographic stories.
- Free from being a slave in any way to masturbation.
- Free from the game of comparison with other women.
- Free from our old sinful nature with all its sexual lusts.

He wants us to stop living in the bondage of the standards of the world, of our twisted interpretations of purity, of our painful experiences, and break free so we can celebrate, love and serve! It is in purity that we will experience the fullness of all that God intended our sexuality to be.

It is for freedom that Christ has set us free. Stand firm, then and do not let yourselves be burdened again by a yoke of slavery (**Galatians 5:1**).

God also wants us to enjoy Him, the one who made us this way. We don't want to get tricked into worshipping the thing that He created (sex). We need to enjoy worshipping the Creator Himself. After all, He is pretty creative!

Sexual Temptations: Understanding Them

James 1:13-14

When tempted, no one should say, "God is tempting me." For God cannot be tempted by evil, nor does he tempt anyone; but each one is tempted when, by his own evil desire, he is dragged away and enticed: Then after desire has conceived, it gives birth to sin; and sin, when it is full-grown, gives birth to death.

Concept

When a lustful thought comes into our heads (which for most women is often hard to recognize), it is not a sin according to James. It is a temptation; it only becomes a sin when, by our evil desire, we allow it to pull us into dwelling on the lustful thought. When we continue thinking about it, the thought is conceived in our mind and becomes sin.

Before we go on, it is important to make clear what lust looks like in women's lives. This clarity is necessary because lust in a woman's life looks different than it does in a man's, and it usually goes unnoticed. For many of us, we have often been confused about what lust is or have not even considered that this is an issue for women. *One of the greatest ways the evil one has kept women in bondage to lust is by deceiving us into thinking we simply don't struggle with it.* For many Christian women, when we think about lust we think of what we need to do to protect the men around us from it. First of all, we don't have the ultimate power to do that because their lust is beyond our control. It is a battle that can only be won by men as they fight against it spiritually first.

Secondly, we need to recognize the lust in our own lives and deal with it with power and consistency. It is then that we are able to live in purity and serve ourselves and one another out of freedom and celebration.

I think one of the easiest and best definitions of lust is the one we already quoted by Miles McPherson, *"Lust wants to please self at the expense of someone else because lust wants to get."* The definition isn't, "Lust is constantly envisioning or looking at naked people and having an uncontrollable urge to fantasize about having sex with them."

No, that may be what lust ends up looking like for some, but the root issue is much deeper. Another great way to define lust is " a desire (which is a good and natural thing) becomes what we think is a need." Youth Specialties put out a book called

"Good Sex," and they did a great job of making it clear when a desire becomes unhealthy, gives birth to temptations, and then becomes sin. Follow this description:

> *Desire is so easily twisted.*
> *"I like it" becomes "I want it".*
> *"I want it" becomes "I need it".*
> *"I need it" becomes "you owe it to me".*
> *Which becomes "never mind, I'll just take it".* [2]

When we look at that in terms of our attitude towards God regarding our desires and the way our flesh works (temptation), it makes things pretty clear. We have these God-given, healthy desires that turn into what we think of as needs that we meet through our own efforts and control.

So, because of how God created us as women, some of our natural and deepest desires are to be *beautiful, chosen, needed, adored, protected, irreplaceable* and *valued*. When we feel all of those things, we are very stimulated in every way. *This is a good thing!*

But the dilemma is that in our world today it is pretty hard to feel that way in a pure and healthy sense. Part of the reason is because men are incapable of meeting those desires without Christ. Sometimes, even if the men are healthy and serving or loving us through Christ, we struggle to receive what they have to offer us because our expectations and ideas are distorted. Let's look at the distorted "stuff" a bit.

The world has done a great job of distorting beauty to "sexiness," so we have no clue that what defines our beauty really has nothing to do with outward appearance (although in our freedom, that beauty will shine all the way through to the outside).

Your beauty should not come from outward adornment, such as braided hair and the wearing of gold jewelry and fine clothes. Instead it should be that of your inner self, the unfading beauty of a gentle and quiet spirit, which is of great worth in God's sight . (**I Peter 3:3-4**).

We also have believed the lie that if we want our desires to be fulfilled, we have to *do something* or *be something*. Because we associate beauty with "sexiness," we make (or are tempted to make) many attempts on a daily basis, consciously and subconsciously, to exude this sex appeal with our bodies. We do this in hope of filling our desire to be chosen. There are many women who simply feel hopeless because they don't think they fit the *standards of "sexy" in our culture. This often leads to self-destructive behaviors in one way or another.*

Another thing we do to meet our desire ("need") to be chosen, is feed into men's lust. Sometimes it is in their lustful response to us that we feel *chosen, needed, adored,* etc. And if that's the best we can get, we'll settle for it. I'm sure by now you are following the twisted web. From this perspective, if we are honest with ourselves, probably most of us can say we have lived our lives far beyond the temptation stage and deep into the sin of our thought-life, self-image and lifestyle.

Ultimately, when you put all of this together and look at our sexual temptations as women, we most definitely struggle with physical temptation and lust, but even above that is the temptation to have power and control in order to have our desires met. All of this is sexual sin – *lust*. Wow, how crazy is that? God's creation of us as women to be uniquely sensitive and gentle has been absolutely messed up by the evil one. He has deceived us into thinking that we are to be powerful and controlling in order to get what we desire. This is such a mask to our true heart!

Incidentally, we can be fairly confident that most of these thoughts and thought processes are not even ours, but are pushed into our head by and evil source. It might just be our old habits (the flesh). The source doesn't really matter. The point is we need to "capture all of these thoughts and turn them over to Jesus." I know it is hard, because those thoughts are very deep and consuming, but we need to begin to pinpoint them, pull each one out and deal with each one in the light of Christ. The Steps to Freedom in Christ is an awesome too for this!

Fighting

Let's look at the verse in Corinthians again. *For though we live in the world, we do not wage war as the world does. The weapons we fight with are not the weapons of the world. On the contrary, they have divine power to demolish strongholds. We demolish arguments and every pretension that sets itself up against the knowledge of God, and we take captive every thought to make it obedient to Christ* (**2 Corinthians 10:3-5**).

Where do arguments and pretensions and thoughts take place? In our minds! The battleground is in our minds! Remember to always fight spiritually first. Self-discipline, emotional awareness and intellectual understanding all come later. This definitely goes against what is most natural for us, but God wants us to be warriors too. We need to take our thoughts captive and make them obedient to Christ *before* we get all caught up in our emotions. A lot of times we can spare ourselves pain when we fight this way first. We quickly discover when a thought is a lie, and it's over before the emotions even begin!

The fight described above could look like this: When you wake up in the morning and look in the mirror, what is the first thought that comes into your head about your body? Whether it's positive or negative, we need to offer a prayer of praise: "Dear Heavenly Father, You have created me a beautiful woman. I belong to you, and I thank you and praise you for your creation. I'm holding on to you, Jesus, my Lord and Savior, to help me enjoy my beauty and respond throughout my day with love and not lust." For most of us, many lies and temptations stem from the thoughts we have when we first glance at ourselves in the morning. Beginning right away, we need to fight spiritually and take captive many thoughts that we have always just bypassed as "normal".

The prayer should also be prayed as you look at a man who you consider beautiful. We too can be tempted and enticed into fantasy, or other sinful responses to our temptations, when we look at a man. Men aren't the only visual ones, and a big need for all of us as woman is to offer prayers of praise regarding one another.

Sometimes I think we find each other more fascinating and beautiful than men do. Unfortunately, the sin of lust in our lives greatly affects us in relationship with one another. We would radiate true beauty so much more if we were free to enjoy and celebrate our own beauty and the beauty of every other woman around us. *This is a huge battle for us!* Satan has a pretty strong grip on Christian women when it comes to our union, appreciation and love for each other. *Lust* often plays a very intricate and toxic role in our relationships with each other. (Boldly confess, discuss and pray about this now if you can.)

Remember, Satan cannot read our minds, so he won't obey our thoughts. Only God knows what you're thinking. So say the truth and reject the evil one out loud!

It is very important that we learn to immediately recognize when normal enjoyment of our sexuality becomes lustful and sinful. Then we can fight right away, giving no opening for Satan's "legal right" to bug us to try to pull us down with his lies.

So let's say a lustful thought comes to mind. Say out loud (unless you are in a crowded room or something, then say it under your breath), "No. In Jesus' name I reject this thought because I belong to Jesus, and I choose not to think like that. Get away from me Satan and every enemy of my Lord Jesus Christ." The exact words are not that important. The three keys here are to *recognize* the thoughts, *reject* the lies and *bring* them before Jesus.

It is very important to take captive each thought as soon as it hits our minds. Here are some examples from my life: I stand in my closet and think, "I look pretty good today, my body is up to par, my hair looks good, so I can wear that certain outfit. It will get me the attention I want." Or I used to see a guy and think, "He is good looking. I wonder what it would be like to kiss him." Or I see another woman and think, "She is so pretty. Why can't I have _____ like her?" If I don't take thoughts like that captive, later that day the thought from earlier will be dragging me away and enticing me before I even know it. A lot of times at this point, I'm not even consciously aware of the original thought. I usually don't become aware of it until after I have already given into the temptation.

This is why we need to take our thoughts captive as soon as they come into our minds. For a lot of us, it is hard to even know when these thoughts first come, so it will be good for you to practice openly discussing your thoughts and struggles with women. As you confess and bring them to light, you will become more aware of the thoughts the moment they come and you can begin to practice taking them captive.

Important Stuff

Most of the Christian writings I have read on the subject of sexual purity focused on what I call a defensive strategy. What I consider a defensive strategy is teaching people to look away when they see someone or something that might make them have lustful thoughts. There are defensive moves that all of us can make that I think are a must –basic fighting—such as a filter on our internet service or getting away from situations where we might be tempted too much. I think every battle plan must have a defense, or we will not win the fight. But if that is all we have then we are in trouble. We cannot and will not win without a good offense.

Our offensive plan laid out in LFL is to learn to fight *spiritually first*. Our offense is to fight with the truth of the Word of God, to renounce lies, accept truth and take every thought captive to Jesus –drawing our swords and fighting in the spiritual realm.

We need a great offense and defense. Both are needed; don't be fooled into thinking that obeying the defense plan alone will win this battle. Attack the lies of the enemy with the power of Jesus, and when the counter attack comes, then you can use some defensive strategies as well.

[1]*Dr. Neil T. Anderson,* Victory Over Darkness *(California: Regal Books – a division of Gospel Light Publications, Ventura, CA 93006), p 43.*
[2]*Jim Hancock with Kara Eckmann Powell,* Good Sex *(Michigan: Zondervan –Youth Specialties Books 2001), p 91.*

Questions for Reflection and Discussion

- How might really believing you are "God's girl" impact sexual issues in your life?

- What impacted you in the chapter on celebrating sexuality?

- The section on understanding sexual temptation included some important thoughts on the ways that our culture and the Devil distort sexuality in our lives and ways to respond to these distortions. Which distortion(s) or lies do you feel impact you the most? What step(s) would you like to try to counteract these distortions?

- During your prayer time, begin sharing with God any thoughts you have regarding anything that touched you through the reading. This could be healing you need, conviction you are sensing, practical wisdom that would help you, or some combination.

📖 Spiritual Reading (For Men)

Our reading this week comes from a program called *Lust Free Living*, an eight-week course designed to help Christian men find freedom in the area of sexual lust. There are several excerpts taken from the program's workbook, *Dangerous Men: the Process of Lust Free Living*. In these excerpts, you will begin to see that the area of sexual lust goes beyond mere resistance to temptation; it is a deeper issue. These excerpts will not address all of these deeper issues, but will provide a good start.

You will notice that the language that is used is quite straightforward. This is a book written by men for men.

The area of sexual lust is a struggle for many Christian men. If you struggle in this area, you are not strange or alone. This struggle does, however, create a stumbling block for many men who are trying to grow in their relationship with God. With this in mind, if you are struggling in this area, you are encouraged to share it with your group if you haven't already. This is an important area in which men can support one another.

For further information on the program, go to www.LustFreeLiving.org. If your group finds that this issue is a struggle for several members, you may want to take some time to focus on this area by going through the *Lust Free Living* materials. The group can take a break from the discipleship materials to complete the program or complete it in the future.

A great website for online accountability is www.covenanteyes.com. This program enables an accountability partner to have access to a listing of the websites you visit each week.

Identity theft

Yet all who received him, to those who believed in his name, he gave the right to become children of God (**John 1:12 NIV**).

And that's the way it was with us before Christ came. We were slaves to the spiritual powers of this world. But when the right time came, God sent his Son, born of a woman, subject to the law. God sent him to buy freedom for us who were slaves to the law, so that he could adopt us as his very own children. And because you Gentiles have become his children, God has sent the Spirit of his Son into your hearts, and now you can call God your dear Father. Now you are no longer a slave but God's own child. And since you are his child, everything he has belongs to you (Galatians 4:3-7 NLT).

Concept

"Understanding your identity in Christ is absolutely essential for your success at living a victorious Christian life. No person can consistently behave in a way that's inconsistent with the way he perceives himself."[2]

Who we are and how we see ourselves determines how we act and live. That is why this question of identity is of extreme importance to us. This seems to be the missing chapter in our thinking.

I will give you an outline view of the concepts, but I think you should do more reading on the subject later. One of the best books and teaching on this subject is *Victory Over Darkness* by Dr. Neil T. Anderson. I highly recommend that you read it. I also recommend Donald Miller's book *Searching for God Knows What*, which gives some interesting thoughts about identity.

Fighting

Read the following statements that I copied from a bookmark from Freedom In Christ Ministries. See if you can tell which statements are God's truth and which ones are lies of the Evil One.

- You are a sinner because you sin.
- You are a saint (one declared righteous by God) who sins.

- Your identity comes from what you have done.
- Your identity comes from what God has done for you.

- Your identity comes from what people say about you.
- Your identity comes from what God says about you.

- Your behavior tells you what to believe about yourself.
- Your belief about yourself determines your behavior.

Yes, the first lines are all lies. But the sad fact is that most of us believe or at least live by them. When we gave our lives to Jesus and started following Him there wasn't a "reset" button that we could push to make all our old habits (or what the Bible calls our flesh) go away. *We have to learn how to renew our minds.*

Do not conform any longer to the pattern of this world, but be transformed by the renewing of your mind. Then you will be able to test and approve what God's will is – his good, pleasing and perfect will (**Romans 12:2 NIV**).

We have to choose to believe the promises of God about us. We have to get God's truth into our minds. Not only do we need to think as we should about who we are, we must also let these truths filter into our hearts (easier said than done).

God's Boy

Sometimes familiarity is a problem with those of us who have grown up in the Christian church. Growing up we hear about a concept or truth so many times that it fails to become a reality for us.

The reality is that we really are God's children, adopted into his family. Our identity in Jesus Christ is one of the most basic principles in the Bible. We seem to intellectually know it but it does not permeate our lives like it should. We need our hearts to soak in this truth. We need our minds renewed.

Here is the truth (read these out loud):

His unchanging plan has always been to adopt us into his own family by bringing us to himself through Jesus Christ. And this gave him great pleasure (Ephesians 1:5 NLT).

I love that last part, "*this gave him great pleasure.*"

But to all who believed him and accepted him, he gave the right to become children of God. They are reborn! This is not a physical birth resulting from human passion or plan – this rebirth comes from God (John 1:12-13 NLT).

But he who unites himself with the Lord is one with him in spirit (I Corinthians 6:17 NLT).

It is difficult to sink this truth into our hearts and minds. We have all heard it said before that we are a child of God, but somehow we still don't get it. Identity is a concept that we have to get from the head to the heart in order to live it out every day. If we change one word, maybe it can become new to us. It can start to mean something again. Let's change the word "children" to "boy." Say it out loud, "*We are God's boys; I am God's boy. I am his son, adopted into his family, he is my dad and I am his boy.*" How does that feel and sound to you, any different? Even if our relationship with our earthly father didn't fit this idea, if we are honest, we all have that desire somewhere in us. We are God's beloved boy.

I heard a saying once and I adapted it to this: *Be a man to men, a warrior to demons, and always a child to God.* You are God's boy!

The more you say that out loud, the more it becomes believable for you. However, it is not true because you say it to yourself many times; it is true because the Bible says that it is true. It is also spoken to your heart from the Holy Spirit, and it becomes real in your soul.

We often seem to go to lesser gods to satisfy our wants, needs and desires, but in the end it never satisfies our deeper longings. We turn to rebellion, cynicism, alcohol, lust and other gods for comfort. We have trouble learning how to go to the true Comforter as our true source of comfort.

Jesus talks to us about how to abide in his love.

"*I am the vine; you are the branches. If a man remains in me and I in him, he will bear much fruit; apart from me you can do nothing. If anyone does not remain in me, he is like a branch that is thrown away and withers; such branches are picked up, thrown into the fire and burned. If you remain in me and my words remain in you, ask whatever you wish, and it will be given you. This is to my Father's glory, that you bear much fruit, showing yourselves to be my disciples. As the Father has loved me, so have I loved you. Now remain in my love*" (**John 15:5-9 NIV**).

We seem to wander from his love so easily and without much of a fight. Hopefully as you go through the rest of this study you will learn how to fight and how to remain in your true identity. You are truly God's boy! Satan is always opposed to God's truth and will always try to trick us into thinking that we are unacceptable, unworthy and will never be seen by God as important. We need to abide in who we are in Christ, abide in Him who is in us. We need to truly accept ourselves as his boys.

Sexuality: Celebrating It!

So God created man in his own image, in the image of God he created him; male and female he created them (Genesis 1:27 NIV).

Concept

Because we probably have been deceived about this subject, it is extremely important that we know how the Bible views healthy sexuality. Here are some truths.

- We are created in God's image.
- God created sex.
- God created us as sexual people.
- God created us male and female.
- God wants us to have great sex (after all He invented it).
- God intended sexual intercourse to be one of the greatest expressions of marital intimacy.

Of course, something that is this positive and good for humans, Satan will try to mess up. Satan twists sex from something wonderful, as God intended it to be, into something shameful and lustful. *We need to rethink how we think about our sexuality.*

What I am going to say next may be on the edge for you, but I want you to see clearly how to view our male sexuality in a healthy way.

As men, God created us to be strongly aroused sexually – it is a normal and positive thing. Enjoy being sexual; that is how we were created! Enjoy the positive sexual things, the excitement you feel when you are sexually stimulated! It is a natural and positive experience. I am not saying to lust and be stimulated with lustful thoughts. What I am saying is that we are sexual people, and it is fun when our bodies work the way God intended them to – within the boundaries that He gives us.

Along with desiring us to enjoy how we were created, God also wants us to be free. Free from addictions, free from lusts, free from pornography, free from being a slave to masturbation free from our old sinful nature with all its sexual lusts. *It is for freedom that Christ has set us free. Stand firm, then, and do not let yourselves be burdened again by a yoke of slavery* (Galatians 5:1 NIV).

God also wants us to enjoy Him, the one who made us this way. We don't want to get tricked into worshiping the thing that He created (sex). We need to enjoy worshipping the Creator Himself.

Fighting

Sex is like soccer. I know because I have played and coached soccer for many years. Sex is like soccer because it is fun to score! But, like soccer, if you don't play by the rules or stay within the boundaries, the game ceases to be fun.

Let's say a soccer player picks up the ball, runs around the bleachers and behind the goal, then drops the ball, dribbles in front of the net and when the goalie comes out, punches him in the face and scores. What fun is it to play with him? Of course it would be no fun at all. None of us would allow him to play with us any more because he's breaking the rules. That's the way it is with sex. If we go outside of God's boundaries and break His rules, the scoring ceases to be fun. It turns negative and creates bondages that control us instead of us being in control.

The rules for sex were created with the same purpose that the rules for soccer were created: maximize the players' enjoyment of the game and keep the players safe from injury.

So what are the rules and boundaries God has given us for great sex? As many athletes understand, the fewer rules the better. In this case, great sex is to be played within the boundaries of marriage, keeping us safe emotionally, physically and spiritually. It's much more fun to play the game this way. We need to be very thoughtful about how far we go physically with a woman before marriage. The farther we go, the more potential for damage: lust, loss of control, diseases and countless other negative forces.

The rules are few. The main rule is to do everything in love, God's love. Not just our love, but the same unselfish and unconditional love that Christ showed toward us. I once heard Miles McPherson talk about sex and he said, *"Love desires to please someone else at the expense of self because love wants to give. Lust wants to please self at the expense of someone else because lust wants to get."* When we choose to live outside God's boundaries, we are not choosing love. I think that is a good way of thinking about it. Memorize it!

Funny how the enemy switches sides so quickly. One minute it seems that he is whispering in our ear, "Go ahead and do it, who cares if it is healthy or not, it won't hurt you." So we go ahead and lust. Then the enemy shows up again, except this time on the other side with, "You really screwed up. You are so stupid – you did it again! See, I told you that you aren't good enough to be a Christian." Lies, lies and more lies, always accusing us: One of Satan's greatest desires is to keep us away from God and from the enjoyment and freedom that come from living within God's boundaries for us.

Important Stuff

Marriage should be honored by all, and the marriage bed kept pure, for God will judge the adulterer and all the sexually immoral (**Hebrews 13:4 NIV**).

"To define sexuality in mere physical terms misses the most important dimension of human sexuality – the spiritual. Sexuality is not just something that joins our bodies;

it also involves the joining of our spirits. (Meeting) our physical needs...is not all we want. We also want spiritual union. We want "belonging." We want to be the object of someone's interest and care. We want reciprocal faithfulness and trust, and we want the assurance and peace that those bring. Any definition of sexuality that excludes those things is inadequate. Sexuality should be defined, therefore, as the human potential for the complete sharing of our whole selves, both body and spirit, with a person of the other sex. Because our sexuality links the spiritual to the physical, no amount of mere physical activity can create the wholeness for which our hearts long."[2]

As sexual boys and men, it may seem like "scoring" outside of God's boundaries is what we were meant to do to meet our sexual needs and have fun. Those ideas, however, are simply more of Satan's lies. What Jones is saying above is that sex with another person outside the God-created boundary of marriage will never be fulfilling. In the next lesson we will learn about how to deal with the enemy's accusations and lies.

Say this out loud: "In the holy name of Jesus I reject the lie that sex outside of your boundaries is healthy or acceptable to me. I accept the truth that you have created me a sexual man, and I can enjoy my sexuality within your plan."

Sexual Temptations: Understanding Them

*When tempted, no one should say, "God is tempting me." For God cannot be tempted by evil, nor does he tempt anyone; but each one is tempted when, by his own evil desire, he is dragged away and enticed. Then, after desire has conceived, it gives birth to sin; and sin, when it is full-grown, gives birth to death (**James 1:13-15 NIV**).*

Concept

When a lustful thought comes into our heads, it is not a sin according to James. It is a temptation; it only becomes a sin when, by our evil desire, we allow it to pull us into dwelling on the lustful thought. When we continue thinking about it, the thought is conceived in our mind and becomes sin.

So it goes like this: we see a pretty woman with a great body and we have this thought come into our head, "What a great body; she really looks great." The mere thought going through our heads, is not sinful. It reflects the healthy sexuality referred to in Lesson 2. We can enjoy the beauty of an attractive woman. However, when we take it further and say to ourselves, "Boy, I would like to sleep with her." Now that thought is lustful and needs to be taken captive and made "obedient to Christ." It becomes sinful if we keep going with the, "Boy, I would like to sleep with her," thought and start lusting in our minds about having sex with her.

Incidentally, the thought may not even be ours, but pushed into our head by an evil source. It might just be old habits (the flesh). The source doesn't really matter. The point is that we need to capture the thought and turn it over to Jesus.

Fighting

Let's look at the verse in Corinthians again.

> For though we live in the world, we do not wage war as the world does. The weapons we fight with are not the weapons of the world. On the contrary, they have divine power to demolish strongholds. We demolish arguments and every pretension that sets itself up against the knowledge of God, and we take captive every thought to make it obedient to Christ (**2 Corinthians 10:3-5 NIV**).

Where do arguments and pretensions and thoughts take place? In our minds! The battleground is in our minds. Remember to always *fight spiritually first*. Self-discipline, emotional awareness and intellectual understanding all come after.

Fighting described above could look like this: As soon as you see the beautiful woman and have the first thought about how great she looks, you can offer a prayer of praise: "*Dear Heavenly Father, You have created this beautiful woman. She belongs to you, and I thank you and praise you for your creation. I'm holding on to you, Jesus, my Lord and Savior, to help me enjoy this beauty and respond to this situation with love, not lust.*"

It's very important that we learn to recognize immediately when normal enjoyment of our sexuality becomes lustful and sinful. Then we can fight right away, giving no opening for Satan's "moral right" to bug us and try and pull us down with his lies. So, let's say a lustful thought (like the one above, "Boy, I would like to sleep with her.") comes into your mind. Say out loud (unless you are in a crowded room or something, then say it under your breath), "No! In Jesus' name I reject this thought because I belong to Jesus and I choose not to think like that. Get away form me Satan and every enemy of my Lord Jesus Christ." The exact words are not that important. The three keys here are Recognizing, Rejecting and Bringing: recognizing and rejecting the thoughts and bringing them before Jesus.

It is very important to take captive each thought as soon as it hits our minds. Let me illustrate. We are in class in the morning or at work and the thought comes to our minds, "She is hot, I could lust about her," and we do not take it captive. Later that day when we are alone, the thought that we had earlier in the day is already dragging us away and enticing us. We will usually give in to the temptation by this point. We need to take our thoughts captive as soon as they come into our minds.

Important Stuff

Most of the Christian writing on the subject of sexual purity that I have read has focused on what I call a defensive strategy. A defensive strategy is like teaching people to look away when they see something that might make them have lustful thoughts. There are also defensive moves that all of us can make that I think are a must – basic fighting – such as a filter on our internet service or avoiding or running away from situations where we might be tempted too much.

I think that every battle plan must have a defense or we will not win the fight. *But if that is all we have, then we are in big trouble*. We cannot and will not win without a good offensive plan.

Our offensive plan that I am laying out in LFL is to learn to fight *Spiritually First*. Our offense is to fight with the truth of the Word of God, to renounce lies, accept truth and take every thought captive to Jesus. Draw our swords and fight in the spiritual realm.

We need a great offense and defense. Both are needed; don't be fooled into thinking that obeying the defensive plan alone will win this battle. Attack the lies of the evil one with the power of Jesus and when the counterattack comes, then you can use some defensive strategies as well.

Flee! When we are in a sexually tempting situation there is one good way to deal with it – run away! Flee the evil desires of youth, and pursue righteousness, faith, love and peace, along with those who call on the Lord out of a pure heart (**2 Timothy 2:22 NIV**).

Flee from sexual immorality. All other sins a man commits are outside his body, but he who sins sexually sins against his own body (**1 Corinthians 6:18 NIV**).

Remember, Satan cannot read our minds, so he won't obey our thoughts. Only God knows what you are thinking. So, say the truth and reject the Evil One out loud!

[1]*Dr. Neil T. Anderson*, Victory Over Darkness *(California: Regal Books – a division of Gospel Light Publications, Ventura, CA 93006), p 43.*
[2]*Jim Hancock with Kara Eckmann Powell*, Good Sex *(Michigan: Zondervan –Youth Specialties Books 2001), p 91.*

Questions for Reflection and Discussion

- How would really believing that you are "God's boy" that he deeply loves impact any challenges you might have in the area of sexuality?

- What ideas in the chapter on celebrating sexuality did you find helpful?

- In the section on sexual temptation, how did defining what sexual sin is and what it is not help you? What do you think about the idea of fighting spiritually?

- During prayer, take some time to open yourself up to God in this area. Is there any area he wants to bring his light and conviction to? Any issue you want to ask for his help in? Remember that you are his boy that he loves and wants to help through this.

As we continue looking at areas relating to inner transformation, we come this week to an often overlooked but very important topic: emotional health. This area is so important that one could grow deeply in many of the topics covered in this discipleship process and still be greatly stunted in their spiritual maturity and in their relationship with God. Sadly, this is precisely what happens to many Christians.

When we are unaware of how the wounds, pain, and unhealthy patterns we have experienced from others in our past affect us now, it can severely undercut our efforts to be transformed into the people God desires for us to be. Where God desires for us to walk in joy, freedom, confidence, and healthy relationships, we can instead find ourselves experiencing frequent sadness, low self-esteem, anger, and repeated struggles in relationships. A lack of emotional health and maturity will also make it difficult to grow deeper in the fruit of the Spirit. Most importantly, a lack of emotional health will have a direct impact on our relationships with God.

Fortunately, God has both the desire and power to bring us the understanding and healing we need. Healing, however, is a process. This session cannot accomplish all of what God wants to do in his healing process, but it can be a beginning (or can help you continue in your process). The goal of this session is to help you become aware of the need for healing and the significant benefits it brings. Another goal is to point you toward resources to help you go further in your healing process. These will be listed as part of the Spiritual Reading section.

For this week, I would encourage you to look at the Spiritual Reading and the Spiritual Practice sections early in the week. The reading will provide a frame of reference for some of the other sections, and looking at the spiritual practice (Sabbath) early will help you in carrying it out.

God bless you as you learn more about the healing heart of your Father.

Spiritual Practice
Sabbath

A spiritual practice that has been lost for many people is the practice of the Sabbath. The Sabbath is God's gift to his people to help them experience his rest in an intentional way.

The idea is to set aside a day that is focused on God, rest, enjoying other people, and doing things that replenish us. God knew that we would need our batteries recharged physically, mentally, and spiritually. Through this practice, we have a better chance of living the healthy, God-centered life he intended for us.

Here's how it works. Most Christians that observe the Sabbath do it on Sundays, because that's when they attend worship. The day begins by focusing on God and being with his people. This might be followed by lunch with family or friends. Part of the meal might be spent sharing about things you are thankful to God for as you look back on the week or how your worship experience that morning impacted you.

195

The afternoon might be a time for taking a nap, reading a book, playing a game with your family, if you have children, going to the park, or spending extended time with family or friends. Whatever brings rest and replenishment to your body and soul.

'In order to experience this kind of rest, it is important *not* to do some things. These would include those things that involve work or stress. The most obvious is not going to work. Beyond that, however, would be not doing work-related things at home, such as bringing work home, checking work email, or making work-related phone calls. Other things to avoid would be work related to home or family. These would include grocery shopping, errands, cleaning, and yard work. There may be some things, such as gardening, that you find enjoyable, which is fine. The criteria should be, "Does this drain me or replenish me?"

The point is not to be legalistic about the Sabbath, like the Pharisees. Jesus clarified the purpose of the Sabbath when he said, "*The Sabbath was made for man, not man for the Sabbath*" (Mark 2:27). The point is to be intentional about clearing out the normal routine and work of life and setting aside a day that is different. This does require being very intentional. If you are married, you will want to discuss this as a couple. If you have older children, you will want to discuss this with them as well and get their ideas. Once they begin to experience it, they will really enjoy it.

You may want to begin your Sabbath on Saturday evening and conclude it before Sunday evening, if you need to begin doing things on Sunday evening to prepare for the week. If your job requires you to work on Sundays, you may want to consider doing the Sabbath on Saturday or another day.

This week, make an effort to try out the Sabbath. Make a plan for yourself or with your spouse. Afterward, reflect on and discuss your experience. This is one practice that you should seriously consider incorporating into your life. It is one of God's means of bringing his healing and rest.

Spiritual Reading
The Great Healer

What Just Happened?

The scene is way too familiar. A couple who has been involved in the church for years, committed to their relationship with God, active in ministry...takes a seat on the pastor's couch. "We don't think our marriage is going to make it. We are thinking about divorce." What? How can this be?

How can people who are sincerely committed to God end up with such problems? Isn't this the type of thing that a life with God is supposed to change? Aren't things supposed to be different?

Yes, they are. And that's why it is so mystifying for those going through it. One of the key blind spots for many followers of Christ is the need for emotional healing in their lives. When this healing does not occur, the deep wounds and lies of their past can derail even the best of spiritual progress that they have made. How does this happen?

Generational Sin

Many people tend to think that the hurts of the past don't affect them today. That would be great, if it were true. The reality is that our families of origin greatly impact the people we become. Many of these effects are positive, but there is no getting around the fact that we live in a broken world, and our parents and others who impacted us most deeply are broken people. And their parents were broken, and so on, and so on.

The result of this is like a waterfall of brokenness cascading down the generations. This is why you can often trace back through your generational family tree and see patterns: addiction, divorce, depression, adultery. The Bible refers to this as generational sin, and there are many examples of it in Scripture.

The hard part is that we often don't connect the dots of the challenges we are experiencing today to the wounds we experienced growing up. We may struggle with how we feel about ourselves, controlling our anger, developing close relationships with our spouses or children, overcoming depression or addictive patterns, or a host of other things. These are often symptoms of long-buried hurt or things we didn't receive in our past. In some cases, we end up blaming those around us rather than finding healing at the root of the issue.

Sources of Brokenness

If these are the symptoms, what does the root look like? It can take many forms.

One or both parents (or a caregiver or other key family members) may have regularly lashed out in anger toward you or even been abusive (verbally, physically, or sexually). They may have been emotionally distant, rarely opening up and sharing their feelings. They may have had difficulty showing affection.

Their love or approval may have been conditional (or at least seemed that way), being based on how well you performed or achieved or followed their rules, rather than being unconditional. Abuse of alcohol or drugs may have brought chaos, inconsistent behavior, and pain into the family and into your life.

You may have experienced the divorce of your parents and all the pain that accompanies that or the loss of one or both parents.

These and other wounds or losses impact us on a deep level. Unfortunately, they don't just fade away.

Breaking the Cycle

Fortunately, we know the Great Healer. As we will see in our Scripture study this week, *"The righteous cry out, and the LORD hears them; he delivers them from all their troubles.*

The LORD is close to the brokenhearted and saves those who are crushed in spirit" (Psalm 34:17-18). He cares deeply about us and longs to bring his healing into our lives.

The key is opening ourselves up to his healing and taking the steps that are going to bring real help. This will nearly always involve the body of Christ: others coming alongside us who have been down this road themselves. This may be a class or retreat offered at your church that focuses on God's healing and restoration; a Christian counselor; a pastor; trusted friends; or, most likely, a combination of all of these. In addition, prayer, Scripture, and other resources you pursue on your own can be very instrumental.

The journey you will discover typically follows a simple but profound pattern: honestly identifying and facing the pain or loss, receiving God's love and comfort, and seeking to forgive those who hurt you. Each of these steps requires the help of God and others to know what we need to do and how to do it—and to have the courage to follow through.

When we do the hard work of pursuing healing, it will, over time, begin to transform our relationships, our view of ourselves, and our view of God. It will not only benefit ourselves, but those around us, including our children and their children, and so on. With God's help, we can break the generational cycle of pain and dysfunction and begin a legacy of freedom and wholeness in Christ.

Questions for Reflection and Discussion

- What do you think about the idea of past sin or pain from our families of origin impacting us now?

- Do you see examples of how your family history may be affecting you today?

- What was helpful to you in the area of breaking the cycle?

- During prayer, ask God to begin to show you what the next step in your healing process might look like.

Soaking in Scripture

Jeremiah 29:11

"For I know the plans I have for you," declares the LORD, "plans to prosper you and not to harm you, plans to give you hope and a future."

This is one of the most hope-filled passages in all of Scripture. When it comes to finding healing from our past, we often need hope!

- This is an important passage to memorize, because God can use it during times when you may be struggling to have hope, especially in the midst of a healing process. Discouragement and lack of hope are some of the Devil's most often-used tactics. Take some time to read over this passage in an effort to memorize it. This also may be one you want to post somewhere you will see often to remind you of the hope you have in God.

- How hard or easy is it to believe that God has hope-filled plans for you in the future?

- What does this passage tell you about God's heart toward you?

- During your prayer time, share with God any feelings this passage has brought up. You may also want to share any hopes you have around his healing in your life.

Digging into Scripture

King David experienced his fair share of pain and trauma. This is a good passage when considering God's healing work in our lives.

Psalm 34:4-10, 15-18

4I sought the LORD, and he answered me; he delivered me from all my fears.
5Those who look to him are radiant; their faces are never covered with shame.
6This poor man called, and the LORD heard him; he saved him out of all his troubles.
7The angel of the LORD encamps around those who fear him, and he delivers them.

8Taste and see that the LORD is good; blessed is the one who takes refuge in him.
9Fear the LORD, you his holy people, for those who fear him lack nothing.
10The lions may grow weak and hungry, but those who seek the LORD lack no good thing.
15The eyes of the LORD are on the righteous, and his ears are attentive to their cry;
16but the face of the LORD is against those who do evil, to blot out their name from the earth.

17The righteous cry out, and the LORD hears them; he delivers them from all their troubles.
18The LORD is close to the brokenhearted and saves those who are crushed in spirit.

Observation
- In relating this passage to God's healing work in our lives, what do you notice about God's heart toward us and his desire to help us?

Interpretation

Application

As a part of our exploration of inner transformation last session, we looked at the emotional health that God desires for us. This week, we begin looking at the area of spiritual health. What is this? For starters, it is the recognition that there are ways of following God that may seem good, but are, in fact, unhealthy. There are a number of expressions of spiritual unhealthiness that we will lump under "Pharisaism," because the Pharisees of Jesus' day seemed to exhibit all of them!

If there was anyone who could get Jesus upset, it was the Pharisees and their sidekicks, the teachers of the law. What was it that upset him so much? Well, there were a number of things, but one was that they focused on outward behavior, but neglected the important heart change that needs to happen within all of us. This resulted in all kinds of unhealthy spiritual behavior, such as hypocrisy, legalism (over focusing on rules), pride, and judgmentalism. It's no wonder that Jesus' words to and about the Pharisees were so strong.

This may all sound obvious, but it is trickier than we might think. Pharisaism can sneak in without us realizing it. It is very important that we identify this kind of thinking early on in our journey; otherwise, we can end up going down the wrong track spiritually. In fact, because of this way of thinking, entire churches have pursued an unhealthy "brand" of the Christian faith, which has led to the name of Christ and the Church gaining a negative image in the eyes of many. All of this is motivation to understand the healthy expression of our faith that Jesus modeled and taught.

The good news is that emotional health and spiritual health often impact one another. As we begin to become healthier emotionally, this will begin to lead to greater spiritual health. Two for the price of one!

Spiritual Practice
The Practice of Secrecy

One of the temptations of Pharisaism is doing things to get noticed or to impress others. This can be very subtle—something that often happens on a subconscious level.

A good practice for counteracting this temptation is the practice of secrecy. In this practice, we consciously perform acts of kindness or generosity toward others and, just as consciously, choose not to tell anyone about it. It is between us and God. This helps underscore the idea that our behavior should flow from our hearts for the purpose of bringing joy to God and others, not for bringing attention to ourselves. It also helps us become more intentional about giving to others, kind of like being a secret agent of kindness.

This week, look for opportunities to intentionally bless others: friends, family members, work colleagues, neighbors, servers where we shop or eat. This could be through a kind word (written or spoken), a material or financial gift, serving someone in a practical way, or listening to someone in an effort to care for them. Then, don't tell anyone else about it—except God. Share your feelings with him about it and listen for what he may be expressing to you. Reflect on how it feels to share it only with God and not with others. What feels good about it? What, if anything, feels hard? It is okay to share with your group how you felt about this practice.

Note: In the case of a financial or material gift, it is okay if the person on the receiving end knows it is coming from you, unless anonymity is more appropriate in the situation.

Soaking in Scripture

This week, we will be focusing on Pharisees and teachers of the law who didn't seem to "get it," spiritually speaking. In a conversation with Jesus, there was a teacher of the law who seemed a little different. Below is his response to a question from Jesus. After the man's response, Mark 12:34 says, "Jesus saw that he had answered wisely."
- First, read about the conversation between Jesus and this teacher in Mark 12:28-34.
- Read Mark 12:33 again, slowly:

"To love him with all your heart, with all your understanding and with all your strength, and to love your neighbor as yourself is more important than all burnt offerings and sacrifices." **(Mark 12:33)**

Questions for Reflection and Discussion

- What do you think the teacher is saying here?

- Why do you think Jesus saw this as wise?

- Burnt offerings and sacrifices were rituals that the people of God at that time could perform without having any true love for God or others. In other words, it could be an empty spiritual practice. What are spiritual practices we might do today that could be done without any true love for God or others?

- During your prayer time, ask God to show you if there are any of these practices that have become empty in your life or more important than loving him with all your heart and loving your neighbor as yourself.

Digging into Scripture

This encounter between Jesus and the Pharisees is like a head-on collision. Jesus doesn't pull any punches. He clearly shows how he feels about the way that the Pharisees and teachers of the law have chosen to live out their life with God. As you study this passage, note not only what Jesus says, but also the strength with which he says it.

Luke 11:37-46, 53-54 (NLT)

37As Jesus was speaking, one of the Pharisees invited him home for a meal. So he went in and took his place at the table. 38His host was amazed to see that he sat down to eat without first performing the hand-washing ceremony required by Jewish custom. 39Then the Lord said to him, "You Pharisees are so careful to clean the outside of the cup and the dish, but inside you are filthy—full of greed and wickedness! 40Fools! Didn't God make the inside as well as the outside? 41So clean the inside by giving gifts to the poor, and you will be clean all over.

42"What sorrow awaits you Pharisees! For you are careful to tithe even the tiniest income from your herb gardens, but you ignore justice and the love of God. You should tithe, yes, but do not neglect the more important things.

43"What sorrow awaits you Pharisees! For you love to sit in the seats of honor in the synagogues and receive respectful greetings as you walk in the marketplaces. 44Yes, what sorrow awaits you! For you are like hidden graves in a field. People walk over them without knowing the corruption they are stepping on."

45"Teacher," said an expert in religious law, "you have insulted us, too, in what you just said."

46"Yes," said Jesus, "what sorrow also awaits you experts in religious law! For you crush people with unbearable religious demands, and you never lift a finger to ease the burden. 53As Jesus was leaving, the teachers of religious law and the Pharisees became hostile and tried to provoke him with many questions. 54They wanted to trap him into saying something they could use against him.

Observation
- Note the key characteristics of the Pharisees and teachers of the law you see in this passage.

- What might this look like for us today if we were to follow their lead?

Interpretation

Application

Spiritual Reading
The Way of Jesus

Would it matter if you moved to a small rural town in Texas and sported your new Save the Whales bumper sticker, asked where you could find some good vegetarian food, and then researched the best place to get your lip pierced—again? It just might...

Without realizing it, we have outward, often superficial signs that identify whether or not we are a part of a certain group or culture. These help to determine who is "in" and who is "out." Types of dress, ways of communicating, certain interests or activities all play a part. Whether young or old, human nature naturally drifts in this direction.

What does this have to do with spirituality and our relationship with God? A lot. These types of outward, superficial markers have influenced followers of God throughout history and continue today. And they absolutely smother healthy, vibrant spirituality. In fact, it can keep people from knowing what that even looks like.

John Ortberg calls this "boundary-marker spirituality." This is where Christian churches and communities choose certain outward markers to determine who is "in" or spiritually mature, and who is not. Depending on what church tradition someone is a part of, it could be one of the following: outward appearances, such as types of clothing, hair length, tattoos/piercings or the lack thereof; frequency of attendance at church services/activities; using Christian media, such as music, books, or radio; political affiliation; a focus on behaviors to be avoided, such as smoking or bad language; and many more.

Most of these things aren't bad in and of themselves. It's not bad to listen to some Christian music or try to be a regular part of things going on in the life of your church. The problem is when these external behaviors become the central, defining marks of what it means to really know and follow God; when what should be central is missing.

What Should Be Central?

What should be at the center of what it means to know and follow God? Hopefully by now in our discipleship process, that has begun to become clear. When we truly, deeply know the Father's love for us and that love has begun to change us on a deep level and especially has begun to shape how we love and treat others, then we are starting to find the "real" stuff.

The problem happens when the outward signs are focused on without these inward, central changes happening. If Jesus were talking to the Church today, he might say to some:

> "You go to church regularly, you give financially, and you are active politically and have strong feelings on the issues of the day. You listen to Christian radio, and you don't smoke or swear. The only small problem is you don't know how deeply I love you. Your heart is small and shriveled when it comes to loving those who are so important to me—those who are hurting and aren't a part of the Christian "in" group. Those who have very different opinions and lifestyles from you... Your children know about the dos and don'ts, but do they know how much you love them? Do you respect them? Spend time with them? Model genuine love for all kinds of people to them? Do you serve and love your spouse sacrificially, the way I have loved and served you?"

When we don't live out of this central place of knowing the Father's love and pouring it out to others and instead focus on the externals, it is very damaging to us and to others. The spiritual life can become quite boring and deadening. It simply does not bring life or joy. It also leads to a focus on the negative, because of the tendency to judge others who are not following "the plan." However, when our focus is truly on loving God with all our heart and loving our neighbors as ourselves, then our life is marked by joy and life-giving love toward others.

It's not hard to imagine how the boundary-marker life impacts those who are in the "out" category. They see Christianity, or at least this form of it, as all the things we just described: boring, joyless, rules-bound, and judgmental. Not a very big draw. On the other hand, when they see those who are filled with the Father's love and live with true joy and peace and freedom and have huge hearts toward all types of people, this gets people's attention.

This was precisely the contrast between Jesus and the religious leaders of his day. The nonreligious and the Pharisees didn't seem to have a lot of contact, and that seemed to suit both groups just fine. Notice the difference with Jesus.

I was struck recently by a reaction of the people to Jesus that I read about in Mark 9. Jesus and several of his disciples are joining the rest of the disciples. When they find the others, they discover that a large crowd is surrounding them. Why? Because the teachers of the law were arguing with them, and the crowd wanted to see what would happen. Isn't it interesting that the religious leaders were arguing with them? Do you think it might be because Jesus' disciples weren't following all of the rules of the religious "in" group? The focus turns to who is right and wrong and is negative in nature.

Now listen to the verse describing the people's reaction to Jesus: "As soon as all the people saw Jesus, *they were overwhelmed with wonder and ran to greet him*" (Mark 9:15). *Overwhelmed* with wonder. Ran to greet him. It sounds like people were kind of drawn to Jesus. Yes, he did amazing stuff, but was this the only reason people were so drawn to him? I believe it was because he taught and lived out a life in such stark contrast to the religious leaders of the day. He was like a magnet to the people.

Later, in Mark 12, it says that a large crowd "listened to him with delight." His words were fresh and genuine and full of the true heart of God. Interestingly, the next words out of Jesus' mouth are these: "Watch out for the teachers of the law" (Mark 12:38).

A Picture of the Un-Pharisee

In college, I went to a church with good people. Looking back, I realize that some of these Pharisee tendencies were at play. We weren't supposed to have dances (so we suddenly became good friends with the Methodist group, who had great dances). Listening to secular music was frowned upon. We were expected to be at church several times a week.

Then I met our college pastor, Nick. As I got to know him and listened to his teachings, I realized that he didn't seem to focus on these things. Instead, he seemed to talk a lot about Jesus, as if he actually knew him. He talked about what Jesus is like and his love for people—all kinds of people. He had a joy and freedom about him.

He also seemed okay with people's doubts and questions. We would sit around and debate issues, and he wasn't rattled at all. He would just keep pointing us back to Jesus. He modeled this in his life as he was honest about his own questions and real about his struggles.

I remember one evening, at one of our large group times together, he told us, "I want you to go to one side of the room or the other, based on your answer to this question. Don't consult with your friends, just go." Pretty intriguing. The question? "Is it okay to go to one of the dance clubs in town?" Because of the college, there were a lot of these. Immediately, half the group went to one side of the room and one half to the other side. It was pretty evenly split. The interesting part was that several couples were split, including my girlfriend and me!

Then we debated, with people going to the microphone to defend their position for why it was or was not okay. At the end, I thought, "What is Nick going to say? This could be a mess!" What he essentially said was that the Holy Spirit within you needs to guide you. For some, going to a club would not be a good idea, because they would be tempted to drink too much or be overly influenced by those there. For others, it might not be an issue and might be a good way to connect with others.

Afterward, I thought, "That sounds like something Jesus might say." Live by the Spirit, not by rigid rules.

Nick's life with God seemed real. If you had asked me how my spiritual life was going, the first thought for me would have been, "How often did I read the Bible or pray this week?" But for Nick, it didn't seem mechanical like that. He would share about something new he felt God was showing him about himself or his life or how he saw God speaking through music or art or movies or other people or the Bible. God wasn't sectioned off into one part of his life on a Sunday morning or times of prayer (although these were a part of the relationship), but instead God was infused in all of his daily life.

He also related easily to people who were far from God. There didn't seem to be some huge relational gap between them (unlike what I, myself, sometimes felt at the time). He wasn't so confined to a religious world that he couldn't relate to them. Because he was real with his own challenges, shortcomings, and questions, he could relate to theirs. He didn't judge them—he befriended them.

Moving Toward Jesus

Nick and others in my life have given me a good picture of what it looks like to live more like Jesus than like a Pharisee. To be honest, living like a Pharisee is less complicated. I think that's why it has been so popular throughout the centuries and still is today. It's simpler to decide who is in and who is out, to choose certain boundary markers and stick to them, to judge others and keep your distance. Doing the opposite is messier, less clear- cut at times, and gets you in trouble with people (mostly religious people, as Jesus discovered).

But it's really the only way to live, especially if we want to be like Jesus and be close to him. It's the only way that brings real life. It's the only way that draws others to him.

Believe that the Father delights and believes in you as his kid. Share that love and joy and freedom with others. Since you know he loves you so deeply, be honest about your struggles and your pain with others. Bring your honest questions to him; he's not afraid of them. Move from judging others to identifying with those who struggle in life just as you do, whether in different or possibly similar ways. Know that he is alive and speaking to you throughout all kinds of things and people throughout your day and your life.

Leave the way of the Pharisee. Follow the way of Jesus.

Questions for Reflection and Discussion

- What "boundary markers" have you either experienced or observed in churches or Christian groups?

- Do you know someone who is a good picture of living out the central expressions of knowing God: an un-Pharisee?

- In prayer, ask God to show you any areas of Pharisaism or boundary markers in your life that he might want to bring to light.

One of the key differences between Jesus and the Pharisees was the issue of grace. Jesus offered grace and mercy to others, including the irreligious or sinners; the Pharisees separated themselves from the less religious and judged from a distance. This flowed from their view of God as One who primarily emphasizes the law. Jesus, on the other hand, experienced a relationship with his Father that emphasized the love of the Father for him, and that love and grace then flowed to others.

At the same time, in the midst of that grace, Jesus also spoke truth to others—truth that would give them life. Both grace and truth flowed from his love for the people he encountered.

Today, we often struggle with this mixture of grace and truth. There may be individuals or groups of people we struggle to truly love and show grace. Instead, we judge and separate ourselves like the Pharisees did. In addition, we may focus on what we see as wrong about a particular *issue*, but forget that there are *people* involved. On the other end of the spectrum, we can seek to show love and grace, but be afraid to share truth with others. It may be uncomfortable, or we may be afraid to offend, but this truth may be the most loving thing we can offer—if it is offered in the midst of a grace-filled relationship.

Grace and truth. How did Jesus offer both, and how can we?

Note: You may need a little more time for the Spiritual Practice section this week.

Spiritual Practice
Researching Grace

One of the key things that can lead us away from grace and into judging or criticizing others is a lack of understanding. We often simply don't know much about the situations and challenges of those we may be tempted to judge. Take some time to think about a group of people or an individual that you may be tempted to judge. You may want to ask God to bring this group or individual to mind.

Next, do some research on the background, issues, and challenges faced by this group of people. You can do this by searching on the internet, reading, or ideally by talking to someone from that group. This process will take a little bit of time, and it could be tempting to not do it. If we will dive into it as the Spirit guides us, God could use it in a significant way in our lives.

Here are some examples:

- Immigrants (legal or illegal)
- Someone who is gay or lesbian
- Transgender individuals
- Particular ethnic group or race
- Members of other world religions or other Christian denominations
- Criminals or someone with a criminal background
- Individuals or groups who have different views on an issue important to you (such as abortion, the environment, war, or guns)
- Republicans or Democrats

Session #20
Spiritual Health: Living in Grace and Truth

(continued)

- Non-Christians (this might be a particular individual or family with different values from yours)
- Gang members
- Different economic or social group

When finished, reflect on what you have learned.

- How does it increase your grace and understanding for this group or individual?

- Does it lead you to confession about previous attitudes you have had?

- What would it look like to express grace and truth to this group or individual with both flowing out of love?

Soaking in Scripture

At the beginning of his gospel, the apostle John described Jesus and his mission in coming to our world. Read part of his description below.

John 1:14

The Word [Jesus] became flesh and made his dwelling among us. We have seen his glory, the glory of the one and only Son, who came from the Father, full of grace and truth.

Jesus was filled with both grace and truth.

- From what you know about Jesus, what are some examples of how he expressed grace to others?

- Similarly, what are some examples of how he expressed truth to others?

- What is more difficult for you to express to others: grace or truth? Why?

- During your time of prayer, express your praise to Jesus for his grace and truth. Ask him to show you if you need to express either grace or truth to someone in your life right now.

Spiritual Reading
Being Filled with Grace and Truth

Pop Quiz

Let's start with a little quiz. How many of these sound like you?

1. You have friendships with people who have pretty different lifestyles or values from yourself.
2. You find yourself disagreeing with some people who are very religious.
3. You enjoy listening to people who have different opinions than yourself.
4. You are aware of your own shortcomings, which helps you relate to many different types of people.
5. While larger societal or political issues may be important to you, you often find yourself drawn to real-life people and their needs.

Why these questions, you might ask? Because these are the types of things that help us determine if we are moving toward the life of grace that Jesus exhibited or away from him. You see all of the above in Jesus' life, minus the shortcomings, and, in fact, several of them in the passage for this week.

Jesus had little difficulty relating to people who had wildly different lifestyles from himself. The woman in our passage this week was most likely a prostitute, but was so touched by Jesus that she was spilling her tears on his feet. He invited tax collectors to lunch and accepted their invitations to parties. And yet, we never see the religious leaders doing this. Why?

Why is it that, today, the same is often true? Why is it that those who consider themselves very committed to Jesus have very little to do with those who have different lifestyles or values? The reason is the same as it was for the religious leaders of Jesus' day: a heavy emphasis on truth. When truth or "being right" comes to strongly define our Christianity or relationship with God, we can expect an ever-growing separation between us and those who are different from us. Another way of saying this is that, if I think that the truth side of the equation is the *most important thing to God*, then this is where my focus will be, and it will lead to separation.

For example, if I believe that living together and having children outside of marriage is wrong, and I believe that these types of issues are the most important things to God, and I have a neighbor or co-worker in this situation, how close do you think I will be to them? At best, I will probably not pursue much of a relationship with them; at worst, I will judge them.

What did Jesus do in these types of situations? It's pretty simple: he focused first on the person, not their actions. He approached them with grace, not judgment. He pursued friendship with them. He shows us that *God's greatest concern is restoring and developing a relationship between the people he created and himself.*

Yes, Jesus spoke truth to people, but *he always led with grace.* It has been said that grace is when you expect a slap and instead receive a kiss. It is amazing and beautiful. The woman at Jesus' feet clearly had already experienced his grace before, and that is why she was there weeping. You can bet she expected a slap, and that's just what the Pharisee wanted to give her, but from Jesus she experienced a kiss: love, acceptance, forgiveness, respect.

Issues or People?

The other area that can separate us from people is a fixation with issues. When we believe that truth or correctness is the chief concern for God, then it is natural to focus primarily on the larger moral or political issues of the day.

A current example would be homosexuality. Some Christians get very passionate about this issue. Is it wrong to wrestle with this issue? No.

What is wrong, however, is that many Christians only see it as an issue being promoted by "those people." They often do not have personal friendships with those who have a homosexual orientation. If they did, their grace meter would very likely increase. They would have greater understanding and compassion. They would realize that this isn't just an *issue*, but real *people* we are talking about. People that God loves deeply. People that God has relationship with or wants to have relationship with.

Another way of saying this is that issues are important, but our relationships with people need to inform *how* we approach these issues. Without these relationships, our meter will peg out on the truth side with little grace.

In his book *What's So Amazing about Grace?*, Philip Yancey writes about Mel White, one of his closest friends for many years. White was also a well-known author in evangelical Christian circles, having written biographies of key figures, such as Billy Graham.

One day, he shocked Yancey by informing him that he was gay and had wrestled with his homosexual orientation from a young age. This turned Yancey's world upside down, because in the past, he had judged homosexuals and their "agenda." He hadn't known anyone personally that was gay and had little understanding of what they might be struggling with in their lives.

This all changed after Mel's announcement. Over the coming months and years, he began to learn about the pain and confusion and abuse his friend had experienced. He discovered that his assumptions, such as the belief that homosexuals simply chose to be gay, were way off base. Over time, he listened and struggled and prayed with his friend; at one point, he literally talked him off of a ledge as he contemplated suicide.

After this, do you think homosexuality was simply an issue to Philip Yancey? No. These were real people, like his friend Mel. People in need of God's grace—and ours.

Jesus and Issues

Again, think about Jesus. Were there key issues in his day? Of course. A huge one was the Roman occupation and those Jews seen as cooperating with the Romans in various ways, including collecting taxes on their behalf and pocketing some of the profits. Other Jews were enraged by this.

Was Jesus upset about this issue of the day? It's hard to say, because we don't read about him saying anything about it. What we do see is him inviting a tax collector to be one of his disciples. The Pharisees, who were very issue-oriented people, just about fell over when this happened.

We see a similar response from Jesus to issues of sexual immorality. We find the Pharisees dragging a woman caught in adultery before Jesus. We know that adultery was an important moral issue that they focused on, because they wanted to get Jesus' reaction to this issue. The woman in this week's passage was most likely known for some type of sexual immorality.

How does Jesus respond to these issues? That's just the thing: he doesn't. He doesn't respond to issues; he responds to people. He doesn't see the women as simply representing an issue, but as real people that God cares about. Even though they have made mistakes, he treats them with dignity and grace.

Is it okay to be concerned with the moral issues of the day? Of course. But we need to also be asking ourselves two questions: Am I spending a lot of time with real people and experiencing God's heart for them and the issues they face? Are these relationships informing how I approach key issues? Put another way, if there is an issue you feel strongly about, do you know someone personally who is impacted by that issue?

What about Truth?

Is there still room for truth, or is it all about grace? If it were all grace, all the time, then God would not be a God of love. You see, both grace *and* truth flow from God's love. His truth leads to the kind of life he intends for us: the joy and freedom we've been talking about.

In our passage this week and the account of the woman caught in adultery, Jesus, in both cases, encourages the women to leave their path of sin. Out of his love, he speaks truth to them. He knows where their current path will continue to lead them, and it's not toward life—the kind of life he wants for them.

It also won't lead them toward the kind of person God has called them to be: beautiful, righteous, noble beings reflecting his beauty and righteousness with greater and greater clarity. If he simply left them where they were at, that wouldn't be very loving.

The key in speaking truth to others is to ask yourself, "Why?" Why do I want to speak truth? Is it because I feel right about something, and it's my duty to set someone straight? Or is it out of genuine concern for them, out of grace? When truth comes out of a real concern and love for someone, they will know it. The truth still may not be easy to hear, but they normally won't feel like they are being criticized or judged.

Grace and Truth in Everyday Life

Once you begin understanding grace and truth and how they work together, you will see ways to apply them everywhere. They act as a filter to see life through.

If you are a parent, for example, do you see your kids through God's lens of grace and truth? Have you leaned too hard on the side of truth, focusing primarily on discipline and correction, and neglected grace? If so, your relationship, along with having joy and fun with your child, has probably suffered.

Maybe it's the opposite situation: you have majored in grace and given your child a pretty wide latitude in his life, but now he is suffering because of it. He needs some clearer boundaries—some truth that will not be fun to live with at first, but that will serve him well throughout his life.

Grace and truth even show up at fast food restaurants. I was at a hamburger place recently, and they got my order wrong—twice. I was definitely leaning toward the truth side of things at that point! What does it look like to respond with grace and truth in this situation? I tried to step back and think about the challenges of working in a fast-paced environment like this one and the number of difficulties they must face in getting every order right and the complaints they get every day. I was trying to understand their perspective in order to lead me toward grace.

At the same time, I really did want what I ordered! The truth part. Having thought about their perspective, I calmly went to the counter and politely let them know about the mistake and asked if they could replace it. They not only replaced it, but gave me a free sundae. Score! Of course that wasn't my motive. The more important result was that they seemed appreciative of the respect (the grace) they received, and I still got what I needed (truth).

Grace and truth. It's needed all throughout life. Seek to understand their situation *first* so that you can express grace. Lead with grace. It doesn't matter if it's your child, your parent, your neighbor, the person working at McDonald's, or the president of the United States, seek to understand their situation and express grace and then explore any ways that truth may need to be communicated.

> **John 1:14**
> *"The Word became flesh and made his dwelling among us. We have seen his glory, the glory of the one and only Son, who came from the Father, full of grace and truth"*

Grace and truth. This is the way of Jesus, and it needs to be our way, too.

Questions for Reflection and Discussion

- Which statements on the quiz did you find yourself identifying with? Which ones were harder to identify with?

- How do you feel about the idea of looking at issues through the lens of relationships with people dealing with those issues?

- Have you had a relationship with someone that impacted how you saw an issue (similar to Philip Yancey's friendship with Mel White)?

- During prayer, share with God how this reading impacted you personally.

Digging into Scripture

This passage offers an excellent contrast between Jesus and a Pharisee in how they treat a woman known for her sinful life. Some questions are provided after the passage to assist you in your observations and interpretation.

Luke 7:36-50 *(NLT)*

36 One of the Pharisees asked Jesus to have dinner with him, so Jesus went to his home and sat down to eat. 37 When a certain immoral woman from that city heard he was eating there, she brought a beautiful alabaster jar filled with expensive perfume. 38 Then she knelt behind him at his feet, weeping. Her tears fell on his feet, and she wiped them off with her hair. Then she kept kissing his feet and putting perfume on them.

39 When the Pharisee who had invited him saw this, he said to himself, "If this man were a prophet, he would know what kind of woman is touching him. She's a sinner!"

40 Then Jesus answered his thoughts. "Simon," he said to the Pharisee, "I have something to say to you."

"Go ahead, Teacher," Simon replied.

41 Then Jesus told him this story: "A man loaned money to two people—500 pieces of silver to one and 50 pieces to the other. 42 But neither of them could repay him, so he kindly forgave them both, canceling their debts. Who do you suppose loved him more after that?"

⁴³Simon answered, "I suppose the one for whom he canceled the larger debt."

"That's right," Jesus said. ⁴⁴Then he turned to the woman and said to Simon, "Look at this woman kneeling here. When I entered your home, you didn't offer me water to wash the dust from my feet, but she has washed them with her tears and wiped them with her hair. ⁴⁵You didn't greet me with a kiss, but from the time I first came in, she has not stopped kissing my feet. ⁴⁶You neglected the courtesy of olive oil to anoint my head, but she has anointed my feet with rare perfume.

⁴⁷"I tell you, her sins—and they are many—have been forgiven, so she has shown me much love. But a person who is forgiven little shows only little love." 48 Then Jesus said to the woman, "Your sins are forgiven."

⁴⁹The men at the table said among themselves, "Who is this man, that he goes around forgiving sins?"

⁵⁰And Jesus said to the woman, "Your faith has saved you; go in peace."

Observation
- What contrasts do you see between the responses of Jesus and the Pharisee?

Interpretation
- What might this woman have been through in her life before this event takes place, and why might she be responding to Jesus in this way?

Application

This week, we shift gears a bit. The last section we looked at covered areas that dealt with inward transformation in our lives. Now we begin looking at various spiritual practices that tap into God's heart for others. We will look at practices, such as compassion and justice, using our gifts to serve others, and helping others through the supernatural power of the Spirit. The hope is that this section will be practical and will set us up for a lifetime of loving others in a way that brings purpose and further connects us to the heart of God.

The first area we will look at is one that is often misunderstood by those who follow Christ, as well as those who don't. It is usually referred to as evangelism. Evangelism means to share the "good news" about Jesus with others. Regardless of what we call it, many Christians are intimidated by it and, as a result, are not too excited about doing it. These feelings often are a result of having a false picture of what it means to share our love for Jesus with others. If we can gain a clearer and more compelling picture of what is involved, then we can feel more confident and even excited about sharing Jesus with others.

We will look at two parts of sharing Jesus with others. The first part, which we will discuss this week, is examining whether we are connected to the world in which we live. One false picture of living the Christian life is to increasingly *dis*connect ourselves from meaningful relationships with those who are not followers of Christ, whether it is in our workplace, our neighborhoods, or even our extended families. In addition, this picture often encourages us to engage primarily in influences and events that are expressly Christian, such as Christian readings, Christian music and media, Christian conferences, and sports and hobbies that we do with Christians. While these influences can certainly be helpful, the combination of disconnecting relationally from those who are not Christians and focusing only on Christian influences can have a significant impact on our effectiveness in relating to and sharing Jesus with others.

If you are new in your journey with Jesus, the above picture may sound strange or unfamiliar, but it is one we can easily pick up as being the most "spiritual" or "Christian." If we are farther along in our journeys and have been living out this picture, this week may raise some challenging questions to wrestle with. To help us, we will look at the life of Jesus and see how he related to his world. We will also look at some reading, which will hopefully inform and stretch our thinking in this area.

In our Spiritual Practice section, we will look at how to address questions that our seeking friends might have. *Also, a bonus section has been included this week to help us begin thinking about potential disciples that we can be praying for in our lives.*

Soaking in Scripture

In this section of Scripture from 1 Corinthians, we get a chance to see the apostle Paul's heart when it comes to being connected to others who do not know Jesus.

1 Corinthians 9:19-23 (MSG)

19-23Even though I am free of the demands and expectations of everyone, I have voluntarily become a servant to any and all in order to reach a wide range of people: religious, nonreligious, meticulous moralists, loose-living immoralists, the defeated, the demoralized—whoever. I didn't take on their way of life. I kept my bearings in Christ— but I entered their world and tried to experience things from their point of view. I've become just about every sort of servant there is in my attempts to lead those I meet into a God-saved life. I did all this because of the Message. I didn't just want to talk about it; I wanted to be in on it!

- What strikes you as interesting or important in this passage?

- Think about an individual or group of people in your life who doesn't know Jesus. What would it look like to keep your bearings in Christ, but enter their world and try to experience things from their point of view?

As a part of your time in prayer, ask God to show you his heart for others who don't know him and what it might look like to be connected with them. Is he placing any particular person or group on your heart at this time? Are there any practical steps he is encouraging you to take to connect with that person or group?

Digging into Scripture

You can find out a lot about a person from observing a brief encounter. This is the case in Jesus' calling of Levi to be one of his disciples. This is a short passage, but take the time to closely observe the scene. As in past accounts from the gospels, this would be another good one to imagine. As you picture the scene and then study the passage, reflect on what it tells you about Jesus and how he related to the irreligious and how that compares to the religious leaders of that day.

Mark 2:13-17 (NLT)

¹³*Then Jesus went out to the lakeshore again and taught the crowds that were coming to him. ¹⁴As he walked along, he saw Levi son of Alphaeus sitting at his tax collector's booth. "Follow me and be my disciple," Jesus said to him. So Levi got up and followed him.*

¹⁵*Later, Levi invited Jesus and his disciples to his home as dinner guests, along with many tax collectors and other disreputable sinners. (There were many people of this kind among Jesus' followers.) ¹⁶But when the teachers of religious law who were Pharisees saw him eating with tax collectors and other sinners, they asked his disciples, "Why does he eat with such scum?"*

¹⁷*When Jesus heard this, he told them, "Healthy people don't need a doctor—sick people do. I have come to call not those who think they are righteous, but those who know they are sinners."*

Observation

Interpretation

Application

When we begin connecting more regularly with those who do not know Christ, often one of our fears is in knowing how to respond to questions about God or the Christian faith that our friends might have. This anxiety can be greatly reduced, however, if we can become better at answering two questions: *why* is the person asking the question, and *what* are the key questions that people often ask?

First, why is the person asking the question? For some people, they are not sincerely seeking to understand, they are simply asking out of cynicism or indifference. In these cases, answering their questions won't really matter all that much, because they aren't all that interested in understanding; you can often end up feeling frustrated. This isn't to say that they are bad people, but rather that discussing questions may not be the right step at this point. The Spirit may lead us to focus on praying for our friends and caring for them until they are ready and interested in sincere discussion.

Others, however, have genuine questions that are barriers to further belief. Trying to help these people could be very helpful to them and rewarding for you. These conversations usually feel energizing rather than combative. Knowing where someone is coming from is key in knowing how to respond.

How can you find out where they are coming from? Ask. You may already have a pretty good idea if they are sincerely asking or not, but if not, you can ask questions such as the following: "Why is that question important to you? If this question is answered in a way that resolves the issue for you, would you be motivated to know more about what it means to have a relationship with Christ?" These can be asked simply and respectfully, and they will help you understand the motivation behind the questions.

Secondly, what are the key questions that people often ask? Often people think that there are numerous questions that others might ask, and that we couldn't possibly know how to respond to such a vast array of questions. In reality, however, there are about half a dozen questions that most people ask.

- How can I trust or believe the Bible?
- How can God allow evil and suffering?
- Why is there such hypocrisy in the Church or in individual Christians?
- What about other religions? How can you say that Christianity is the only true religion or true path to God?
- What about contradictions between science and Christianity related to evolution and creation?
- Why are Christians against homosexuality or other current social issues?

Most questions will flow from the ones above. While it's helpful to know this, you may be thinking, "But those are pretty tough questions!" The key is not to have all of these questions completely figured out, but rather to have at least a basic understanding of the issues surrounding the questions and to know where to go to find out more. What this will probably mean is doing some reading in the near future (resources are listed below) and then returning to that reading when specific questions come up for people. You can also refer them to the same resources and discuss their feelings about what they are reading.

When you are talking to someone who is genuinely interested, two tips can be helpful to know. First, express your opinions and feelings in terms of how they have been helpful to *you*, rather than in terms of what *they* should believe. For example, "The Bible is true, because it is inspired by God." Inference: you should believe that, too. Here is another option, "I know that trusting the Bible to be accurate is challenging for many people. I have come to a place of believing that it is reliable and that I can trust it." The first approach puts people on the defensive, while the second invites them to consider your experience or feelings without having to defend themselves. This often opens people up to increased dialogue.

The second tip is to validate and discuss their questions, but to also point to Jesus as *the* question to consider. After discussion on other questions, you may want to ask them what their thoughts are on Jesus. You might say something like, "My experience has been that coming to a deeper understanding of who Jesus is has helped me understand some of these other important questions. For me, I have come to a place of believing that Jesus is the Son of God and that has helped me understand what God is like and how to know him and how he might respond to many of these issues." If they are open to it, you might suggest that they read more about Jesus in one of the gospels in the Bible and discuss their thoughts with you.

Taking a Step

A great step would be ordering one of the resources below and beginning to read about some of the key questions. If that's too much at this time, it might be helpful to look up one or more online and scan the description and table of contents to get an idea of what they offer. Also, you may want to look at the Alpha Course website. Alpha is a ten-week introduction to the Christian faith and offers an ideal discussion-based environment for your friends who have questions. Alpha is offered all over the U.S. and across the world. You can search for an Alpha Course near you.

Resources

- *The Alpha Course: www.alphausa.org*
- Searching Issues: The Most Common Questions Encountered in the Search for Faith, *by Nicky Gumbel, Alpha Resources. Top questions asked about the Christian faith in short, easy-to-understand chapters.*
- Letters from a Skeptic: A Son Wrestles with His Father's Questions about Christianity, *by Dr. Gregory Boyd and Edward K. Boyd, David C. Cook Publishing. A pastor and theology professor corresponds through letters with his agnostic father over a three-year period. Provides very helpful thoughts on key questions and models how to respond in a sensitive and respectful manner.*
- The Reason for God: Belief in an Age of Skepticism, *by Timothy Keller, Riverhead Trade. The pastor of a large, growing church in the heart of Manhattan uses his significant experience teaching and relating to urban skeptics to address key questions and counter the arguments of recent atheist authors. Particularly helpful for those who desire more intellectual but accessible responses to challenging issues.*

📖 Spiritual Reading

The reading this week is two short chapters from two books by John Fischer called *Real Christians ~~Don't~~ Dance! - Sorting the Truth from the Trappings in a Born-Again Christian Culture* and *True Believers ~~Don't~~ Ask Why*. Fischer was a pioneer in contemporary Christian music, recording and performing for many years.

With this background, Fischer writes about our need to avoid or break out of an isolated Christian world in a chapter called, "Only One World." As we discussed in the introduction this week, some of you may not identify with what he writes—it may be something rather to stay aware of. For others, it may be thought provoking and even stretching.

It's taken me a long time, but I think I'm starting to get it. I live in one world.

One world: an ugly one filled with war, disease, terrorism, rape, exploitation, hunger – I could fill the page – but that is the world. I have read my Bible from cover to cover, and I have not found any mention of another one. In fact, the world I find in the Bible seems to be basically the same as the one I live in.

The glorious news of the Gospel, of course, is that God came into this world in human flesh. He came in the person of His only begotten Son, Jesus Christ. Jesus did not come to create a little world within a world; He came straight from His Father in heaven to bring love, mercy, healing, and forgiveness into *this* world.

To do that, He lived in this world – you know, the ugly one, the only one we have, the one full of prostitutes, criminals, soldiers, lepers, and crazy maniacs. He lived in a world of people with wild eyes and smelly bandages, people who, if they moved in next door, would definitely bring down the property values.

The world Jesus came into the same world He sends us into as His followers. He prayed, "My prayer is not that you take them out of the world but that you protect them from the evil one. They are not of the world, even as I am not of it. Sanctify them by the truth; your word is truth. As you sent me into the world, I have sent them into the world" (John 17:15-18).

But instead of going into the world as we have been sent, we have created our own little world within a world. It's a world where "Christian" things are true, where everyone lives happily ever after, and, most importantly, where we can be safe from the "other" world – the big, scary one out there. Furthermore, the safety and security we count on so much in our own little world have less to do with Jesus Christ than with locks, fences, money, and the "right" neighborhood.

It's important to note that the born-again culture has been born and bred in this sheltered world-within-a-world, and that's why it finds itself so limited and so out of touch with the people Christ came to save. We have done just what He told us not to do. We have put our light under the bushel of safe Christian subculture.

But the most distressing problem with this little world we have created is that, through it, we plan to escape the ugliness of the other world. We are glad to be insulated and prefer to watch Christian news, listen to Christian music, and have only Christian friends. We get more excited about the number of Christians who are in our office than we do about the number of non-Christians who are there for us to love. The truth is, we don't love non-Christians; we don't even like them. They swear, they have different values, and they wear smelly bandages.

We like our little world. We feel safe here. But our little world is a fantasy. If you look hard enough, you'll find as many crimes here as you do in the real world; they're just more carefully concealed. The safety of this little fantasy world is a fantasy, too. Why? Because we really live in only one world, and it's an ugly one.

Sooner or later that world is going to come crashing in on our little fantasy world-within-the-world. Sooner or later the rapist is going to break into our house, the riot is going to spill over into the street, or the bomb is going to go off under our car. It's inevitable. There's no way to escape the danger of life in this hostile world because, after all, the world is our address.

We have to get beyond being shocked and horrified by what we see in the world and get on with walking into it with the love and mercy of Jesus Christ.

When we do, we will finally realize that safety has nothing to do with locks, that security has nothing to do with fences, that joy has nothing to do with the absence of pain, and that peace has nothing to do with comfort. We will no longer confuse the securities of our subculture with the presence of Christ.

We will know the real Christ sustaining us in the real world, where He once sustained himself by doing the will of His Father. We will also hurt with the world, bleed for it, and cry over it just as Jesus did. We will be in danger and touch the unclean bandages.

The question is simple and straightforward: Are you in the world of are you escaping it? The issue is black and white. You are either walking into the world and into reality or you are walking away from it and into fantasy – because there's only one world and it's an ugly one.

In the second essay, Fischer demonstrates some of what he encourages in the first reading through a conversation he has on a plane ride. Take note of what you see as effective in his approach.

Any seasoned traveler should be well acquainted with the sinking feeling associated with first discovering that he or she has been reluctantly assigned a B or an E seat for a three-hour flight. I'm a C-D person myself – most comfortable with the aisle seat. Even if the plane is full, I still have one open side and free access to the lavatory without having to crawl over any bodies.

With travel agents routinely preassigning seats, this usually gets taken care of; but occasionally plans change or computers break down, and I sometimes have to suffer a B or an E seat. And you can be sure, if you are 11B, that all the other window and aisle seats are taken – including, of course, 11A and 11C. The middle seats are the last to go.

It's illogical to think – sealed and strapped in a tiny fuselage screeching through the sky at a frightening speed – that an aisle on one side and an empty seat on the other would give a person a feeling of autonomy, but it does. The middle seat, shoulder to shoulder and elbows vying for armrests, is, in my opinion, the epitome of entrapment. I will do anything, even sit in the smoking section, to avoid a B seat.

But on this particular evening, I was on standby for a late trip from Dallas to San Francisco and had to take what I got. What I got was 11B. Oh boy, three hours in Claustrophobia.

As I boarded the already-crowded plane, I noticed 11C was standing by patiently at his seat. Obviously a frequent flyer, he knew he would eventually have to get up for two people, so he chose to stand and wait.

223

We made eye contact and he moved away to let me pack my carry-ons in the overhead bin and enter my assigned cubicle. "Welcome to Sardine Airlines," he said. Well, at least he has a sense of humor, I though. We stood next to each other, waiting for 11A to show up, and carried on typical small talk.

Suddenly his eyes widened and I followed his studying gaze to a very attractive woman who was making her way up the aisle toward us. When she passed, he sighed, "How come they never end up next to me? Some guys get all the luck."

"Well, thanks a lot!" I replied.

Seconds later, however, she was back. "Excuse me. I think that's my seat," she said, nodding toward 11A, and 11C and I eagerly scrambled out to let her in. As we did, I stole a glance at him and found his eyebrows in a raised position. "Some guys get all the luck," he repeated in a whisper, indicating that stock in 11B had suddenly shot up in value.

I had a premonition: This was going to be *some* trip.

There are subtle ways that people have of indicating, early on in a flight, whether or not they are interested in engaging their fellow passengers in conversation. Burying one's head in a book or a briefcase is a signal easily read by all but the most indiscreet of travelers. Usually you can tell in the first minute or so what to expect, and the woman next to me let us know right away that she was up for conversation.

I say "us" because from the start I had 11C hanging over my right shoulder making sure I never had one private moment with the brunette in 11A. I considered giving 11C my seat, but he would never have gone for such an obvious tactic. Besides, that would have put me on the outside; and I knew if I was in 11C, I would dip into the conversation cordially, and then excuse myself to my ubiquitous yellow legal pad.

I don't usually seek out this kind of animated dialogue unless I'm the center of attention. It comes from all those years on stage, I guess. This was definitely outside my comfort zone. I wanted to fly with this experience even though I was scared. Being in 11B was going to force me to relate as a human being – something that as a "Christian" singer, author, and songwriter" I can avoid doing if I so choose. In the "Christian World" I can get away with thinking I'm something more than human; but on this plane to San Francisco, I was just the guy in 11B. This was one time when "Fasten Your Seat Belt" has other implications. For the next three hours, I leaned my seat back, and 11A and C leaned into a lively exchange that had my head rotating between two bright and captivating people. I kept my seat belt fastened the whole flight.

Those three hours went a long way toward changing my concept of what Christians commonly call "witnessing." Believe me, when you're strapped into a 600-mile-an-hour conversation in 11B at 30,000 feet, all those neat books and seminars on "How to Share Your Faith" go flying out the airplane window. If I could re-write those seminars and books, I would try something like, "How to Be Normal," or "How to Enjoy People," or "How to Be a Part of What's Happening Around You."

Half an hour into the flight and halfway into finding out what each of us did for a living, the flight attendant came by with beverages.

"I'd like a beer," said 11C, leaning for his wallet.

"White wine, please," said 11A, reaching for her purse.

"I'm buying," said 11B, pushing back both the wallet and the purse.

I can't believe I'm doing this, I thought. Is this anything like the wine at the wedding, Jesus? Something tells me you won't find this part in the witnessing book.

We had already found out that 11A represented an interior design firm that specialized in decorating corporate offices. Now we discovered that 11C represented a furniture company that specialized in furnishing corporate offices, which immediately set of a mad exchange of business cards, brochures, and ideas. My neck felt as if someone had turned up the water pressure on the sprinkler.

"And what do you do?" they asked inevitably.

I knew it was coming, but there was no way I could have been prepared.

"Uh... music. I write and perform my own music. I have a couple of books published as well."

No, I didn't tell them I wrote Christian music or Christian books. It was difficult, but I found ways around it. I wasn't ready to tell them I was a Christian. Not when they were just starting to like me, and not when I was finding out I could actually carry on normal conversation with normal people.

We followed my lead into discussing music, writing, and the arts, then on to a brief dip into politics, and finally the subject of religion came up. Halfway through the flight, my moment came. 11C set me up perfectly.

"Would you believe the uncanny luck I have?" he said. "It seems as if almost every flight I'm on, I end up sitting next to some minister who wants to talk to me about God!"

"Well, brace yourself," I said, "'Cause it's going to happen again!"

(Rule #1 in John Fischer's book on how to witness: Be a knowledgeable person. Have something to talk about. Don't just read Christian books and Christian magazines. It's a big world out there, and the Lord is the Lord of it all. If Jesus is the way, the truth, and the life, you should be able to start anywhere and end up with Him. Paul did this in Athens. He started with an idol to an unknown god and ended up with the resurrected Christ.

Rule #2: Don't tell them you're a Christian too soon; they might just happen to like you. And then when you finally do tell them you're a Christian, they might decide to like you anyway, which means that because of you, they will have to reexamine their whole idea of Christianity in the first place.

In this case, they had to like me because we were all having too much fun.)

"No! You're a minister and you bought the drinks?"

"Ever hear of the first miracle of Jesus?" I asked.

"Wasn't that when he changed the water to wine at a wedding?" asked 11A.

"Yes. How'd you know that?"

"I used to be a Baptist." And we were off.

For the next hour and a half we talked about miracles, Christians, TV evangelists, Catholicism, Baptists, faith, family, relationships, living together, life death, Jesus Christ, and 11A's boyfriend who was waiting for her in San Francisco – the one she couldn't decide about because she left one in Dallas, too. (We understood how this could happen.)

By the time we landed at San Francisco airport, there wasn't one thing that I wanted to say about the gospel of Jesus Christ that I hadn't said. Yet none of it was forced, planned, rehearsed, or manipulated. And none of what I said was received as a sermon.

I'll never forget saying goodbye and walking away from baggage claim realizing that I had just been the best witness I could be by simply fastening my seat belt in 11B and going along for the ride. For in the energy, excitement, and sensuality that was flying around row 11, there was also a Holy Spirit very alive and well in the middle of it all.

Questions for Reflection and Discussion

- What did you find interesting or challenging in the first reading, "Only One World"?

- How did you feel like he lived out what he wrote in the first reading in his encounter on the plane?

- What steps could you take in your life to avoid being isolated in a "Christian world" and intentionally build relationships with those who don't follow Christ? What changes would it mean for you? Are there changes you would need to make to help you find common ground with people (see Fischer's Rule #1 for witnessing)?

- Take some time to pray. Ask God to reveal any of his thinking on these issues.

Bonus Section
Praying for Potential Disciples

At the end of the discipleship process, we will discuss the specifics of how to disciple someone, but now is a good time to begin to pray about who God might leading you to for discipling. Although there is the possibility of people being directed to you by others in the Church, the primary way you will find others to disciple is through your own relationships.

Jesus provides a good model for us in identifying others to disciple. In the gospels, we find that Jesus spent a period of time in relationship with a large number of his followers. After spending a night in prayer, he asked twelve of them to be with him in a closer, mentoring relationship. Through prayer he was directed by his Father as to who to invite into a discipleship relationship.

At this point, you don't need to talk to anyone, although that's fine if the opportunity arises. You simply need to begin praying and asking God to show you how he may be leading. He may lead you to people you are already in relationship with or into new relationships.

How do we know what to look for in a potential disciple? Here are a few things:

- It may be someone you know or will meet who is currently not a follower of Christ, but may be seeking. This is why this week's discussion on being in relationship with spiritual seekers is so important.

- When someone is eventually invited into the discipleship process, they will need to have made a decision to follow Christ in their lives. Otherwise, the process could be confusing for them.

- A key characteristic is that the person is eager to grow and welcomes the opportunity to have help from someone else. As you know, this process is a significant investment, so the person will need to be pretty motivated.

Over the coming weeks, you can discuss with your group the people you feel that God may be leading you to and get the group's input. An additional factor to consider is where the people are at in terms of emotional health in their lives. If they are experiencing significant pain, addiction, or relational challenges in their life, they may want to consider going through Restoration or a similar program before beginning the discipleship process. You may want to consider getting them started or even going through it with them.

The first step is prayer. Begin praying regularly throughout the rest of the course, asking God to guide you. Pray with a sense of expectation and adventure, trusting that God will begin to lead in surprising ways. If possible, take some time to pray right now. Let the adventure begin!

If we are becoming or continuing to be connected to the world as we discussed last week, we should begin to have opportunities to talk with others about our journey with Jesus. One of the things that can stifle our sharing with others is fear: fear that they will reject what we have to say or simply be indifferent, fear that it will create awkwardness in the relationship, or fear that we will look foolish. It may sound "spiritual" to say that those things shouldn't matter, but in reality, they do. They are valid feelings and concerns. These types of fears stop many people from sharing their faith with anyone.

Fortunately, God has provided a way to address these fears and help us become effective in sharing our faith and, as a result, find great joy and adventure in the process. When done God's way, sharing our faith can be one of the most exciting and fulfilling things in our lives.

What God has provided is the Holy Spirit. When it comes to sharing Jesus with others, we must learn how to follow the leading of the Spirit. When we don't, the whole process can seem like a random activity that can easily end up in failure. However, when we learn to recognize how the Spirit is working in their lives and their openness to his work, and we are sensitive to how the Spirit may be prompting us, then the likelihood of a good experience for *both* you and them goes way up.

To help us in this, we will look at the example of Jesus and hopefully gain some practical help from our reading. In our Spiritual Practice section, we will look at some simple and specific ways to share the gospel message itself, should the Spirit be leading us to do so.

Soaking in Scripture

This is a very interesting passage in which Jesus describes the way his ministry relates to the work of his Father. It is also a great passage to consider in our ministry of sharing Jesus with others.

John 5:19-20

19 Jesus gave them this answer: "Very truly I tell you, the Son can do nothing by himself; he can do only what he sees his Father doing, because whatever the Father does the Son also does. 20 For the Father loves the Son and shows him all he does. Yes, and he will show him even greater works than these, so that you will be amazed.

- What do you think Jesus means by "the Son...can do only what he sees his Father doing"?

- How could this relate to our trying to help others come to know Jesus?

- Personalize the following portion of v. 19 and read it a number of times in an effort to memorize it:

  "I can do nothing by myself; I can only do what I see my Father doing."

As a part of your prayer time, ask God to bring one or more people to mind whom you know that don't currently follow Jesus and ask him to show you what he is doing in their lives. Ask him how you could join him in what he is doing.

Digging into Scripture

This encounter between Jesus and Zacchaeus is a great example of recognizing God's activity in the life of a person who is spiritually seeking. As you make your observations, note the various actions of the different people in the account. What do you notice about Zacchaeus? Jesus? The crowd? In particular, how does the reaction of Jesus to Zacchaeus compare to the response of the crowd to Zacchaeus?

Luke 19:1-10

¹Jesus entered Jericho and was passing through. ²A man was there by the name of Zacchaeus; he was a chief tax collector and was wealthy. ³He wanted to see who Jesus was, but because he was short he could not see over the crowd. ⁴So he ran ahead and climbed a sycamore-fig tree to see him, since Jesus was coming that way.

⁵When Jesus reached the spot, he looked up and said to him, "Zacchaeus, come down immediately. I must stay at your house today." ⁶So he came down at once and welcomed him gladly.

⁷All the people saw this and began to mutter, "He has gone to be the guest of a sinner."

⁸But Zacchaeus stood up and said to the Lord, "Look, Lord! Here and now I give half of my possessions to the poor, and if I have cheated anybody out of anything, I will pay back four times the amount."

⁹Jesus said to him, "Today salvation has come to this house, because this man, too, is a son of Abraham. ¹⁰For the Son of Man came to seek and to save the lost."

Observation

Interpretation

Application

Sharing our faith story and the gospel can seem a bit overwhelming, but it doesn't need to be. Below are some helpful handles that can make it easier for you and the person you are sharing with. If these don't work for you, feel free to go with what does.

Read the following illustrations. When your groups meets, take turns role-playing the bridge and pie chart illustrations with one another. This may seem a bit contrived, but it is often very helpful to have practiced sharing the gospel story. Draw the illustrations as you share. If there is anything worth becoming more comfortable with, this is it!

The Bridge

In the reading for Session 11, we discussed the idea of Jesus and his death being a bridge between us and God the Father. It may be helpful to review that part of the reading.

Adding the visual to that description is often very helpful to people when they are trying to understand the role of Jesus and his death. Here is an example of how a conversation might go:

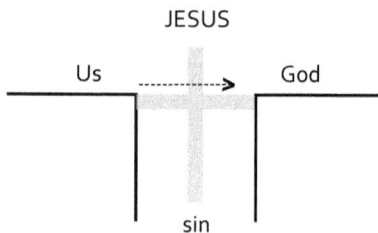

"It sounds like you may be interested in having a closer relationship with God. Here is a visual that was helpful to me in understanding how to start this kind of relationship with him. [Write "Us" on one side of the page, and then write "God" on the other side of the page, with a large gap in between.] God deeply desires to have a relationship with us. In fact, he created us in order to have that type of close relationship with him, like a Father with his son or daughter, but there is a huge gap separating us and God.

"That gap is caused by our sin. [Write "sin" in the gap area.] We have a sinful nature, and God is pure—free of sin. It is not possible for us to have a relationship with a holy God. That sinful nature has caused us to do life on our own, apart from God.

"Most people try to bridge this gap by their own effort: being a good person, doing things for others, or going to church, but there is no way for us to bridge that gap on our own. Nothing we can do is going to create a pure, sin-free nature within us. There will always be a huge separation between us and God.

"The good news, however, is that God so strongly desires to have a relationship with us, that he did something about the problem. He sent his Son, Jesus, to bridge the chasm between us and the Father. Specifically, Jesus took our sin nature and the consequence of that nature, separation from God, on himself and crucified it on the cross. [Draw a cross in the gap, creating a bridge between "Us" and "God."] It is Jesus' death that creates the bridge that we can walk across into relationship with the Father and with Jesus [Draw an arrow across the bridge].

"When we accept Jesus' death on our behalf, we can begin the type of relationship we've been looking for. Does this make sense?"

After discussing their understanding so far, you can continue by saying, "But this is only the start of the relationship. There is a 2nd picture that might help you see how this relationship with God can impact your life."

Pie Chart

The pie chart that we discussed in the reading for Session 12 is a great way to help someone see how this relationship with God plays out in their life. It is helpful for them to know from the beginning that our relationship with God doesn't stop with salvation; in fact, that's just the beginning! We want them to have the expectation of God working in all areas of their life as they surrender to his leadership.

Again, the pie chart represents the different areas of one's life: family, work, finances, etc. The key question is, "Who is at the center of the pie, directing things?" Here is an example of how someone might use this illustration when sharing, continuing on from the bridge visual.

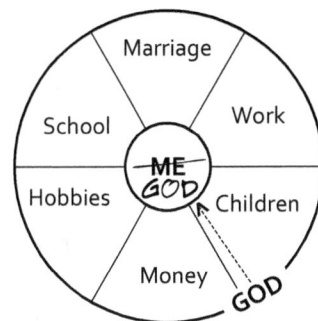

"If the bridge visual shows how to start a relationship with God, this visual helps us see what a life with God looks like.

"This circle or pie chart represents our life. [Draw a circle with pie wedges in it.] We have our family, work, money, friendships, hobbies, serving others, etc. [Write one in each pie section.] At the center of it all, who is calling the shots? Most of us, if we're honest, would have to say, "Me". [Write "me" in the center.] We are usually deciding how *we* will handle each area of our life, and what *we* think is best. We may believe in God, but he really is on the edges of our life. [Write "God" at the inside edge of the circle.]

"But God wants to be at the center of our lives, directing things. [Cross out "me" and write "God" at the center.] He wants to be giving us *his* wisdom, *his* perspective, and *his* priorities, in all areas of our lives [draw arrows from God out to the different areas of life]. He wants to lead us, and when we follow him, we begin to experience a wonderful relationship with him, and life as he intended it to be. Does that kind of make sense?"

This illustration can be very helpful for those who have had a *religious* view of God, but very little understanding of a *relationship* with God that is meaningful to the important areas of their lives. It is also a good opportunity to share how God has impacted your life in real ways.

If they seem open, you can ask, "Would you like to have this kind of relationship with God in your life?" If they do, ask them if they are ready to cross the bridge and accept what Jesus has done for them and start a relationship with God at the center of their lives.

You can offer to pray with them using the prayer below or something similar. In a time of prayer, you can guide them by saying the words for the first area ("Sorry"), and then allowing them to pray; then move on to the next area. Begin by saying something like the following:

"Let's pray together, and I will help lead you through the prayer if that would be helpful."

Sorry
"Express anything you feel sorry for from the past. This may be specific sins, as well as generally living apart from God in your life." (Then they pray.)

Please
In your own words, ask God to please forgive you through Jesus' death for you and share your desire to live life in relationship with him. (They pray.)

Thank You
Thank him for his forgiveness and his promise to come and live within you through the Holy Spirit. (They pray.)

Express your desire for him to come and lead you in all areas of your life. (They pray.)

To close you can pray something like the following:

Father, thank you so much that _____ has begun a new relationship with you today. I know you must be thrilled to have him/her come home to you and experience your love and leadership in their life. Thank you so much that I could be a part of this amazing moment. Amen.

If they are more comfortable, they can pray something similar to the above on their own when they are alone. Either way, it is good to encourage them to take this concrete step to solidify their commitment. A good metaphor is marriage: we may be interested in someone for a long time, but it is when we take the concrete step of proposing marriage that both parties know that a life-long commitment is being made (and to extend the analogy, baptism is like the wedding in terms of being a public declaration of that commitment).

Do versus Done

One last visual can be helpful, particularly to those who are trying to understand how Christianity is different from other religions. The difference can be summarized in two words: *do* and *done.* Other religions teach that we can be accepted by God because of what *we* do: being a good person, helping others, following certain rules or religious practices, avoiding doing bad things. In the end, it's all about *our* efforts. This approach is spelled D-O. If you are sharing this with someone, write "Do" on a piece of paper.

Christianity, however, is spelled D-O-N-E (write "Done" on the paper). It is about what *Jesus* has done for us through his death on our behalf. He has paid the penalty for our sin and made it possible to have relationship with the Father. He has done what we could never do.

As a result, we can get off the treadmill of trying to earn God's acceptance and instead receive what Jesus has already done for us and begin a relationship with him and the Father.

This simple explanation, along with the accompanying visual, can make a big impact on those who have been confused about this critical truth.

Losing the Anxiety

Even with these helps, you may feel anxious when imagining sharing these types of things with people in your life. Hopefully, the reading from this week will be helpful in this regard. When you know that someone is open to God and receptive to you personally (a "person of peace," as described in the reading), then discussions like the ones above will feel good and natural.

You don't have to worry about getting it exactly right, because this is someone you have a relationship with and who is open spiritually. It may take several conversations or things that they hear from others or read somewhere to bring it all together for them.

When you share your own story and the basics of how we can have a relationship with God through Jesus in a simple way, a person who is spiritually receptive will often be ready to take the next critical step. It will be one of the most exciting days of your life.

Spiritual Reading
How to Follow the Spirit's Lead

Understanding the Spiritual Spectrum

One of the mistakes that can be made in evangelism is taking a one-size-fits-all approach: assuming that people are all in a similar place and that a similar approach will be effective. The reality is that people are at very different places in terms of spiritual openness, and this should impact how we try to help them.

It may help to think of it in terms of a continuum, with those who are less interested spiritually on the left side of the continuum and those who are more interested moving toward the right.

Indifferent or Angry

To the far left, we have those who are indifferent to God or spiritual things. This is the most challenging, because there is no interest, no awareness of any need for God. Trying to share about Jesus or discuss spiritual questions usually has little impact. In these situations, praying for them and being present in their lives is the most important. Should something in their lives change that causes them to become more interested, if they have someone in their lives that they trust and respect that has been open about faith but not pushy, then they will often turn to that trusted friend.

Others may be more angry than indifferent when it comes to things related to Christianity or Christians or the Church. Often this is a result of a bad experience they have had as a child or adult with Christians. It could have been with their parents or other family members, a pastor or priest, or a coworker.

Many times, it's a church experience that turns them off. It could have been a legalistic environment or people who seemed hypocritical or inauthentic.

In these situations, the most helpful thing is to provide the opposite picture. A picture of a Christian who is genuine, humble, caring, full of life and joy, and honest about personal shortcomings—all of these things can begin to shift the image of what a Christian is. This will not automatically cause others to begin to seek after God, but it can at least begin to lower some of the resistances they have had.

Curious or Seeking

Moving along the continuum, some go from indifference or anger to curiosity. This could be because something challenging has happened in their lives that caused them to begin to look for something for help or stability. This could be a divorce or marriage problems, job loss, a financial struggle, addiction, or emotional wounds. Or it could simply be a desire to find more meaning and fulfillment in life.

Regardless, they are now more interested and open to spiritual things, which may go beyond Christianity. They begin to notice Christian books and articles, Christian music, the Bible, and they may begin to be curious about churches.

This is where it is most fruitful for a Christian to be actively engaging with them, trying to answer questions, directing them to resources, inviting them to church, introducing them to other Christians.

It is important to remember that, at this point, they may have a range of beliefs about spiritual things, some that line up with biblical truth and some that do not. Do not overreact to these views, but continue to walk alongside them and gently point them toward Jesus and truth.

As they begin to understand more about God and who he really is, they will hopefully begin to actively seek more of him and what it means to know him. In this phase, they will begin to attend church regularly on their own, attend a small group, read the Bible, and pray.

It is important to know how to simply and clearly share the gospel and what it means to have a relationship with God, as opposed to having "religion." This is where the visuals and explanations we looked at in our Spiritual Practice section can be helpful.

Movement is the Key

You are trying to help people move along the spectrum. By your authentic, humble example of someone trying to follow God in your life, you may be able to help someone move from angry to curious (or, at least, less angry). Someone may come along later in their lives when they are more open and help them move to seeking or committing their lives to Christ. They key is to be obedient to help them move in the right direction.

"You Weren't Ready"

A friend of ours, Jamie, came to Christ as an adult a few years ago. She told us about how that journey began for her. She had a close friend named Samarra that she had known for about ten years. She knew Samarra was a committed Christian, but they hadn't talked about that much over the years.

Then Jamie entered a very difficult period of her life and in her marriage. One day, when Jamie and Samarra were discussing the situation, Samarra simply asked, "Have you thought about reaching out to God?" Jamie was a bit surprised and said, "Why have you never asked me that before? I've known that you were a Christian." Samarra responded, "Because you weren't ready."

Samarra was aware of where Jamie had been on her journey: indifferent. But she had been a good, caring friend and a positive example of Jesus along the way. Samarra followed the lead of the Spirit and sensed that Jamie might now be open to God. She was right. Samarra hadn't forced the conversation in the past, being sensitive to the Spirit in this way, but when she sensed possible openness, she had the courage to simply extend an invitation: an invitation that Jamie could receive or dismiss.

This awareness of someone's openness to God is key. In Jesus' instructions to his disciples when he sent them out to villages ahead of him, he told them to look for a person of peace (Luke 10:6). What he meant by that was someone who was open to them relationally and open to the message they were bringing about Jesus and his kingdom. "When you find someone like that," he told them, "Stay with them. Spend time with them."

Similarly for us, we need to invest time with those who seem open to God and to us. We still want to be in the lives of those who are not open, but mainly as a healthy, loving example of Jesus in their lives. The great part is we don't have to feel like we have to somehow force those who are not ready to believe or do some masterful sales job. Like Samarra, we need to be in their lives, but to trust God to be at work and to alert us when they are becoming more open.

What can you do to know whether someone you are getting to know is a person of peace—someone that is open to God? One of the main things is sharing naturally and intentionally from your life and seeing how they respond. Depending on how well you know the person, it may be mentioning a challenge going on in your life and how you are seeking God for help. It could be something you recently did with others from your small group or church community.

It can also be letting people know that you see God playing a role in your life. My wife, Jacki, is a photographer. As she gets to know clients, it is often natural to mention that we moved to Minnesota from California. That is usually followed up with something along the lines of, "Why would you do that?!" (Note that this question is coming from Minnesotans!) There are a lot of ways she could respond to the question, but she intentionally—and accurately—responds, "Well, it's kind of a crazy story, but we believe that God led us to move here." That is like handing them an invitation to ask more, isn't it? Some do and some don't. If they are intrigued, it often indicates openness.

Another way to discern if others are open is to be aware of needs in their lives. This means you need to get to know them well enough to hear or observe those needs. This is when people are most open to God. When they are struggling in their marriage, with their kids, their work, a relationship—this is when they *may* be open. Like Samarra, this is a good time to offer help of some kind (how God might help them, prayer, an invitation to a group, a helpful book). If they are open, great. If not, don't push it; simply pray for openness in the future.

Spread the Net Wide

All of the ideas discussed above only make a difference if we are applying what we learned last session. We have to be connecting with many people in our lives who don't know God. If we are isolated in our Christian activities and relationships, there will be no need to pray about how we help or respond, because there won't be anybody to respond to!

Seek not just one or two people in your life, but many. These may not all be deep relationships, but you need to be connecting with a number of people from the various parts of your life. The key is to take small but intentional steps toward connecting with others. This may mean spending more time in the front yard in hopes of seeing a neighbor, talking to someone at work during a break, or putting down the phone at a kid's practice or game to talk to another parent.

When you cast a wide relational net, what you will find is that people are all along the spectrum we discussed above. Some, not usually a lot, will be open. It may be one or two people at any given time, but if you are only connecting with one or two people in your life who don't know God, the odds aren't in your favor!

Take intentional steps toward others, open up your life, and see how they respond. Know that God is already at work in their lives, and he will be guiding you, too.

Questions for Reflection and Discussion

- How does understanding our role with people at different places on their journey help you?

- What do you find helpful about the "person of peace" principle?

- During your prayer time, ask God to give you a sense of where different people in your life are at in their journeys. Indifferent? Open (a person of peace)? Pray to see how he might lead you to help them.

Over the past two sessions, we have been looking outward as we have discussed sharing Jesus with others. This week, we will continue looking outward as we discuss sharing Jesus' love with others through acts of compassion and justice. If we are not careful, we can view the outward sharing of Jesus with others in words only—sharing the message—and neglect the *demonstration* of the message through compassion and justice.

In Scripture, we see God's heart clearly expressed through hundreds of passages that focus on the poor and others in need (compassion) and the oppressed (justice). We will look at passages and readings that deal with both areas: compassion *and* justice. Out of the two areas, we may be more familiar with compassion: sacrificially assisting, and often learning from, those who are experiencing various types of need, often related to poverty.

We may be less familiar with issues of injustice, also referred to in Scripture as oppression. In an attempt to define injustice, Christian author and leader Gary Haugen writes in his book, *Good News about Injustice: A Witness of Courage in a Hurting World*, that "injustice occurs when *power is misused* to take from others what God has given them, namely, their life, dignity, liberty or the fruits of their love and labor." These are issues such as child labor; forced prostitution; violence based on race or religious beliefs; and police, judges, or elected officials looking the other way instead of administering justice.

The topic of compassion and justice is a large one. The readings and other materials this week are designed simply to get us thinking about this important area. If you have not explored this area very deeply, I would strongly encourage you to read *The Hole in Our Gospel Special Edition: What Does God Expect of Us? The Answer That Changed My Life and Might Just Change the World*, by Richard Stearns, as well as the book mentioned in this week's Spiritual Practice, *Good News about Injustice: A Witness of Courage in a Hurting World*, by Gary Haugen.

Obviously, issues of compassion and justice are not usually light or simple. God, through the Holy Spirit, can help us grow in our understanding and show us what it looks like in our lives to live out this important area of his heart.

Soaking in Scripture

In Jeremiah 22, God is expressing his displeasure with Jehoahaz, the king of Judah, and how he is different from his father, Josiah, the former king, who was righteous and pleasing to God. To get the context, it will be helpful to first read Jeremiah 22:11-15.

Jeremiah 22:16

He defended the cause of the poor and needy, and so all went well.
Is that not what it means to know me?" declares the Lord.

- What do you think God means by "Is that not what it means to know me?"

- What would you normally think of when considering what it means to know God? Would it usually include defending the cause of the poor and needy?

- In Jeremiah 22:11-16, what contrasts do you see between what the son focused on in his life and what the father focused on?

- During your prayer time, talk to God about how well you know his heart in this area and seek to listen to what he might say to you.

Digging into Scripture

This week's passage from Isaiah 58 offers excellent insight into what is important to the heart of God, particularly as it relates to both compassion and justice.

This is a longer passage, so a little direction may be helpful. The first section (vv. 1-5), could be titled, *What Frustrates God?* The second section (vv. 6-7), could be called, *What Does God Want?* The third section (vv. 8-10) could be titled, *What Does He Promise?* This may help as you make your observations for each section.

As always, seriously consider how God may be speaking personally to you through this passage and how it might apply to your life. It may also be helpful to think about how this passage relates to the Church. If possible, spend some time in prayer to see what God might be saying to you.

Isaiah 58:1-10

[1]"*Shout it aloud, do not hold back. Raise your voice like a trumpet.*
Declare to my people their rebellion and to the descendants of Jacob their sins.
[2]*For day after day they seek me out; they seem eager to know my ways, as if they were a nation that does what is right and has not forsaken the commands of its God.*
They ask me for just decisions and seem eager for God to come near them.
[3]'*Why have we fasted,' they say, 'and you have not seen it?*
Why have we humbled ourselves, and you have not noticed?'

"*Yet on the day of your fasting, you do as you please and exploit all your workers.*
[4]*Your fasting ends in quarreling and strife, and in striking each other with wicked fists.*
You cannot fast as you do today and expect your voice to be heard on high.
[5]*Is this the kind of fast I have chosen, only a day for people to humble themselves?*
Is it only for bowing one's head like a reed and for lying in sackcloth and ashes?
Is that what you call a fast, a day acceptable to the Lord?

[6]"*Is not this the kind of fasting I have chosen: to loose the chains of injustice and untie the cords of the yoke, to set the oppressed free and break every yoke?*
[7]*Is it not to share your food with the hungry and to provide the poor wanderer with shelter—when you see the naked, to clothe them, and not to turn away from your own flesh and blood?*
[8]*Then your light will break forth like the dawn, and your healing will quickly appear; then your righteousness will go before you, and the glory of the Lord will be your rear guard.*
[9]*Then you will call, and the Lord will answer; you will cry for help, and he will say: Here am I.*

"*If you do away with the yoke of oppression, with the pointing finger and malicious talk,*
[10]*and if you spend yourselves in behalf of the hungry and satisfy the needs of the oppressed, then your light will rise in the darkness, and your night will become like the noonday.*

Observation

Interpretation

Application

Spiritual Practice
Learning about Injustice

As mentioned in this week's introduction, some may be less familiar with issues related to injustice. To help with this, we are going to take some time to look at one organization that is doing great work in the area of injustice. The organization is called International Justice Mission (IJM).

Set aside some time, thirty minutes or more, to research the IJM website (www.ijm.org). Here you can get an overview of the work IJM does across the world, as well as look at case studies and videos, both found under Downloads on the Resources tab. As you read and learn, see how God may be speaking you to about his heart concerning issues of justice. Be aware of how he may be leading you to take further steps to learn more or to get involved. There are practical steps to explore under the Get Involved tab.

Another great resource, written by the president of IJM, Gary Haugen, is a book called *Good News about Injustice: A Witness of Courage in a Hurting World*. This could be a next step for you in your learning process.

If you would like to look at a neat opportunity for helping people become self-sustaining, check out www.kiva.org. Kiva is an organization that provides micro-loans by linking those with resources to entrepreneurs in developing countries.

The Great Divide

Growing up in Texas, I was part of a strong church that taught about the importance of a relationship with Jesus and the role his death played in making it possible to have a relationship with him and the Father. I learned a lot about the Bible and the wisdom it provided for my life, as well as the importance of sharing my faith with others. I learned many other things, but one area that was not discussed much was the topic of God's heart for compassion toward the broken, poor, and often forgotten in our society. I did not learn his passion concerning justice for those who have been mistreated or oppressed due to race, gender, social class, or a host of other reasons.

Interestingly enough, had I walked down the street to another church, it's quite possible that I would have heard a great deal of teaching on these topics. In fact, I might have heard an emphasis on these subjects. However, I may have heard very little on the importance of a relationship with Jesus, both for my salvation and for the transformation he can bring to who I am as a person, or the key role that the Bible can play in my work, relationships, and decisions.

Why would this be? Why would there be such a difference in two churches, both of which are supposed to be Christian?

A (brief) history lesson may be helpful here. Around the turn of the twentieth century in the U.S., a number of church leaders had become very concerned that the broader Church in America was becoming too theologically liberal. By liberal, they meant that the leaders of those churches had begun teaching that many of the things that had been core to historical Christian teaching—the identity of Jesus as the Son of God, salvation being made possible through Jesus' death, the Bible as the inspired Word of God—were now in question. In place of these traditional teachings, an emphasis was often put on our need to show the love of God to others through acts of compassion and justice.

More traditional church leaders reacted to this teaching by distancing themselves and their churches from this liberal teaching and placing even greater emphasis on historical beliefs. As a result, the areas of compassion and justice were often seen as liberal issues and de-emphasized or even seen as efforts to "earn" salvation. There was a great divide within the larger Church. There were certainly exceptions, but many churches and Christians were impacted by this split in thinking.

The consequences of this divide have been huge. On the liberal side of the divide, these leaders and Christians have often had a great impact on their communities and the world by helping the poor, the hurting, and the homeless. They advocate for those suffering from racism, unfair laws, forced labor, slavery, and other injustices. However, at times, the personal transformation and closeness that can comes through a relationship with Jesus based on his grace can be missing. It can mean great outward impact, but an inward emptiness.

On the other side of the divide, it has sometimes meant those who are very committed to their beliefs and a personal relationship with Jesus have been isolated from critical needs in the community around them. It has also meant sometimes being on the wrong side of very important issues of justice, such as slavery and civil rights. Remarkably, many Christians and Christian leaders were vocally opposed to the abolition of slavery and later to civil rights. When the inward, personal nature of our faith is emphasized to such a great extent, the outward impact we can have on the world around us can be greatly diminished.

God's Heart

With all of this in mind, we need to ask the important question: How does God feel about all of this? Which side of the divide is important to him? I bet you have a hunch.

If you look across the full sweep of the Bible, you will find that God feels deeply about both sides of the divide. Clearly, from the very beginning, he has desired relationship with those he has created. That has been his plan all along. He has gone to great lengths in sending his Son to repair the relational divide and, through that restored relationship with him, to see deep change happen within us and peace restored to our lives.

It is also clear that he is not satisfied with a relationship that simply benefits us and those closest to us. In literally hundreds of passages, we see his heart and command to love the lonely and forgotten, the orphan and the widow, and to defend those who are being oppressed.

We see God's heart and fierce passion in passages like the one that we studied this week from **Isaiah 58:6-7**:

> *Is not this the kind of fasting I have chosen:*
> *to loose the chains of injustice and untie the cords of the yoke,*
> *to set the oppressed free and break every yoke?*
> *Is it not to share your food with the hungry*
> *   and to provide the poor wanderer with shelter—*
> *when you see the naked, to clothe them,*
> *   and not to turn away from your own flesh and blood?*

God appears to be saying that all the practices of personal faith don't mean much to him when we are ignoring the needs and injustices of those around us that he cares about so much.

Getting a Picture

What does it look like when both parts of God's heart come together in the Church?

John Wesley was a dynamic Christian leader in England during the eighteenth and nineteenth centuries. Those who followed his leadership went on to become known as the Methodists. Wesley would preach powerfully about the need for people to come to know Christ, receive forgiveness for their sins, and begin a new life with him. He also urged them to share their new faith with others, and thousands of people across England and later America began to follow Jesus as a result.

Wesley, however, didn't just lead individuals to Christ; he began a movement. This movement of people began to dramatically impact the society around them. At the time, the slave trade was in full swing, and others worked in horrible conditions, particularly in mines and factories. Children were forced to work at an early age, and poverty was rampant. Wesley and those he helped come to know Christ began to serve these groups and advocate on their behalf.

In the end, Wesley's followers "not only played a major role in the abolition of the slave trade but also had an effect on prison reform, labor laws and factory working conditions, and the availability of education for the poor" (*The Hole in Our Gospel Special Edition: What Does God Expect of Us? The Answer That Changed My Life and Might Just Change the World*, Richard Stearns). Wesley and his followers understood both parts of God's heart, and it changed an entire country.

Making It Personal

What might this look like on a more personal level? First, it means having God's heart—having the desire—to love those in difficult situations. This is easier said than done, because our natural tendency is to focus on our needs and those closest to us. This isn't a bad starting point, but our compassion needs to venture farther out.

As our hearts begin to grow and align with God's heart, we will often need help in knowing whom to help and where to start. Often, those with greater needs don't cross our everyday paths.

Consider those in the following situations and think about whether you encounter them on a regular basis:
- A child from an at-risk family in need of a mentor or foster parents
- A young, unwed mother with few resources
- A newly arrived refugee family with no friends or family
- Working parents who regularly run out of food before the end of the month
- Families who don't qualify for federal assistance because they earn too much money, but are in danger of losing adequate housing
- Teenage girls forced into prostitution
- Children enslaved as laborers for years
- Orphans in need of parents

If you do experience any of these situations through your family, your work, or your neighborhood, then you have a wonderful opportunity right in the midst of your life. That would certainly be a great place to start, asking God to lead you into the next step.

You may find it rare, however, to come across these types of needs. In that case, a few things can be helpful.

First, find organizations that are already engaged with some of the problems or needs mentioned above (and many others). Become aware of what is happening in your community, surrounding area, and globally. These groups are actively engaged on a daily basis with people in need. This can be a bridge from your daily experience to those who are living in very different circumstances.

Next, take time to reflect on your *passions*. Think and pray about your past life experiences. Often, God will use challenges, pain, or positive experiences from your past to ignite your passion.

Living through the divorce of your parents might make your heart tender toward a child in a similar situation that needs a mentor. Wrestling with addiction in the past may motivate you to help others with a similar challenge. Maybe a past mission trip experience stirred your heart around adoption or helping refugee or immigrant families.

Rather than a past experience, God may help you see how he has wired you—your gifts and passions—to connect with a particular need. We will look at this more closely in a few weeks.

Lastly, look for *people* to partner with. You don't have to do this alone. You may want to partner with a like-minded friend. If you have a family, talk about these things with your spouse and your children. Your family could explore some of the needs and groups that are working with these needs and then discuss what you might be excited about doing together. How exciting to think about your kids growing up sharing the love of Jesus with others in this tangible way and seeing this as an important part of what it means to be a follower of his: being a family on mission together.

If you are a part of a group at church, it could mean discussing your passions as a group and the resources you bring to the table (skills, talents, finances, networking) and dreaming about what you could do together. A group of people working together can make a tremendous impact. The side benefit is that it will pull you closer together than ever before as you are on mission together.

First Steps

What is your first step? It may simply be beginning to ask God to give you more of his heart surrounding this area of compassion and justice. Ask the Spirit to alert you when you come across Scripture passages revealing God's heart or see something on the internet or in conversation with friends or family. It could also be more specific.

When you begin to connect God's heart and your passion, you will be surprised at the places it will lead you. Places full of challenge and adventure. Places that will change the lives of those you are serving and change yours in the process as well.

Questions for Reflection and Discussion

- Have you experienced either side of the "divide" in your church experience?

- What is a barrier to reaching out in compassion or justice for you? Is there anything discussed in the reading that would help overcome that barrier?

- During your prayer time, share your desires, as well as any struggles, when it comes to being a person of compassion and justice.

The Church, as God intends it to be, is an amazing thing. It has the ability to be a potent force in the world and in our lives. But what exactly is the Church? Do we have a clear picture of the Church and its purpose? Its potential? It is easy to have some ideas about the Church from our past that are inaccurate—or simply too small.

One key aspect for us to understand is that the Church, by its nature, is intended to be *missional*: on a *mission* that is impacting others. For many, the picture of the Church is that of a group of people who simply care for those within the Church. However, it should be clear from the past few weeks that he wants his Church to be looking outward, caring for the world around it.

A special focus as we look at the Church will be the practice of Christian community. Why is community so important to our lives and to our spiritual growth? How does community help us live out what the Church is meant to be for one another? How can we impact others *through community* in the ways we've been discussing over the past few weeks, through sharing Jesus with others and practicing compassion and justice?

In the weeks ahead, we will look at some other aspects of being the Church in more detail, including worship and using our spiritual gifts.

Soaking in Scripture

In this passage, we get a chance to see the relationship between Jesus and the Church and between the Church and the world, both of which are important to understand. Ephesians 1:20-21 has been included to provide some background. We will focus on vv. 22-23 for our reflection.

> **Ephesians 1:20-23** (MSG)
>
> 20-21*All this energy issues from Christ: God raised him from death and set him on a throne in deep heaven, in charge of running the universe, everything from galaxies to governments, no name and no power exempt from his rule. And not just for the time being, but forever. He is in charge of it all, has the final word on everything.*
>
> 22-23*At the center of all this, Christ rules the church. The church, you see, is not peripheral to the world; the world is peripheral to the church. The church is Christ's body, in which he speaks and acts, by which he fills everything with his presence.*

- What do you think it means when it says that Christ rules the Church?

247

- Write v. 23 in your own words, particularly reflecting on the Church as Christ's *body*.

- What would it look like for the church you are a part of to be "Christ's body" to the world around it?

- As a part of your prayer time, express your thoughts and ask God to share his on the importance of his Church in this world.

Digging into Scripture

Acts 2:41-47 is a key New Testament passage, because it is one of the best descriptions of life in the early Church. It is a brief snapshot that can be very helpful to us today.

As always, read and study the passage slowly several times. There is a lot packed into this short section. As you make your observations, consider what overall feeling you get from this description. What is your general impression? What strikes you about the different elements of community life they were experiencing? How does it impact your view of what the Church should or could be like today?

Acts 2:41-47 (NLT)

41Those who believed what Peter said were baptized and added to the church that day—about 3,000 in all.

42All the believers devoted themselves to the apostles' teaching, and to fellowship, and to sharing in meals (including the Lord's Supper), and to prayer.

43A deep sense of awe came over them all, and the apostles performed many miraculous signs and wonders. 44And all the believers met together in one place and shared everything they had. 45They sold their property and possessions and shared the money with those in need. 46They worshiped together at the Temple each day, met in homes for the Lord's Supper, and shared their meals with great joy and generosity—47all the while praising God and enjoying the goodwill of all the people. And each day the Lord added to their fellowship those who were being saved.

Observation

Interpretation

Application

Spiritual Reading
What is Church?

Many Different Pictures

What comes to mind when you hear the word *church*? It probably depends on what you are currently experiencing, if you are a part of a church, or what you experienced growing up if you were a part of a church at any time. It could be influenced by what part of the country or world you grew up in.

The variety of church experience is amazing. Formal, casual, small, huge, strict, relaxed, expressive, reserved, diverse, not-so-diverse, rural, urban, Catholic, Protestant, Orthodox, church buildings, public buildings, home, and on and on.

If you were in China, you most likely would gather with other believers in an underground house church (non-state approved churches are illegal). In England, you might be in a historic church or cathedral that is hundreds of years old. In Africa, you might be under a simple covering in an outdoor village church. In the U.S., you might be in a mega-church, a school auditorium, or anything in between.

With so much variety, can we get at the essence of what church is? What it is supposed to be? What is the purpose of the Church? Is the Church optional for us? What is my role in the Church?

God's Invention

A good place to start might be recognizing that the Church is God's idea—his invention. It is not something early or later Christians came up with.

In an intense moment with Peter, Jesus informs him, "Now I say to you that you are Peter (which means 'rock'), and upon this rock I will build my church, and all the powers of hell will not conquer it" (Matthew 16:18, NLT). Ultimately, Jesus is the head of the Church, but Peter was to be the key human leader to launch the Church when Jesus returned to heaven.

Jesus also says that the Church will not be defeated by the forces of hell. In other words, the Church is God's plan for bringing his kingdom to earth, for changing the world, and Satan will not defeat it. As church leader Bill Hybels puts it, "The Church is the hope of the world; it's God's Plan A, and there's no Plan B."

Right away, this should help us see that the Church is very important to God and should be very important to us. It is not some optional thing to do; it is a critical piece of God's plan.

It is also critical to understand that the Church is the people. It's not a building or a location, but the people. God chose to create a community of people to carry out his purposes in the world. This is not a religion of individuals worshipping God on their own; it is a community of people on a mission from God.

Acts 2: Up, In, and Out

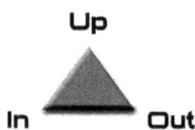

The picture given in Acts 2 gives us a good snapshot of the early Church and some of its core ingredients. What we find in this description is not just the facts, but the "feel" of the early Church. You get the feeling that it was an exciting thing to be a part of. People were in awe of what God was doing. They were enjoying one another. Their lives had purpose as they saw other lives being changed. Things were hopping!

What were the key elements that made that happen and could result in the same excitement and impact today? The Church can take on a lot of forms, but when it has the mix of ingredients found in the biblical picture of the early Church, odds are that it is going to make a difference in its people and the world around it.

A simple way to look at the early Church is using three points of a triangle. This comes from Christian leader Mike Breen and his friends at 3DM, a Christian organization that works with church leaders.

Up

At the top of the triangle, we have *Up*. Up is the pursuit of our relationship with God. In this picture of the early Church, we see that they were *devoted* to teaching, prayer, and worship. They took this new life as followers of Jesus seriously. They wanted to know how to grow in this relationship.

Healthy, vibrant churches take seriously the challenge of helping people grow in their relationship with God in order to have a close, intimate relationship with him. Practical, clear teaching that people can understand and apply to their lives is important. Helping people learn skills, such as studying Scripture, prayer, and other practices that foster a deepening relationship, is key. Offering opportunities to worship God in meaningful ways is vital.

Ensuring that people have a healthy and accurate understanding of who God is and his love for us is critical. Churches need leaders that have a clear understanding of God's grace and, as a result, are free to be authentic and honest about who they are, including their challenges. These leaders tend to foster environments of freedom and authenticity. This authentic environment creates a "greenhouse" for optimal growth in one's relationship with God. When considering a new church, this is a key element to look for: authentic, grace-filled leaders. These efforts to help people grow Up in their relationship with God can be in large and small settings.

In

In is the relationship between those in a church community. If Up is the vertical relationship with God, In is the horizontal relationship between people. In some churches, there is a strong emphasis placed on Up, but little emphasis on In. You attend a large gathering on Sunday, hear a teaching, sing some songs, pray, and go home. That's it. Come back and do it again next week.

Compare that with our picture of the early Church. They had larger gatherings at the temple, but they also met in homes, eating together, enjoying one another. They became so closely connected that, when needs arose, they sold their possessions and gave the money to use for one another.

This wasn't a group of polite acquaintances or a social club. Even "community" might not be the right word. They were family. An extended family is probably the best term to describe what these followers of Jesus became, except that this was a family not defined by blood, but by the common bond of following Jesus, their Lord.

We see this sense of family even in their physical environment. At the close of many of Paul's letters, he sends greetings to various people (this is the part most people skip over). At the end of his letter to the Christians in Rome, he gives instructions to "Greet Priscilla and Aquila, my fellow workers in Christ Jesus...Greet also *the church that meets at their house*" (Romans 16:3-5).

During the first two centuries, most churches met in homes. If you think of extended family gatherings at holidays you have had, this probably gives you a good idea of what it felt like, but with a focus on God. A houseful of people eating together, laughing together, singing together, praying for one another, caring and sacrificing for one another, and learning from one another.

Because of meeting regularly like this, it was natural to know the needs that others were facing, whether it was related to money, health, or relationships, and to meet those needs together.

It was also a perfect environment for newer believers to be discipled by more mature believers. This is one of the highest goals or mission of the Church: for disciples of Jesus to disciple new and growing followers of Jesus so that they can go on to disciple others. We will look at this important area more closely in a few weeks.

Many churches today have begun to rediscover the critical need for family. There is a need to meet beyond Sunday mornings in smaller gatherings and to share life together. Not only to look at the Bible together (a "Bible study"), but to eat and have fun together, to share the true challenges and joys of our lives, and to get together in other casual, informal ways. To be a family.

Out

The third point on our triangle is *Out*. For many people, if they could be a part of a church that was doing the first two elements, Up and In, well, they would be thrilled. They would be growing in their relationships with God and seeing that impacting their relationships, their family lives, their identities, and their decisions. They would be enjoying rich, meaningful relationships with others; friendships that brought real support in life.

Sounds pretty good, doesn't it? I think we're done here. There's one more piece to the puzzle. One more leg to the stool. One more metaphor, in case you didn't get it.

A key part of God's desire for his Church is that all this good stuff doesn't stay bottled up. This is the God of love, remember? In our picture of the Church in Acts 2, you get the sense that all of this amazing stuff that the people were experiencing with God (Up) and in this new family with one another (In), began to overflow into love for others outside their community (Out). The end of the passage says that they were "enjoying the goodwill of all the people. And each day the Lord added to their fellowship those who were being saved" (Acts 2:47).

People began to see the powerful community that was happening and were impacted by it. Many wanted in! This kind of love—this kind of life—was *contagious*. Daily, people were becoming followers of Jesus. The influence of one individual who sincerely follows Jesus can be significant, but a family of people who truly love one another and begin to actively invite others into that loving environment is truly powerful.

Today, this looks like groups in which we have become extended families purposely reaching out and loving others together. We talk and pray about how to reach others as a family; a "family on mission," you might say. It could be planning social events and inviting persons of peace from our lives (those who are spiritually open, as we discussed in our session on evangelism). It could be inviting those who are ready to our group gatherings and warmly welcoming them and being sensitive to questions they might have.

It could also look like serving others together, as we discussed last week in our session on compassion and justice. Here we are not only trying to meet practical needs, but praying that God would help us build ongoing relationships with those we serve in the hopes that they would be spiritually open.

When a group—a family—is looking outward, it gives them purpose. It draws them closer together (In) and draws them closer to God (Up), because they are connecting with his heart for others.

Out also happens in our larger gatherings as people come to hear messages that God uses to speak into their lives, as they hear stories of what God is doing in the lives of others, and as they encounter God through worship. The combination of larger and smaller gatherings can pack a wonderful one-two punch (in a good way!) in people's lives.

Our Role

When these three elements of Up, In, and Out come together in a church's larger and smaller gatherings, it can be really exciting. Of course, we have to invest ourselves in order to be a part of that excitement. When we see the potential that a church family has in growing close to God, blessing one another, and helping change the course of someone's life, most of us will want to invest in something like that. In a couple of weeks, we will look at the role our gifts and passions play in the life of the Church and broader community, which just adds to the fun.

The Church in Action

I want to finish our reading with an email from a woman who experienced the love of a church family: a group of people, an "extended family," trying to grow closer to God, be family to one another, and love others in their lives.

> *Wow. I'm really speechless. I can hardly believe how generous everyone has been to us. Thank you. Thank you for your prayers, for your acceptance, for your patience with all my silly questions. Thank you for all your help, financial, emotional, and just being there.*

> *When we were invited to this "church group" several years ago, I really was not sure it was something I wanted to get involved in. Mark and I started dating in high school and made many bad choices. We were lost and confused and just trying to make the most out of everything. We were confronted by multiple "Christians" who seemed to go out of their way to share their disapproval in our choices. It seemed to only get worse when we had our first child out of wedlock. That was a big no-no. We got used to people looking down upon us, treating us differently. It got to the point where I started viewing us the way I though everyone else viewed us. Screwed up and worthless. Never going to amount to much. Nice people that went down the wrong path.*

> *I really started closing myself off. But I so desperately wanted to make some new friends. Friends with good values, good beliefs. So we took a chance. We came to one of these get-togethers to see what it was all about. I can't speak for my husband, but I was very surprised at how accepting everyone was. I didn't feel judged or looked down upon even though my views were (are), quite liberal.*

> *So again, thank you. Thank you for welcoming us in and making us a part of your*

God family. Thank you for showing me that where you come from does not pave the way to where you are going. That choices we make do not make us who we are. Thank you for helping me open my heart and allowing me to be okay with just being myself. Thank you for showing us the light and demonstrating what being a Christian is really about.

Love,
Kathy

That is the Church.

Questions for Reflection and Discussion

- What did you find interesting about the Up, In, and Out elements of the Church described in the reading?

- How does this picture of the Church compare to church experiences you have had?

- How does the truth that the Church was created by God and is important to him impact you?

- For prayer ideas, see the Spiritual Practice section for this week.

Spiritual Practice
Praying for Your Church

When we pray, we may not always think about praying in a focused way for the church we are a part of. Consider some of the following ways to pray:

- **Pray for the Leadership of Your Church**

  Pray for pastors and church staff, for elders, and for volunteer ministry leaders. Often leaders are a target for the enemy to attack, because he knows they are strategic to the life of the church. Pray for God's protection for them and their families against temptation, harassment, and discouragement. Pray that God would give them fresh vision and wisdom.

- **Pray for the Ministry of Your Church**

  Pray that God would help your church become an Acts 2 type of church: vibrant, alive, rich in community, and impacting the world. It may help to pray along the lines of the reading for this week of what a church can be like. Look at the current ministries in your church and pray for God's direction and power to flow through them. Pray for God's fresh leadership in helping your church advance his kingdom in your community and around the world.

- **Pray for the People of Your Church**

  A great way to pray is for the unity of the body. Again, one of Satan's primary strategies is to create conflict and disunity within a church. Pray against his schemes. Pray for the specific needs you are aware of that people have or for those the Spirit may lead you to pray for, even if you are not aware of particular needs at this time.

In addition to the power that comes with praying for different areas of your church, it can also give God the opportunity to speak to you about what's on his heart for *you* related to these needs. For example, he might lead you to send an encouraging note to a pastor or leader or prompt you to get more involved in a ministry.

Try it out now. Spend some time praying for one or more of the areas mentioned above for your church. On a practical note, if your church has a website, it may be helpful to look at it to remind you of the names of leaders and the different ministries of the church.

For the future, you may want to look at incorporating this practice into your prayer time. One idea is to take some of your prayer time on a particular day each week to pray for your church.

This week, we are going to look at the practice of worship. Worship can be like other practices we have looked at, for example, prayer: we know that it is key to our lives with God (in fact, it may be our highest calling), and yet we may not know a lot about how to do it. Sure, we get the main idea, but there may be things holding us back from fully expressing ourselves in worship. What are some of these things?

It may be limitations in understanding *who* we are worshipping. When our picture of God is too small or too distorted, then our worship becomes thin or lethargic.

We may be limited in *how* we worship. We may have only seen certain expressions of worship or may be limited by our own personalities.

Finally, we may be limited by *where* and *when* we worship God, thinking it needs to be within the four walls of a church building.

These are some of the limitations we will try to address this week as we seek to worship God with all our hearts in the midst of all of our lives.

Soaking in Scripture

There are a few instances in Scripture of individuals directly encountering God. In these encounters, the individuals respond not only in worship, but outright shock and complete awe, because they are encountering a Being who is beyond anything they have ever experienced in their lives. This reminds us of the awe-inspiring nature of the One we worship.

The prophet Isaiah had this type of encounter with God. For context, read Isaiah 6:1-8. To put it mildly, Isaiah was "blown away" by the presence of God.

After reading the passage, we will then focus on Isaiah 6:3, which are the words of the angels who were worshipping God. This is instructive because we would expect angels to know how to worship God!

Isaiah 6:3

And they were calling to one another:
"Holy, holy, holy is the LORD Almighty; the whole earth is full of his glory."

- "Holy" is a key term for God used throughout the Bible. We normally think of it in terms of being pure. While this is true, it also has a different, broader meaning. Holy also refers to being different and special. For example, in the Ten Commandments, when God says "Remember the Sabbath day by keeping it *holy*" (Exodus 20:8), he is saying that the Sabbath day is holy, because it is set apart from the other six days of the week; it is meant to be different from the other days. It is special.

When we then apply the term holy to God, we are recognizing that he is different from us. While he has made it possible to relate to him, we must remember that, in countless ways, he is different from us. It is the differentness of God that evokes awe in those who have encountered it and can evoke true worship in us when we are reminded of it.

With this in mind, what are some of the ways that God is different from us—ways that he is holy? Reflect on this and list some of these differences below.

- What does it mean that the *whole* earth is *full* of his glory? How does this expand your understanding of where, when, and how we can worship God?

- Repeat Isaiah 6:3 a number of times in an attempt to memorize it. Because this passage leads us to worshipping God in the midst of our lives, it might be a good one to post somewhere that you will see in the midst of your day.

- As a part of your prayer time, take some time to express your worship of God to him for the things that you wrote that were different about him.

Note: *For another awe-inspiring picture of God and those worshipping him, see Revelation 4-5. Keep in mind that the book of Revelation is symbolic in nature, which can make it challenging to understand at times. Nevertheless, this gives us another picture of God's awesome, holy nature and of worship.*

Spiritual Practice
Creation Walk

In our Soaking in Scripture section, we looked at Isaiah 6:3, which says that "the earth is filled with his glory." The practice of taking a Creation Walk is a great way to appreciate God's glory as it is displayed in his world and in his creation. Because God created the world, it tells us a lot about who he is. Observing his works closely is a great pathway into worship.

With this in mind, plan a time this week that you can take a walk outside. It could be in your neighborhood or somewhere in nature that you would enjoy. As you walk, take in all that you see from God's creation. As you feel drawn, focus on one particular part of his creation (the sky, a bird, a flower, etc.) and reflect on what it tells you about who God is. Worship him for the qualities you see reflected in what you are observing. In addition, listen to see if there is anything he may be saying to you or about your life as you reflect. If you have time, you can focus on to other parts of his creation as well.

Give it a try. You may discover that this is one of your favorite expressions of prayer and worship!

Note: If you would like to extend your reflection on God and his creation, you may enjoy looking at a video that discusses the grandeur of the universe. Go to www.crazylovebook. com, and under the Videos tab, click on *The Awe Factor of God*.

Digging into Scripture

Not surprisingly, the Psalms are filled with examples of and instructions about worship. It is easy to read these in a generic way. For this psalm, however, we will look at it closely to see what it can teach us about worship.

As you closely study this passage and make your observations, here are some questions to consider.

- *What* about God are they worshipping or being encouraged to worship?
- *How* are they encouraged to worship? What kind of attitudes or emotions, what kind of physical expressions?
- How does this impact your own experience of worship? Is there anything that keeps you from worshipping in these ways? (Bonus point: What does "extol" mean?)

Psalm 95:1-7

[1]*Come, let us sing for joy to the LORD; let us shout aloud to the Rock of our salvation.*
[2]*Let us come before him with thanksgiving and extol him with music and song.*

[3]*For the LORD is the great God, the great King above all gods.*
[4]*In his hand are the depths of the earth, and the mountain peaks belong to him.*
[5]*The sea is his, for he made it, and his hands formed the dry land.*

[6]*Come, let us bow down in worship, let us kneel before the LORD our Maker;*
[7]*for he is our God and we are the people of his pasture, the flock under his care.*

Observation

Interpretation

Application

Spiritual Reading
What Does God Want in Our Worship?

Which Would You Prefer?

In his book *The Air I Breathe*, Louie Giglio begins one chapter by asking a series of questions, kind of like the game *Would You Rather?*

> **Which would you prefer?**
>
> *A dad who tells you how important you are*
> *Or . . .*
> *A dad who actually shows up for the important stuff in your life?*
>
> *A "significant other" who makes you really cool, homemade cards telling you you're the best thing that has ever happened to them*
> *Or . . .*
> *One who respects you, keeps your trust, and doesn't cheat on you?*
>
> *Friends who keep reminding you how "tight" you are*
> *Or . . .*
> *Friends who are there when you need them most, never stabbing you in the back?*
>
> *Someone who tells you how special you are*
> *Or . . .*
> *Someone who shows you?*

If we really think about it, most of us would say we wanted both. It feels good to hear someone say that they care about us, that we are important. But if those words aren't backed up by real action, then they can become hollow and even painful.

Here's the thing: God is not so different from us in this regard. He loves to hear the words, whether it's our words of praise during a prayer time on our own or singing songs with others. But when those words are not backed up by our hearts and by our lives...well, I'll let him tell you how he feels about it.

Isaiah 1:13-17 (NLT)

¹³*Stop bringing me your meaningless gifts; the incense of your offerings disgusts me! As for your celebrations of the new moon and the Sabbath and your special days for fasting—they are all sinful and false. I want no more of your pious meetings.*
¹⁴*I hate your new moon celebrations and your annual festivals. They are a burden to me. I cannot stand them!*
¹⁵*When you lift up your hands in prayer, I will not look. Though you offer many prayers, I will not listen, for your hands are covered with the blood of innocent victims.*
¹⁶*Wash yourselves and be clean! Get your sins out of my sight. Give up your evil ways.*
¹⁷*Learn to do good. Seek justice. Help the oppressed. Defend the cause of orphans. Fight for the rights of widows.*

How do you *really* feel, God?! It is clear that he doesn't like empty praise any more than we do. Isn't it true that empty or false praise is irritating or even a burden?

He isn't saying that our lives have to be perfect or that we need to feel guilt any time we pray or sing to him, but it does mean that we need to be sincerely living our lives for him. Our hearts' desire should be to follow him and love others.

The positive side of this is realizing that the small, everyday things we do to follow God in our lives are seen by him as worship. It is one of the key ways we show our love for him.

My wife, Jacki, writes the most tender, beautiful notes on the cards she gives me throughout the year, but the reason they are so meaningful is that they are backed up by countless small acts of love and commitment, day in and day out. She really listens as I share about something from my day that's probably not the most fascinating topic for her. She drives one of the kids to a sleepover when I'm beat. She forgives me when I've been impatient or sarcastic. I still love to hear and read the words, but I experience and *feel* the love in those everyday actions.

It is similar to our relationships with God. When, out of our love for him, we genuinely listen to the needs of a co-worker or ask our child for forgiveness or roll up our sleeves and help at a workday at our church, God feels the love. He recognizes that we genuinely love him and are trying to follow his heart in our everyday lives. This is worship to him.

Cultivating Gratitude

In addition to loving God through our everyday actions, we can love and worship him through gratitude. Cultivating the habit of gratitude can go a long way toward making us worshippers.

Gratitude is basically noticing. Noticing the countless gifts God gives us and recognizing the heart of the One who is behind those gifts. This is particularly important to point out in our culture. We have received so much that it is very easy to take much of it for granted.

The other day, my wife informed me in a lighthearted way that I sometimes overreact in certain situations, and she was concerned that I would turn into a crotchety old man.

"Yep," my two wonderful children chirped in unison.

"What?!" I responded, realizing I was in danger of overreacting, thus proving their point.

"Yeah, like the other day in the drive-thru, when you started getting irritated at the woman because she couldn't understand you and asked you to repeat yourself a couple of times," my son helpfully noted.

It *was* irritating. She asked me like five times! Okay, maybe three, but still. Being the reflective person that I am, however, I later realized that this might be yet another wake-up call. In this case, it was a clue that I might be getting a tiny bit ungrateful in my life. A smidgen. Teensy-weensy.

The antidote to irritability and ungratefulness is to make gratitude a regular practice. You might call it intentional noticing.

As mentioned in the session on prayer, one of the best practices for this is the yesterday practice. This is where you take a few minutes to reflect on the previous day. As a part of this reflection, you will bring to mind things that have happened that you are thankful for.

This is helpful in remembering the small things that God is doing in your life all the time: a good meeting at work, a fun meal with friends, a hard but good talk with a child, a refreshing workout, helpful drive-thru ladies.

Remembering—noticing—these types of things in your life and turning them into thanks to God will begin to help you see God's fingerprints throughout your day. It will help you realize just how good this God is.

Imagine how it feels to God when we notice his many gifts, his goodness, in our lives. Noticing is worship.

Say it. Live it. Notice it. Worship our awesome God.

Questions for Reflection and Discussion

- What did you find interesting about the idea that God wants our words and our actions?

- How do you think noticing might help you in your relationship with God? Have you experienced this in the past?

- During your prayer time, think over the previous day and thank God for the small things you notice.

In 1 Corinthians 12:1, the apostle Paul says to his readers, "Now about the gifts of the Spirit, brothers and sisters, I do not want you to be uninformed." It is possible to be a follower of Christ, but be ignorant—unaware—of spiritual gifts and how they work in our lives and in the Church. When this happens, it is a great loss to the Church and to us as individuals.

Spiritual gifts are those abilities that God has given us for the purpose of ministering to others within the Church and enabling the Church to be effective in serving others in the community around us and beyond. Passion is discovering *where* and with *whom* to share those abilities.

Session #26
Discovering
Spiritual Gifts
and Passions

In this week's materials, we will look at the variety of gifts and passions seen in Scripture and the ways in which God leads us in gaining greater understanding of what these are in our lives. This is an exciting and at times challenging process that usually unfolds with greater clarity over time and often involves the help of others who know us well.

Next week, as a part of our session on the voice and power of the Spirit, we will take a closer look at some of the supernatural gifts that can sometimes be confusing.

Note: *A part of the Spiritual Practice section is providing reflection for others in your group concerning their gifts and passions. This should be prioritized in your group time, because it can be very helpful. If you run out of time for this, it would be worth taking a second week to discuss it further.*

Soaking in Scripture

This week, we are trying to gain a better understanding of the spiritual gifts and passions that God has given us. In addition to this practical knowledge that we need, we also have to have the right attitude, the right heart—the heart of a servant. Otherwise, all of the practical knowledge won't really matter.

Shortly before Jesus' death, two of his disciples, James and John, made a request of Jesus to sit at his right and left hand when he returned to heaven. In essence, they asked to be his right-hand men in order to have influence. Even after they had been with Jesus for several years, they still had a lot to learn! Their hearts still weren't in the right place. Here is how Jesus responded.

Mark 10:42-45 (MSG)

41-45 *When the other ten heard of this conversation, they lost their tempers with James and John. Jesus got them together to settle things down. "You've observed how godless rulers throw their weight around," he said, "and when people get a little power how quickly it goes to their heads. It's not going to be that way with you. Whoever wants to be great must become a servant. Whoever wants to be first among you must be your slave. That is what the Son of Man has done: He came to serve, not to be served—and then to give away his life in exchange for many who are held hostage."*

- In your own words, how would you describe the difference between the approach to power and influence that Jesus describes above and the common approach of the world ("godless rulers")?

- "He came to serve, not be served." How do Jesus' words about himself challenge you in terms of your attitude toward serving others in general?

Serving in the Church?

- The next time you are at a church service, small group gathering, or social event with family or friends, say these words to yourself and to God: "I have come to serve, not to be served." See how God leads you. Try to make this a regular part of your attitude toward others. During prayer, express your desires and confessions concerning having a servant's heart.

Digging into Scripture

This week, our study will be a little different. Below are several key passages concerning spiritual gifts. As in the past when we have had longer passages, some direction may be helpful.

First, identify and list the various gifts that are mentioned. You do not need to have a complete understanding of each gift. These will be defined in the Spiritual Practice section this week. This will, however, begin to give you an idea of the variety of gifts.

Next, note anything you see concerning the purpose of spiritual gifts. Why does God give these gifts?

Lastly, list any observations you have concerning how we are to use these gifts, that is, with what attitude. Of course, note any other types of observations you find. This is a good example of where you may have questions that you would want to place in the interpretation section and bring up to discuss. It also might help to look up the definitions of some words.

1 Corinthians 12:1, 4-11, 27-31

¹Now about the gifts of the Spirit, brothers and sisters, I do not want you to be uninformed.

⁴There are different kinds of gifts, but the same Spirit distributes them. ⁵There are different kinds of service, but the same Lord. ⁶There are different kinds of working, but in all of them and in everyone it is the same God at work.

⁷Now to each one the manifestation of the Spirit is given for the common good. ⁸To one there is given through the Spirit a message of wisdom, to another a message of knowledge by means of the same Spirit, ⁹to another faith by the same Spirit, to another gifts of healing by that one Spirit, ¹⁰to another miraculous powers, to another prophecy, to another distinguishing between spirits, to another speaking in different kinds of tongues, and to still another the interpretation of tongues. ¹¹All these are the work of one and the same Spirit, and he distributes them to each one, just as he determines.

²⁷Now you are the body of Christ, and each one of you is a part of it. ²⁸And God has placed in the church first of all apostles, second prophets, third teachers, then miracles, then gifts of healing, of helping, of guidance, and of different kinds of tongues. ²⁹Are all apostles? Are all prophets? Are all teachers? Do all work miracles? ³⁰Do all have gifts of healing? Do all speak in tongues? Do all interpret? ³¹Now eagerly desire the greater gifts.

Romans 12:3-8

³For by the grace given me I say to every one of you: Do not think of yourself more highly than you ought, but rather think of yourself with sober judgment, in accordance with the faith God has distributed to each of you. ⁴For just as each of us has one body with many members, and these members do not all have the same function, ⁵so in Christ we, though many, form one body, and each member belongs to all the others. ⁶We have different gifts, according to the grace given to each of us. If your gift is prophesying, then prophesy in accordance with your faith; ⁷if it is serving, then serve; if it is teaching, then teach; ⁸if it is to encourage, then give encouragement; if it is giving, then give generously; if it is to lead, do it diligently; if it is to show mercy, do it cheerfully.

Ephesians 4:11-13

¹¹So Christ himself gave the apostles, the prophets, the evangelists, the pastors and teachers, ¹²to equip his people for works of service, so that the body of Christ may be built up ¹³until we all reach unity in the faith and in the knowledge of the Son of God and become mature, attaining to the whole measure of the fullness of Christ.

Observation

Interpretation

Application

Spiritual Reading
Understanding Our Gifts and Passions

Gifts

Recently, a friend of ours named Becky moved in with another friend, Jessica, for a few months until Becky could purchase a home. Within a day or two of moving in, Becky was telling some of us in the group we are a part of, "Yeah, it's been great. I met the people across the street, and they have visited our church. And it turns out I know another family, and we ended up talking about our church and how Jessica and I met each other there, and they seemed interested in hearing more about it."

Jessica turned to Becky, and was like, "Really? I've barely met any of them, and I've lived there for over a year."

Is Becky more spiritual than Jessica? More friendly? No and no. Becky has been created by God to be a people person. He has given her some spiritual gifting around evangelism. It is simply very natural for Becky to get to know people and to share from her own experience about God and church. Because Becky feels comfortable, others feel comfortable.

When we are aware of what our spiritual gifts are and are not, it can free us up to use those gifts to their maximum potential and not worry about gifts that may not be our strong suit.

God has given every follower of Jesus spiritual gifts to be used for his purposes. It is simply a matter of becoming aware of what these gifts are in our lives. Often, these gifts will have some overlap with things we do in our careers or personal lives, but are used for kingdom purposes.

For example, Becky has used her natural extroversion as a bus driver meeting loads of kids and parents, in the classroom as a teacher, as a soccer parent, and in many other contexts. Since becoming a follower of Jesus, she now uses the way God has created her to share him with others.

What if Jessica sees what Becky does and thinks, "Wow, I am lame at that evangelism stuff. I guess I should love God more or try harder." She might worry about God's disappointment in her.

On the other hand, the following Sunday, Jessica made food and created a nice environment for a newcomers' lunch at the church. The food was great, and it made coming to the event that much easier for these new people, some of whom are new in their faith or still exploring a relationship with Christ.

Jessica doesn't think much about this, because cooking is fun and easy for her. Being new not too long ago, she understands how helpful something like this lunch can be.

Let's say Becky happens to drop by the office while Jessica is finishing the preparations for the lunch and thinks, "I wish I had more of a desire to serve like Jessica does. What's wrong with me?"

You get the idea. On the one hand, our gifts are often so natural to us, so close to us, that we don't even see them as gifts and may not realize the contribution they make. It can just feel like they are part of who we are (which they are), or it can feel like, "Well, of course! Anybody would do this." The truth is everybody wouldn't do it, or at least wouldn't have the natural desire to do it.

Becky might not realize what a gift she has in talking to others about God (doesn't everyone do that?) and Jessica may have similar feelings about cooking (what's the big deal?).

Both could feel guilty about not being drawn to what the other does, but they don't need to. When everyone knows their gifts and uses them, then things get done in God's kingdom, and people enjoy doing them.

Discovering Our Gifts

How do you know what your gifts are? Sometimes it's as easy as thinking about those abilities that you naturally gravitate toward in your life and considering how God might use them. Again, they may be so natural that you don't think of them as abilities or gifts.

Is it natural and enjoyable for you to discuss topics with a group of people? Do you like to organize things? Do you like to plan events? Do you like to learn about new things and share them with others? Do you think about how to improve things? Do you build stuff? Do you listen to people's challenges and help them?

All of these can be used by God. It's simply a matter of recognizing these gifts we have and seeing where they can be used. Sometimes they will be used in more structured settings, such as a program at the church, and other times in less structured settings, like Becky's new neighborhood.

For some, questionnaires can be helpful in identifying gifts. For an example, see http://beresolute.org/spiritual-gifts-assessment/. When combined with time spent reflecting on what we currently enjoy, these inventories can be very helpful.

Simply trying different things can assist us in discovering our gifts. For example, you may enjoy organizing things and are good at details, which is the biblical gift of administration. Perhaps you could try helping your church with their new database system they are setting up.

Maybe you discover that you love this one thing. You're good at it, and it's really helping things move forward in the church. Or...not so much. Maybe you do fine at it, but it's just not very fulfilling and begins feeling more and more like an obligation. This may indicate that, while this is a gift for you, the way in which that gift is used may not be a good fit.

This gets at the second important element, and that is passion.

Passions

If gifts are the abilities God has given us, then passion is understanding how or with whom these abilities are used. In his book *What You Do Best in the Body of Christ: Discover Your Spiritual Gifts, Personal Style, and God-Given Passion*, Bruce Bugbee describes three areas of passion. It's not necessary to categorize our passions, but sometimes these categories can help us identify what we are passionate about.

People

For some, their primary passion is a particular group of people. Let's say someone has a natural affinity for middle schoolers (a rare breed indeed!). They just "get" middle schoolers and love being around them. They understand the challenges they are going through, appreciate their quirkiness, and remember how tricky that time in life was. Middle schoolers are a passion for them.

Over time, you may discover you have a passion for young married couples, those who are grieving, people in recovery, preschoolers, immigrants, or a host of other people groups. Regardless of the group, your strongest desire will most likely be seeing change within the people in that group.

Roles or Functions

Some have a passion for a particular role or function. These typically can be applied to different people groups or efforts. For example, someone may have a passion for helping programs or groups become more strategic or have better systems for getting people involved.

Others might be entrepreneurial and enjoy starting new things. Over time, they might be involved in different kinds of new efforts. Again, often they will be interested in a number of groups or settings where they can use their roles or functions.

Causes

Those who have a passion for causes have deep feelings about particular efforts or issues. They may have strong feelings about human rights issues, financial stewardship, discipleship, or at-risk youth.

When someone has a cause as a passion, they often feel frustrated that others don't see the deep needs they see in that area. They are often willing to sacrifice time, energy, and resources, and usually it doesn't feel like a sacrifice.

Bringing Gifts and Passions Together

For some, their passion may be pretty clear—"I love middle schoolers!" In that case, it might be getting some clarity on what abilities or gifts they want to use within that passion area. Leading a middle school small group? Planning events?

In other cases, they may have some understanding of their gifts—they like to teach, or lead groups, or organize things—but where or with whom do they do it? That may take some time and experimenting with different areas or groups of people to discover.

One of the couples in our church was leading a small group of high school students in our student ministry and did a great job, but over time they begin to realize that they were doing it more out of obligation than passion. It was a significant commitment, so it began to wear on them.

At the same time, they began to reflect on their experience recently in our ministry for emotional healing and how much it had impacted their lives. They begin to realize it was their passion to see others experience the healing they had received in their lives. Now they are using their leadership gifts in our healing ministry and loving it. The commitment level is as high or higher, and yet they feel more energized rather than less.

Throughout this process of bringing our gifts and passions together, God will be leading us. We can lay out descriptions and categories, but the reality is God can lead us in a natural way over time if we are seeking him.

Some Additional Thoughts

A few things to round out our discussion of gifts and passions.

First, there are some things that God calls all of us to do. For example, he calls us all to share his love and message with those who are seeking him. Some, like Becky, will be gifted at this, but in our own way, using our own personality, we are called to walk alongside others. For Jessica, it might look a little quieter, walking with one or two people over a longer period.

Similarly, we are all called to give faithfully, but some may have a gifting and passion for financial giving that results in great faith or sacrifice in giving. We are all called to love and show compassion toward others, but some may have a passion for a particular cause.

Another thought to be aware of is that at times we will need to serve in an area outside of our giftedness. We may not be particularly gifted or excited about setting up for an event, sharing a testimony, or making a meal, but sometimes we need to step up and do things to help. The key is being willing to do these types of things for a short-term commitment. When these become longer commitments is when it becomes difficult and counter-productive.

Lastly, our gifts and passions can be used in larger and smaller gatherings, as we described in our session on the Church. Your gifts may be best used on Sunday mornings in ministry programs, but also can be very useful in smaller gatherings like home-based groups. Gifts such as leadership, hospitality, caring for others, discipleship, and many others can be utilized in this setting, because it is so relational.

Okay, one more. Sometimes the more supernatural gifts (such as healing and words of knowledge) can be a bit difficult to understand. We will spend more time with these in the next session.

If you haven't already, jump in! See how God leads you as you begin to serve. God has designed us with gifts and passions and has created us to use them for his kingdom and his glory. It's just another part of his great adventure!

Questions for Reflection and Discussion

- What did the section on spiritual gifts help clarify for you? What questions about gifts do you still have?

- What did you find helpful in the section on passion?

- During your prayer time, talk to God about any passions or gifts you feel may be emerging in your life.

Spiritual Practice
Exploring Your Gifts and Passions

Hopefully by now you are beginning to get a feel for how spiritual gifts and passions work in our lives. A great way to begin to understand our gifts and passions is to begin serving and see what brings life and what doesn't. To make that process more effective, however, it also helps to do some intentional self-reflection and seek the reflections of others who know you. The following exercises are designed to assist you in this reflection process.

Questions for Self-Reflection

As you answer the following questions, don't be concerned with how you would accomplish these things or whether it would be possible. This exercise is simply to help you begin to identify those passions and gifts within you.

Note: Some of the following questions have been taken from the *Network, Revised, DVD Curriculum* by Bruce Bugbee and Bill Hybels.

Reflecting on Passion

- If you could snap your fingers and know that you wouldn't fail, what would you do for others?

- What do you repeatedly see that annoys or angers you, which, if changed, would be glorifying to God and would help others?

- Is there anything that, when you talk about it, energizes you?

- Are there any categories of people that you care for in a strong way (e.g., children, at-risk youth, disabled adults, parents)?

Reflecting on Spiritual Gifts

- In the descriptions of spiritual gifts on p. 273, which ones did you identify with?

- Are there activities you have seen being done by others within or through the church that you think you might enjoy (e.g., teaching, serving behind the scenes, making meals for others)?

- What are activities you have felt effective at within your home or at work? How could you picture using these skills or talents within or through the church?

Providing Reflection for Others

- Give some thought to what passions and gifts you have observed in the other members of your group. List any passions you have heard each group member talk about or shown interest in. List any gifts you have seen them exhibit or could easily imagine them using.

- During your group time, take turns focusing on each group member, sharing the reflections of other group members concerning that person's passions and gifts. When they share their reflections with you, see how these reflections compare with your own self-reflections from above.

Descriptions of Spiritual Gifts

The following is a list of spiritual gifts found in the Bible with definitions for each gift. The definitions are adapted from the curriculum for Resolute, a ministry focusing on discipleship and leadership development for men. Used with permission.

SPIRITUAL GIFTS	
Leadership	Leadership aids the body by leading and directing members to accomplish the goals and purposes of the church. Leadership motivates people to work together in unity toward common goals (Rom. 12:8).
Administration	Persons with the gift of administration lead the body by steering others to remain on task. Administration enables the body to organize according to God-given purposes and long-term goals. (1 Cor. 12:28)
Teaching	Teaching is instructing members in the truths and doctrines of God's Word for the purposes of building up, unifying, and maturing the body (1 Cor. 12:28; Rom. 12:7; Eph. 4:11).
Knowledge	The gift of knowledge manifests itself in teaching and training in discipleship. It is the God-given ability to learn, know, and explain the precious truths of God's Word. A word of knowledge is a Spirit-revealed truth (1 Cor. 12:28).
Wisdom	Wisdom is the gift that discerns the work of the Holy Spirit in the body and applies His teachings and actions to the needs of the body (1 Cor. 12:28).

SPIRITUAL GIFTS - continued	
Prophecy	God uses this gift to communicate a message to his people. This could be a message in the form of direction, warning, or conviction about a current or future situation. Prophecy can also manifest itself in preaching and teaching (1 Cor. 12:10; Rom. 12:6).
Discernment	Discernment aids the body by recognizing the true intentions of those within or related to the body. Discernment tests the message and actions of others for the protection and well-being of the body (1 Cor. 12:10).
Exhortation	Possessors of this gift encourage members to be involved in and enthusiastic about the work of the Lord. Members with this gift are good counselors and motivate others to service. Exhortation exhibits itself in preaching, teaching, and ministry (Rom. 12:8).
Shepherding	The gift of shepherding is manifested in persons who look out for the spiritual welfare of others. Although pastors, like shepherds, do care for members of the church, this gift is not limited to a pastor or staff member (Eph. 4:11).
Faith	Faith trusts God to work beyond the human capabilities of the people. Believers with this gift encourage others to trust in God in the face of apparently insurmountable odds (1 Cor. 12:9).
Evangelism	God gifts his church with evangelists to lead others to Christ effectively and enthusiastically. This builds up the body by adding new members to its fellowship. (Eph 4:11).
Apostleship	The church sends apostles from the body to plant church or be missionaries. Apostles motivate the body to look beyond its wall in order to carry out the Great Commission (1 Cor. 12:28; Eph. 4:11).
Service/Helps	Those with the gift of service/helps recognize practical needs in the body and joyfully give assistance to meeting those needs. Christians with this gift do not mind working behind the scenes (1 Cor. 12:28; Rom. 12:7).
Mercy	Cheerful acts of compassion characterize those with the gift of mercy. Persons with this gift aid the body by empathizing with hurting members. They keep the body healthy and unified by keeping others aware of the needs within the church (Rom. 12:8).
Giving	Members with the gift of giving give freely and joyfully to the work and mission of the body. Cheerfulness and liberality are characteristics of individuals with this gift (Rom. 12:8).
Hospitality	Those with this gift have the ability to make visitors, guests, and strangers feel at ease. They often use their home to entertain guests. Persons with this gift integrate new members into the body (1 Pet. 4:9).
Healing	Those with the gift of healing bring physical restoration to others through the power of the Holy Spirit (1 Cor. 12:9).
Miracles	Those who the Spirit uses to authenticate the ministry and message of God through supernatural interventions that glorify him (1 Cor. 12:10).
Tongues and Interpretation of Tongues	Tongues is the Spirit-empowered ability to speak in a language unknown to the speaker. Interpretation of tongues is the Spirit-empowered ability to make known to the body of Christ the message of one who is speaking in tongues (1 Cor. 12:10).

Over the past few weeks, we have been talking about the Church: what God calls the Church to do and what worship and spiritual gifts look like in the life of the Church and in our lives. In the New Testament Church, we discover that the power and voice of the Holy Spirit played a prominent role. Yet today, that is not always the case. Some followers of Christ and even entire churches know little of the Spirit's supernatural power and communication.

For example, when we studied the gifts given by the Holy Spirit last session, some may have been more familiar to you, while others, such as knowledge, prophecy, and gifts of miracles and healing, may have been less familiar.

Why is this? There can be a variety of reasons. Some churches teach very little or not at all in this area compared to the New Testament Church, which received specific teaching. For some individuals and even leaders, there is a sense that, in our modern-day society, God's supernatural power and communication don't occur and may not even be needed.

Is that true? Or is it possible that we as individuals and our churches and our world still need the supernatural voice and power of the Spirit to be active in order to lead us and empower us and to bring glory to God? In particular, as we seek to minister to those within the body of Christ as well as to those who do not know him, we need *all* of the gifts, *all* of the means of communication, *all* of the expressions of God's power to be at work.

As with other sessions, this is a big topic to cover. The hope is that you will begin to see how the Spirit speaks to you in a variety of ways for yourself and as you pray for and minister to others. Secondly, I hope that you would start to gain an understanding of how the Spirit's supernatural power works in your life and particularly in ministry to others.

Soaking in Scripture

In this Old Testament book, God speaks through the prophet Joel to his people. God is encouraging his people to return to himself and letting them know what the results will be if they do so. In the passage we will be focusing on, he looks further into the future and makes a significant promise concerning his Spirit and his people.

Joel 2:28-29

28"And afterward, I will pour out my Spirit on all people.
Your sons and daughters will prophesy, your old men will dream dreams,
    your young men will see visions.
29Even on my servants, both men and women, I will pour out my Spirit in those days."

- What do you think the significance is of God saying that the Spirit will be poured out on *all* people? What are the different groups that he mentions in this passage?

- What are the different results mentioned in the passage of the Spirit being poured out?

  Why do you think God would want to see these things happen?

- To see how this promise was fulfilled, read Acts 2:1-18.

- Express your desires to God concerning knowing more about the power of his Spirit and how it might work in your life.

Digging into Scripture

We have seen that God promised through the prophet Joel to pour out his Spirit in power and that he fulfilled that promise at Pentecost. In our study, we will look at an example of the Spirit working in power through someone and the results of that power.

In this passage, the person being used by the Spirit in power is the apostle Paul. In describing the Spirit working in power, the New Testament often says that the Spirit "came upon" someone or that someone was "filled with" the Spirit and then there is a powerful result. This is the case with Paul.

The first five verses will provide some background, with the second half of the passage being the key part we will study. This is another good example of the need for close observation. Who are the key people involved, and what do we know about them? How does the Spirit work through Paul, and what are the results upon the others in the account? What might this mean for us today as we try to share the reality of Jesus with others?

Acts 13:1-12 *(NLT)*

¹Among the prophets and teachers of the church at Antioch of Syria were Barnabas, Simeon (called "the black man"), Lucius (from Cyrene), Manaen (the childhood companion of King Herod Antipas), and Saul. ²One day as these men were worshiping the Lord and fasting, the Holy Spirit said, "Dedicate Barnabas and Saul for the special work to which I have called them." ³So after more fasting and prayer, the men laid their hands on them and sent them on their way.

⁴So Barnabas and Saul were sent out by the Holy Spirit. They went down to the seaport of Seleucia and then sailed for the island of Cyprus. ⁵There, in the town of

Salamis, they went to the Jewish synagogues and preached the word of God. John Mark went with them as their assistant.

⁶Afterward they traveled from town to town across the entire island until finally they reached Paphos, where they met a Jewish sorcerer, a false prophet named Bar-Jesus. ⁷He had attached himself to the governor, Sergius Paulus, who was an intelligent man. The governor invited Barnabas and Saul to visit him, for he wanted to hear the word of God. ⁸But Elymas, the sorcerer (as his name means in Greek), interfered and urged the governor to pay no attention to what Barnabas and Saul said. He was trying to keep the governor from believing.

⁹Saul, also known as Paul, was filled with the Holy Spirit, and he looked the sorcerer in the eye. ¹⁰Then he said, "You son of the devil, full of every sort of deceit and fraud, and enemy of all that is good! Will you never stop perverting the true ways of the Lord? ¹¹Watch now, for the Lord has laid his hand of punishment upon you, and you will be struck blind. You will not see the sunlight for some time." Instantly mist and darkness came over the man's eyes, and he began groping around begging for someone to take his hand and lead him.

¹²When the governor saw what had happened, he became a believer, for he was astonished at the teaching about the Lord.

Observation

Interpretation

Application

Spiritual Reading

Experiencing the Voice and Power of the Holy Spirit

The Spirit Within and Upon

In past sessions, we have looked at the work of the Spirit *within* us. We talked about how the Holy Spirit can speak to us when we are paying attention and how, over time, he can help us experience transformation—help us change to become more like Jesus. This is what the apostle Paul calls developing the fruit of the Spirit.

This week, we are returning to the Holy Spirit, but we are looking at how the Spirit can, at times, come *upon* us to speak in special ways or to empower us to minister to others in special ways.

Understanding both activities of the Spirit, within us and upon us, is important. We need both the Spirit's transformative work in our lives and his empowerment. Let's look at some differences between these two activities.

The Spirit Within

As we know, when Jesus returned to heaven, he promised to send the Holy Spirit as a counselor, teacher, and comforter to his followers who would live *within* them. This wasn't just temporary; the Spirit would live within them and within future followers of Jesus throughout their lives. Over time, if they were responsive to the work of the Spirit, they would begin to change and exhibit the fruit of the Spirit in their lives.

This is a key purpose of the Spirit's work within us: to help us, over time, to become more and more like Jesus in the way we think, speak, and act. To take on his character, his heart, his priorities. The Spirit lives and works within us throughout our lives.

The Spirit Upon

The Bible also talks about the Spirit coming *upon* people at particular times to express the supernatural power of God through them for the benefit of others. In the Old Testament, this is the main way we see the Spirit at work. We don't see the Spirit living within people to change them. That is why Jesus' promise to send the Holy Spirit to live and work within us is so significant.

In the Old Testament, we see a kind of formula that goes like this:

The Spirit came upon _____ (an individual), and the result was _____ (a supernatural act of God).

Let's look at one example.

If you attended Sunday School as a child, you may remember the Old Testament story of Samson, one of the early leaders of Israel. Usually he is pictured with big biceps, because he was known for his amazing displays of strength.

Judges 14:5-6

⁵Samson went down to Timnah together with his father and mother. As they approached the vineyards of Timnah, suddenly a young lion came roaring toward him. ⁶The Spirit of the Lord came powerfully upon him so that he tore the lion apart with his bare hands as he might have torn a young goat. But he told neither his father nor his mother what he had done.

Apparently, tearing apart a young goat was no problem (was this a hobby or something?). God gave Samson supernatural strength through the power of the Spirit to kill a lion, presumably to spare Samson's life.

You see this same formula throughout the Old Testament. Sometimes it is powerful acts like the one above, and sometimes it is God speaking through a prophet or other leader to his people when the Spirit comes upon them.

This continues on into the New Testament with one key difference: instead of the Spirit primarily coming upon leaders, God, through the prophet Joel, promises that all kinds of people will begin to experience the power of the Spirit upon them.

This is what we see when the Spirit comes in power upon the first believers at Pentecost in Acts 2, fulfilling Jesus' promise in Acts 1:8, "But *you will receive power* when *the Holy Spirit comes on you*; and you will be my witnesses in Jerusalem, and in all Judea and Samaria, and to the ends of the earth."

The key distinction of the Spirit coming upon someone in power is that it is *temporary* and for a specific purpose, as compared to the Spirit's work within us, which is *ongoing*.

You can see that in the example of Samson: the Spirit temporarily came upon him for a very specific purpose: to tear apart a lion.

Similarly, in our study passage this week, the apostle Paul was filled with the Holy Spirit when he looked the sorcerer in the eye. Paul went on to speak with great boldness and declared that the sorcerer would be struck with blindness, which is what happened. The Spirit empowered Paul temporarily for a specific purpose.

Note: *The term "filled with the Spirit," which is found a number of times in the New Testament, can be used to describe the Spirit's work upon someone, like the above passage with Paul, or to describe the Spirit's work within us. For example, Ephesians 5:18 says, "Do not get drunk on wine, which leads to debauchery. Instead, be filled with the Spirit."*

In a moment, we will look at how the Spirit comes upon us today in his power.

The Need for Both

The key truth for us to grasp is that we need both the Spirit's work within us and upon us. The reality, however, is that many Christians are strongly imbalanced to one side or the other. Some have church backgrounds that talked a lot about the need to be like Christ (the Spirit's work within us), but may have taught very little about how the Spirit can work in power through us to minister to others. In fact, some churches teach *against* the idea that the Spirit even works in supernatural ways today.

Some, like me, grew up in churches that focused quite a bit on the power of the Spirit. Others may have had exposure as adults to churches or special services that emphasize the supernatural work of the Spirit. In some of these churches, however, the fruit of the Spirit (the Spirit within) is not emphasized enough. The other stuff is too exciting!

This is why you hear about high-profile televangelists or other church leaders who focus on healing and miracles, the power of the Spirit, experiencing great moral failures from a lack of the fruit of the Spirit. Or they seem to try to manipulate people through emotions. In some churches, you see little evidence of love and grace and instead see a focus on the power of God mixed with legalism.

What do you think we need? What might God want? Both! People who are growing in the fruit of the Spirit, seeking the Spirit's ongoing work within them and who are also open to the power of the Spirit working through them in wonderful ways to help others.

Since we've taken time in past sessions to look at the work of the Spirit to develop his fruit in our lives, we will now look at how the Spirit can work in power in our lives. We will look at two ways he works in supernatural ways: he speaks, and he acts.

The Spirit Speaks

We have looked at the way the Spirit speaks through our thought process, the Bible, teachings, and wise friends and mentors. There are additional ways, however, that might be less familiar but are important to be aware of.

Dreams

Most of the time, I can't remember my dreams, or they are just really weird. One morning, however, I woke up and clearly remembered my dream, and it was actually kind of cool.

I was commuting to work, but instead of driving in my car, I was floating in the air on my back. As I cruised along, I noticed I was following the course of a river to work. I did this for a while, and then I woke up. I was bummed that I woke up, because it was such a fun dream! I had no idea what to make of it. I remember thinking, "Why was I going to work in my dream?" After that, I kind of forgot about it.

A few months later, I was in the middle of an interview process with a new church. There were things that seemed to be pointing me in the direction of working at this church, but I was concerned, because the church I was at had just lost its senior pastor (I was an associate pastor at the church).

Suddenly, in the midst of that process, I remembered the dream. Guess what the name of the church was? The full name was The River Church Community, but everyone just called it The River. A dream where I was floating above a river as I went to work. Hmmm...I may be dumb, but I'm not stupid.

As we discussed in our session on God's guidance, I wanted other cords of his guidance, which I received. But this was a strong message that felt direct from God, and it helped me make a difficult decision.

What if I had no awareness that God could speak through dreams and ignored it? What if I thought that dreams were just silly, as some are, of course? I would have missed an important piece of guidance and confirmation from God.

If you scan through the Bible, you will be surprised how many times God speaks through dreams. Of course, we need to exercise wisdom when it comes to dreams. Many dreams are reflections of things going on within us subconsciously, like anxiety or stress. It can be informative to look at these more closely, but that is different than God speaking directly through a dream.

Usually, the dream will have a different quality to it. You often will be able to remember it more clearly, and you may have a sense that there is something unique about it. The dream may be for you or something for you to communicate to someone else.

The best approach is to be open to the idea that this may be from God and then lay it before him in prayer. Ask him to confirm that it is him speaking and to show you any steps you should take. This will usually involve sharing the dream with someone in your life who is wise and asking for his or her input (the "discussion" step of the listening circle).

Visions

"Visions" is such a strong term that may even seem spooky to some people, so I often will use the word "pictures." The biblical term used, however, is visions.

Either way, the idea is the same. Visions are like dreams, except they happen when we are awake. It is a visual image or scene that God places in our minds, often during a time of prayer, although it can happen at any time. Like dreams, God can be trying to communicate for us or for someone else.

A few weeks ago, our home group from church was praying for a couple who was going through some challenges; the wife was undergoing testing for multiple sclerosis. Before we prayed, I mentioned that, if anyone sensed God giving them a picture or message of some type, to share that in prayer. We prayed intently, but no one shared anything related to what I had mentioned.

The next day, the husband of the couple we prayed for shared this email.

> *Hello Family!*
>
> *Vince said to allow whatever images to come to mind as you prayed over us, and at first I became quite scared, for I saw a fire. Not a roaring bonfire just flames flickering.*
>
> *Then as I allowed more of it to come to me, more of the image came. I saw the flame belonged to the tip of a candle. Then near the end of the prayer I got more. A long white candle with a gold ring around its base; I immediately thought of a unity candle—the one Julie and I had at our wedding.*
>
> *At the end of the prayer the image became complete and I noticed the flame was actually quite calm; not flickering, but burning peacefully.*
>
> *A unity candle. God reminded me of my marriage to Julie and that we are one,*

that we must be one together through health and illness. And God confirmed the unity of our group as a whole: one smiling, hopeful family. And lastly, that God brings us together, unified with Him.

Thanks for the hope. I think things will be just fine.

With Love and Blessings,
Todd

God used a simple image, a unity candle, to communicate something important to this couple: that they needed to stay united in their marriage and with God during this scary, difficult time. Soon after, Todd, who was new in his faith, sensed God leading him and Julie to renew their vows. This time around, they would commit their marriage to God, who was not a part of their marriage the first time around.

Words and Impressions

In addition to speaking through visual means like dreams and pictures, God can use verbal means to communicate. One of these is through a word or phrase that comes into our minds, but we have the sense that it didn't come from our own thought process (referred to as a "message/word of knowledge" in 1 Corinthians 12:8). We have the feeling that it "came out of nowhere." Often we will not know at the time what it means. We may sense God showing us who this message is for, if not for us. Sometimes this is obvious, because we are praying for or talking to someone when the word or phrase comes to us.

In his book *Surprised by the Voice of God*, John Deere, a pastor and author, writes about a time when he felt God was encouraging him to lovingly confront a group of leaders who were experiencing conflict. He felt very nervous and awkward about doing this and wasn't sure if he was hearing God right or not. He and his wife prayed about it, and he asked for some kind of sign, because he didn't know if he could move forward without it. Here is what happened next:

> *Within ten seconds the telephone rang. A friend of ours who had been staying in the same hotel said, "Jack, I don't know what this means but I was praying a few minutes ago. I wasn't even praying for you or Leesa, but while I was praying, this particular chapter of scripture came into my mind. I don't even know what's in the chapter, but I am sure God spoke it to me. I had an impression I was supposed to call you and say it's for you.*

The chapter was about confronting others. The same chapter had been prayed over him a few months before, the person praying sensing that he would be using the things from that chapter. God had used two words, the name of a book in the Bible and the chapter number, to speak clearly in an important moment.

Similar to words from God are impressions. This may not be a specific word or phrase, but a strong sense that we are supposed to say or do something. This has the quality of coming from God and not from our own natural thinking processes.

In the story I shared earlier about my dream, a friend of mine also had an impression that was important in my process. During a prayer time, I had told God that I was a bit confused about whether I was supposed to stay at the church I was working at, but that

I didn't want to force anything by looking elsewhere if it wasn't his timing. I said I would be open if it seemed he was opening up something, but that I wasn't going to proactively look for anything.

A few weeks later, a friend of mine said that she had woken up during the night with a strong sense that she was supposed to encourage me to interview at the church she was attending—the same church I mentioned earlier. She wasn't used to this happening to her, so she wasn't sure what to do. After it happened a second time, she thought, "Okay, I'm just going to tell him!" This gave me the confidence to contact the church and start the process.

In both cases, a key component was the person receiving the word or impression being obedient, even when it could have felt a bit foolish, given that they didn't know what it all meant. When we sense that God is showing us something for someone else, the best posture is to communicate that we believe God may be showing us something for them, as opposed to saying, "God told me you should do this." In the end, the person we are sharing with needs to prayerfully evaluate and confirm what God is saying or not saying to them.

Through the power of the Spirit, God can speak to us in these and other ways. We need to be aware and open. We also need to recognize that, like a lot of things, this is a learning process. We will grow in recognizing when God is speaking in these ways and how to respond.

The Spirit Empowers

In addition to communicating, the Spirit also moves in power for us and through us.

A number of years ago, my wife, Jacki, was experiencing severe back and neck pain. The neck pain had gotten so bad that she couldn't move her head to the right or left. She was unable to work and had become very discouraged.

A trusted friend told us about a couple of men who held monthly healing services at a hotel meeting room in the area. We weren't totally sure about it, but we thought we would give it a try. Why not?

I have a pretty strong radar for flaky stuff, so my antenna was up as we arrived, but these guys were very down-to-earth, not flashy at all. In fact, I think they were farmers or something like that. They and their wives simply prayed for people as they sensed God leading them.

At one point, Jacki and I went forward for prayer. Jacki told them about her neck pain. One of the women began praying for her and said she had a picture of Jacki's mom and Jacki as a child. Her mom was speaking harshly to her in the scene. Jacki begin to cry as she shared how she had felt hurt by her mom's alcoholism and harshness. Of course, this woman had no previous knowledge of any of this. God had showed her.

After this, the woman's husband came over and asked about Jacki's neck. Jacki said that they really hadn't even prayed for her neck. He said, "Well, try moving it and see how it feels." She nervously moved her neck, and it was completely free from pain. God had healed Jacki both physically and emotionally.

Notice that the Holy Spirit had brought both his communication through the picture/ scene and his power of healing and had done it through ordinary but open people.

Nothing fancy, no shouting, just the love and power of the Spirit working in a hotel meeting room.

Ways the Spirit Ministers

There are a variety of ways that the Spirit can come upon someone or work through them to minister to others. The above example of physical or emotional healing is one. The Spirit works through people to bring healing. Of course, he often uses natural means to bring healing, but at times he chooses to work supernaturally and often uses others in that process.

The Spirit can come upon someone who is sharing about Jesus with an individual or group to give them the right words and to empower them in a way that speaks to the heart of that person. Similarly, the Spirit can come upon someone who is teaching or preaching to share in a particularly powerful way.

The Spirit can show someone when demonic activity is happening in another person's life. The Bible refers to this as the discernment of spirits. An example would be a person who does not know Christ, but is seeking to know him, who may have unknowingly had contact with evil spirits through various activities in life, such as occult practices.

The Spirit can show a follower of Christ what is happening and, especially with training, know how to best respond in the direction and power of the Spirit. Our study passage is a good example of this, although, in this case, the person is not exactly seeking after God.

These are just a few of the ways the Spirit can work in power.

Understanding the Supernatural Gifts

Most of what we have been discussing can be found in the scriptural descriptions of what are sometimes referred to as the supernatural gifts. All of the gifts discussed in last week's session are from God, so in that sense, they are supernatural, but the expressions of the Spirit we have been discussing tend to have a direct display of the Spirit's power or activity.

When the Spirit seems to work through a person in one of these areas on a frequent basis, we may say they have a gift from God in that area. For example, someone who tends to receive words, impressions, or pictures from God may have the gift of words of knowledge, a gift described in 1 Corinthians 12. In the case of the men who held the healing prayer meetings, God was using the gift of healing through them.

This does not mean someone is more spiritual if God is using them in this way. It is up to the Spirit to decide how he wants to use people. Often it is partly due to those who are open to the Spirit working in their lives and using them in these ways. These gifts are no more or less important than the other gifts of helps, teaching, administration, etc. As it's important to grow in our understanding of how to use a gift we have been given, it is as important to grow in any of the "supernatural" gifts. We can learn about how to use these gifts with wisdom.

It is important to note that the Spirit can use us in any of the ways we have discussed, whether it seems to be a gift for us or not. For example, the Spirit may give us a word or picture for a friend, and that's it. Maybe years later, he gives us a dream that's helpful to someone. It's important to be open to the Spirit's work, whether it is a frequent occurrence or not.

An Initial Experience

A final but important issue to discuss is an initial experience of the Holy Spirit that people may have, especially when made aware of this possibility. This is simply the Spirit coming upon someone, as we have discussed, in a way that makes him real to us: a tangible experience of the Spirit.

A number of years ago, I attended a retreat with teaching on the Holy Spirit similar to what we have been looking at. As a part of that teaching, we looked at biblical examples of people who had an initial experience of the Holy Spirit, such as in Acts when Peter is speaking to a group of Gentiles (non-Jews) about Jesus.

> ### Acts 10:44-46
> *[44]While Peter was still speaking these words, the Holy Spirit came on all who heard the message. [45]The circumcised [Jewish] believers who had come with Peter were astonished that the gift of the Holy Spirit had been poured out even on Gentiles. [46]For they heard them speaking in tongues [other languages] and praising God.*

They had a powerful encounter with the Holy Spirit.

The pastor leading the retreat, Brad Long, taught about how the Spirit still touches people like this today, and it usually results in the person being much more aware of the reality of the Spirit and how he can work in us and through us.

That evening, he and others were going to pray for those who would like to ask for a touch or experience of the Spirit in this way. My pastor friend whom I had come with had to leave early, so we wouldn't be able to be there that evening. Brad offered to pray for my friend and me right then before everyone went to a coffee break.

He prayed a simple prayer for us, asking the Spirit to touch us, and then everyone went to get coffee. As we sat there, both of us leaning forward, I felt a gentle presence on my back. I mentioned this to my friend. "Me, too!" he said. He remembered that part of the definition of God's glory is weight, as in you can sometimes actually feel the weight of God's glory and presence.

Then I said, "I just feel so joyful and peaceful." He said, "Me, too!" The Spirit was touching us in the same way.

Then he said that he thought we should pray, and I felt drawn to pray for people in my life who didn't know Jesus. As I did, I just began to weep. As much as I want people to know Jesus, I knew this wasn't me getting emotional. It was the Spirit grieving and showing us how much God's heart breaks for those who don't know him.
At this point, people began coming back from the coffee break (talk about a non-emotional environment!), and we sang a couple of worship songs. I felt like Jesus said to me, "You teach others about my love, but I want you to experience my love for you." It felt like a fire hose of love pouring into my chest.

The Holy Spirit became more real for me that day. As you can imagine, after that experience, it didn't surprise me that he would speak and act in a variety of ways. I also became more and more involved in evangelism ministries after that.

When someone experiences the Spirit in this way, it is a kind of doorway into an awareness of the Spirit's supernatural work. It makes us aware of just how real he is and how he can work.

It's important to be aware that the Spirit touches people in a variety of ways. For some it's pretty dramatic, and for others, much less so. Some of the common experiences are feelings of warmth, "electricity," deep peace or joy, sometimes even a desire to laugh, spontaneous praise or speaking in unknown languages, and an experience of God's love or healing.

Sometimes, there's not a physical experience, but simply a knowing that the Spirit has touched us and a new awareness and openness to his work in our lives.

Regardless, our part is simply to be open and invite him to touch us any way he chooses and whenever he chooses to do so. We cannot control the Spirit. I certainly was not expecting to experience him that way during a coffee break!

Trusting the Spirit

We cannot control the Holy Spirit, but we can trust him. After looking at how the Spirit speaks and moves in power, you may feel excited, a bit confused or wary, or somewhere in between. It's okay. Just trust him to lead you into good things and to a greater understanding of his work in your life.

Be open and not fearful. He is good, and he loves you.

Questions for Reflection and Discussion

- What did you find helpful about the discussion of the role of the Spirit *within* us and *upon* us?

- Have you experienced God communicating to you in any of the ways mentioned in the reading about how the Spirit speaks?

- Was there anything new for you in reading about the empowerment of the Spirit or the supernatural gifts of the Spirit?

- During your prayer time, share any desire you have to experience more of the Spirit in the ways discussed in the reading.

Spiritual Practice
Practicing Our Listening Skills

As you will see in this week's reading, there are a variety of ways that God can speak to us for ourselves and for others. However, this usually requires us giving him the opportunity to speak, learning more about how this works, and practicing. Whenever we are learning about something new and beginning to practice it, we have to be willing to make mistakes and grow in our understanding. This is true of learning the different ways that God can speak to us.

This week, we will get the chance to practice. First, make sure you have done the reading for this week, as it will give you some ideas of how God speaks. In your group time, take a moment in silent prayer to see who feels led by the Spirit to share something with the group that is going on in their lives that they would like prayer for. Once group members feel led in this way, they can let the group know that they want prayer.

Instead of sharing at length about their needs, however, they should simply share a one-sentence description. For example, "We are struggling with our oldest daughter."

The group should take a few minutes (it doesn't have to be long) to listen to God in silence and to see if he is showing anyone in the group something to pray. This could be a picture that comes to mind, a single word, a particular Scripture passage, or a specific encouragement. One key principle is that you may not have any idea how what you are sensing relates to the need that was shared. That's okay. Go ahead and share what you are sensing and pray along those lines.

Your time might go something like this. After a time of waiting on God in silence, someone might say, "I see a picture of a young girl skipping through a meadow on a windy day. God, if this relates to Mary's need, please show that to her." The next person might say, "The phrase that came to mind was, 'My timing.' Father, if this is from you, please help Mary know what that means." And so on.

After the time of prayer, check in with the person who shared the need and see how what was shared during the prayer time connected with him or her. The key, again, is to remember that you are learning. You may find something connecting in a very clear way. For example, "The picture you had is exactly like a vivid memory from my childhood!" Or, "God said the exact same words to me this morning when I was praying!"

Sometimes, it may not seem clear at the moment, but will later. And sometimes it just isn't connecting, meaning that it may have been our own thoughts. Or we may not have sensed/heard anything at all. This is all okay. We are learning and growing. For many of us, this will be some of our first steps in this area.

One of the goals of this discipleship process is to see God and his ways permeate our lives to a greater and greater degree over time. The way we approach every part of our lives should be impacted by our relationship with God. We have discussed how our relationship with God impacts our relationships, our priorities, the use of our gifts, our emotional health, our sexuality, and more.

We now come to an area in which many people, including long-time followers of Christ, have had a difficult time allowing God to enter into in a deeper way: money. For a host of reasons, people often wall off this part of their lives from God and his influence. This is tragic, because it cuts us off from the wisdom and blessings God has for us and can lead us into damaging consequences.

God knows that money has a huge effect on us and our lives. That is why there are *hundreds* of verses in the Bible about money. We may see money as a mundane, non-spiritual part of our lives. God knows better. He knows that it is connected to some of the deepest parts of our hearts and our characters—in other words, the people we are becoming. He knows that money and possessions directly impact our relationship with him. If it weren't so important—a core issue in our lives—Jesus wouldn't have said things like, "Where your treasure is, there your heart will be also," and, "You *cannot* serve both God and money" (Matthew 6:21, 24).

Here are some of the questions we will explore:
- **Stewardship** Whose money is this anyway, and how does that impact how we use it?
- **Materialism** How does the sin of materialism in our culture impact us, often without us even realizing it?
- **Wisdom** How do we gain God's wisdom in handling finances, rather than blindly following society's "wisdom" that often leads to destructive results?
- **Giving** How we can discover the joy and blessings that come from being obedient to God's teaching on giving, including the deeper relationship we can have with him?

As you can see, that's a lot to cover. Because we will only be able touch on these areas, this will be an important part of your discipleship to pursue further in the future. Fortunately, there are some excellent resources, including books, videos, and discussion groups that you can take advantage of. These are listed in the Spiritual Reading section of this week's materials.

Soaking in Scripture

1 Chronicles 29 is an excellent picture of people giving generously from their hearts. In this case, they were following the lead of King David in giving to the building of a temple for God. In the passage below, David talks about the first area mentioned in our introduction, stewardship. Stewardship is the idea of caring for or managing something of value for another person. This is a very important principle for us to examine, because it will impact how we view money on a fundamental level.

1 Chronicles 29:14, 16-17 (NLT)

¹⁴But who am I, and who are my people, that we could give anything to you? Everything we have has come from you, and we give you only what you first gave us! ¹⁶"O Lord our God, even this material we have gathered to build a Temple to honor your holy name comes from you! It all belongs to you! ¹⁷I know, my God, that you examine our hearts and rejoice when you find integrity there. You know I have done all this with good motives, and I have watched your people offer their gifts willingly and joyously.

- Paraphrase vv. 14 and 16 in your own words.

- How could understanding that it all belongs to God impact how you view money and possessions in your life? (Take your time on this one!)

- What strikes you about the way in which David and the people gave, as described in v. 17?

- We are going to do something a little different. Below, you will find a brief letter written to God. Take some time to read it, and then think and pray about what it might mean for your life. If you feel that it reflects your heart's desire, then sign it with sincerity as a pledge to God. You may not know specifically what it will mean for the future, but it will express your intent to him.

Note: The following is adapted from *Money, Possesions and Eternity*, by Randy Alcorn.
Date: _____

Dear Father,

I hereby grant to you myself, all of my money and possessions, and all else I have thought of as mine, even my family. From this point forward, I will think of them as yours to do with as you please. I will diligently seek to know how you wish for me to use your assets to further your kingdom. In living this way, I realize I will give up some earthly treasures, but in exchange, I will have the opportunity to impact others during this lifetime and for eternity.

Please help me be a faithful steward of your resources for the rest of my life.

Willingly and joyfully yours,

_____

⛏ Digging into Scripture

The Bible has a wealth of wisdom when it comes to money (no pun intended). Because money is such a broad subject, it seems like another good opportunity to look at a range of brief passages that address various issues related to the topic.

For each passage, note any key observations or principles. It also may be helpful to paraphrase the key idea of the passage in your own words. For application at the end, you may want to reflect on which aspect of God's wisdom concerning money you want to pursue further.

Debt

Proverbs 22:7 (NASB)

The rich rules over the poor, and the borrower becomes *the lender's slave.*

Deuteronomy 28:1-2, 12

¹If you fully obey the Lord your God and carefully follow all his commands I give you today, the Lord your God will set you high above all the nations on earth. ²All these blessings will come on you and accompany you if you obey the Lord your God. ¹²The Lord will open the heavens, the storehouse of his bounty, to send rain on your land in season and to bless all the work of your hands. You will lend to many nations but will borrow from none.

Proverbs 22:26-27 (NLT)

²⁶Don't agree to guarantee another person's debt or put up security for someone else. ²⁷If you can't pay it, even your bed will be snatched from under you.

Saving

Proverbs 21:20

The wise store up choice food and olive oil, but fools gulp theirs down.

Generosity

Psalm 112:5

Good will come to those who are generous and lend freely, who conduct their affairs with justice.

2 Corinthians 9:6-7 (NLT)

[6]Remember this—a farmer who plants only a few seeds will get a small crop. But the one who plants generously will get a generous crop. [7]You must each decide in your heart how much to give. And don't give reluctantly or in response to pressure. "For God loves a person who gives cheerfully."

Responsibility

Romans 13:6-8

[6]This is also why you pay taxes, for the authorities are God's servants, who give their full time to governing. [7]Give to everyone what you owe them: If you owe taxes, pay taxes; if revenue, then revenue; if respect, then respect; if honor, then honor. [8]Let no debt remain outstanding, except the continuing debt to love one another, for whoever loves others has fulfilled the law.

Pursuing wealth

Proverbs 23:4-5 (NLT)

[4]Don't wear yourself out trying to get rich. Be wise enough to know when to quit. [5]In the blink of an eye wealth disappears, for it will sprout wings and fly away like an eagle.

1 Timothy 6:6-9 (NLT)

[6]Yet true godliness with contentment is itself great wealth. [7]After all, we brought nothing with us when we came into the world, and we can't take anything with us when we leave it. [8]So if we have enough food and clothing, let us be content. [9]But people who long to be rich fall into temptation and are trapped by many foolish and harmful desires that plunge them into ruin and destruction.

Application

Spiritual Reading
Getting God's Mind on Money

The Big Picture

There are two realities that can fundamentally alter how we look at money. Reality #1: This is not my money. Reality #2: This world is not my home.

As we looked at in our Soaking in Scripture section this week, everything we earn and own actually belongs to God. It's all his. We are stewards, managers, of God's money and things.

This is huge. When we really begin to get a hold of this reality, we begin looking at things a little differently. We start saying things like, "This isn't my money, God, so how do you want me to spend it? How can I use it most wisely? What changes do I need to make in how I handle it? What does giving look like?"

With our material things, we begin saying, "It's not my car, God. How do you want me to use it? How much should I spend on it? Do others need to use it? It's not my house. It's yours. How do I use it in a way that pleases you?"

Along with this, the second reality is that this earth is not our home; heaven is. What this means is that it is easy to get caught up in focusing on material things, which are only temporary. Of course there are things we need—food, clothing, shelter—but our culture goes beyond that and obsesses about the latest and greatest.

When our focus, however, is on seeing God's kingdom breaking into this world, we will begin to look at our money differently. We will begin thinking about what will have eternal impact. In particular, we will begin to focus more on *people* than *things*.

For example, instead of being focused on whether we can find a newer or bigger car, we are trying to save our money to be available to help someone who might be in need or financially support those that God is using in our world in some way or being faithful in our regular giving.

This is a completely different way of looking at money and material items than most of us have been used to. It's a shift away from centering our decisions about money on ourselves to centering on God and his mission in this world. Here's how Jesus puts it.

> **Matthew 6:31, 33**
>
> *[31]So do not worry, saying, 'What shall we eat?' or 'What shall we drink?' or 'What shall we wear?' [33]But seek first his kingdom and his righteousness, and all these things will be given to you as well.*

The Joy of Giving

Here's the thing that many people don't get to discover: giving is fun. When you begin to look at your stuff as being God's and truly are asking him how to use it, it can be really cool.

A number of years ago, I had the chance to walk with a young man who was getting off of drugs, finding stable work, and seeking to know God. After some of these things began to take hold in his life, he met a wonderful woman and got married.

Because we lived in an expensive part of the country (Silicon Valley), housing was very difficult. After doing some research, they realized that they could afford the monthly payments on a prefabricated house, but they didn't have the money for a down payment, which was a few thousand dollars.

My wife and I talked about it and decided it would be a blast to give them the money to make it possible to move into a new home. And it was! It was so fulfilling to be able to help them in this way. Did we have two older model cars in the driveway? Yep. But who cares? It was way more fun to help this awesome couple than to be driving a shiny hunk of metal.

When you hold your money and your stuff loosely, God can do great things with it!

One area of giving that is tough for a lot of people is tithing. Tithing is giving 10% of your income to God through the local church.

In Malachi, God is talking to the people of Israel and offers both a strong rebuke and a remarkable promise when it comes to tithing.

Malachi 3:8-10

[8]"Will a mere mortal rob God? Yet you rob me.

"But you ask, 'How are we robbing you?'

"In tithes and offerings. [9]You are under a curse—your whole nation—because you are robbing me. [10]Bring the whole tithe into the storehouse, that there may be food in my house. Test me in this," says the Lord Almighty, "and see if I will not throw open the floodgates of heaven and pour out so much blessing that there will not be room enough to store it.

God says that the people are actually robbing him by not bringing their tithes to the storehouse (the temple), which provides food and other resources for those in need, as well as providing for the needs of priests. Then he actually encourages them to test him and see if he will not provide for them and bless them abundantly.

This is the same struggle many have today: if I tithe, will God truly provide for me? We look at our incomes and expenses and can't imagine how this could possibly work. That's the problem: no imagination. We only see what we could humanly do. We can't imagine the ways that God could provide in new ways or give us the insight to know how to reduce expenses or both. We forget that this is God we're talking about!

Many people who step out and begin tithing look back on it as one of the most significant steps in their spiritual journey that they have ever taken. This is because they can point to tangible ways that God held true to his promise of caring for them: discovering an idea for a new source of income, finding a better paying position, receiving an unexpected raise, finding new ways to lower or eliminate some expenses. Many Christians have not experienced these things, because they have not stepped out and given God the chance. Rob him or trust him? Those are our choices.

Note: Our Spiritual Practice section this week will look further at the area of tithing.

God's Wisdom

In order to be free and generous with our resources, we need to be using God's wisdom in the area of finances. Otherwise, we will just feel frustrated and anxious when it comes to money. Money is a major source of stress for many people, but you probably already knew that. Most people, including many Christians, do not live according to God's wisdom. These core principles can be found in the passages we looked at this week in our Digging into Scripture section.

Spend Less Than You Make

I know. This sounds pretty obvious, doesn't it? But apparently it's not, because a majority of Americans don't do it. In fact, in 2005, individuals in the U.S. had a *negative* savings rate. That means that, as a country, we spent more than we earned. You might remember what started soon after this—right, a recession.

It's pretty easy: if you spend less than you earn, you will probably be in pretty good shape. If you spend more than you earn, you will sooner or later (probably sooner) find yourself living under stress. Stress that God doesn't want for you or your family.

Why do we do this? For starters, we have a hard time following Paul's advice: "If we have enough food and clothing, let us be content" (1 Timothy 6:8, NLT). Be content with the basic necessities of life, Paul says. It is challenging to be content in a society that intentionally targets us in an attempt to make us feel *dis*contented. Ironically, on the webpage where I found the above statistic on negative savings, an ad for a clothing store was scrolling across the top of the screen with images of various types of clothing.

One of the things that is helpful is shutting down the in-flow of information about things to buy. Statistically, the more TV you watch, the more you will spend. The more you look at websites, magazines, and catalogues, the more you will spend. The more you go to stores and malls to browse, the more you will spend. Shut down the temptation!

In our session on Satan, we discussed that he deceives us into looking down on ourselves. When we do this, we often begin looking to material things to fill this sense of unworthiness. For many people, this is the underlying reason that drives our discontentment and need to buy. Seeking God's help on this deeper level can help root out discontentment.

The combination of our culture and Satan targeting us is a lot to resist. This is the starting point: we must be content in who God has made us to be and our lives with him, so that we don't crave all that comes at us. Designer clothes, premium cable, new cars, bigger houses—do you need these to be content? Let me help you: No! You don't need these or a lot of other things.

There's another practical question here. Do you know how much you spend? Again, a majority of people don't know how much they spend in a typical month or year. They know how much they make, but really don't know how much they spend. How will they know if they spend more than they make? They won't!

This is why, if you go to see a financial counselor, one of the first things they will have you do is work on a financial plan (I'm trying to avoid that dirty word: budget). Yes, it's a pain at first, but it is just getting honest with yourself, and it begins to lead to freedom.

Be Prepared

This is another way of saying, "Save!" As we saw earlier, we are not the greatest at saving in this country. Here's what happens: we spend to the max—or over the max— and then we have an "emergency." Most of the time, it's not really an emergency; it's stuff we should expect to happen at some point. For example, the brakes go out, the water heater needs to be replaced, or a tooth needs to be filled. It's depressing just hearing it, isn't it? But these things are what we call...life. Many people are not prepared for them.

That's why God tells us, "*Precious treasure and oil are in a wise man's dwelling, but a foolish man devours it*" (Proverbs 21:20, ESV). That's what many people do: they devour all they have. The wise store up; they save for inevitable needs.

Those who are wise save for both short-term needs like the ones mentioned above, as well as longer-term needs (replacing a car, for example) and for retirement. A simple rule of thumb that some Christian financial counselors give is the 10-10-80 rule: take your total household income and subtract 10% for the tithe, giving God our *first* fruits. Then take 10% for savings, divided into short- and long-term savings. The remaining 80% is available for regular expenses.

Some of you just went into shock. The thought of giving 10 % and then saving 10% might seem like a pipe dream. If you are determined and have some guidance, it can be done. Without savings, you are going to get shocked anyway, quite often. In addition, a lack of savings will lead you into the area we will discuss next, which is also the most dangerous: debt.

Avoid Debt

Debt is a national pastime. We love debt! Actually, we love to get the things we want, and we love to get them when we want, which usually happens to be—right now!! Because very few people, including Christians, model anything different, we go right along with the rest of society.

Proverbs 22:7 tells us that "*the borrower becomes the lender's slave*". We become enslaved by debt—it rules over us. We have to maintain a certain income, because we owe for things like credit cards, cars, and houses. Often we assume we will maintain the same income level we have or that it will become higher. When a surprise comes along, like getting laid off, having to take a lower-paying job, an unexpected child, or a health issue, things get stressful very quickly.

We waste huge amounts of money on interest and miss out on *gaining* interest. Here's a fun little exercise. Let's say you have a credit card balance of $5,000 with an 18% rate, and you pay the minimum of 4% each month. To pay it off, it will only take you eleven years. Add an extra $3,000 in interest that you will be paying. Now let's say you invested that same $5,000 in a retirement fund that earned 10% for twenty years and just sort of forgot about it. It would be worth about $33,000.

When you put all of this together, you realize why God doesn't want us to live under the burden of debt. What do we do?

A great place to start is by avoiding the two most common forms of debt: credit cards and cars. For most people, these are just assumed. "Of course we are going to have a balance on our credit cards, and obviously we are going to have a car payment or two."

We own two vehicles. Combined, they are twenty-three years old. Both are dependable. Each month, we put money in a savings account to replace them. When we need to replace one, we will take the money we saved and pay cash for a car that is about four or five years old and has a reliable record.

You *don't* have to have these types of debt, and when you don't, you will save a lot of money and stress. Between credit cards and car payments, a family or individual can easily spend $500-$1,000 a month or more, with much of this going toward interest. Imagine being able to move that money into savings and being generous.

Is there any "good" debt? Debt that Christian financial counselors typically say is acceptable meet two criteria: 1) the investment is likely to appreciate, and 2) will not put you at financial risk.

An example of this would be a home mortgage. Over a longer period, a home is likely to appreciate in value (although, as we saw in the recent recession, values can decrease significantly in the short run). The mistake many people make is violating the second rule and purchasing a home that requires too much of their income, resulting in stress.

A good, comfortable guideline is 25% of household income going toward a monthly mortgage payment, including taxes and insurance. The further you go above this percentage, the more anxiety you will experience. Even when this guideline is met, wise counselors encourage paying down mortgages sooner than later. This is because so much is paid toward interest.

For example, if you owe $150,000 on your thirty-year mortgage and have a loan rate of 6%, you will pay $173,000 in interest over the life of the loan. If you were able to pay the loan off in fifteen years (maybe by not having other debt), you would pay $77,000 in interest and, as a bonus, you would not have any house payment after those fifteen years. Again, this may not sound possible, but if you follow a plan laid out by wise counselors, it can be.

Moving Toward Freedom

Steps like getting out of debt and beginning to save may seem overwhelming. In the Other Resources section below, you will find some very helpful options. These are Christian organizations dedicated to helping people take these very steps. They can offer you a step-by-step plan, as well as counselors and groups to help you. This is the combination you will need: a plan and a partner.

God does not want us burdened and stressed out because of money. He doesn't want our marriages strained because of financial anxiety. He wants freedom for us: freedom to enjoy life as he intended and freedom to give generously and further his kingdom.

Questions for Reflection and Discussion

- What did you find interesting or challenging about the two realities described in the Big Picture section?

- Which of the areas under God's Wisdom impacted you the most, and why?

- When have you experienced the joy of giving?

- During your prayer time, ask God what a next step might look like in the area of money. Even one small step—a conversation with a spouse, looking at a website—can be significant.

Other Resources

Taking steps toward reshaping our finances often requires the help of others. The following sites are respected, Christian experts in this area. For many, the most helpful step is joining a group that is working through a process of applying God's financial wisdom in their lives. This structure and support often makes the difference between good intentions and real change. If your church does not offer one of these groups, it is likely that a church in your area does. The sites below can direct you to one of these groups.

- Crown Financial Ministries (crown.org): This organization offers resources (books, articles, videos, etc.), as well as small groups. Its strength is in teaching biblical principles about the deeper issues in our life related to money and giving and also in teaching how money relates to our relationship with God. In addition, they offer practical steps toward financial freedom.
- Dave Ramsey (daveramsey.com): Dave Ramsey has become well known for his engaging teaching on financial principles on radio and TV. His website offers a number of helpful tools, as well as groups/classes called *Financial Peace University*.Particularly helpful is Ramsey's "7 Baby Steps" towards finding financial freedom.

Hopefully, through the reading about tithing and recognizing through Scripture that it's all God's to begin with, you are feeling drawn toward beginning the practice of tithing, if you don't tithe already. How do you get started? Here are some suggestions that might help in taking that first step.

- First, recognize that, if you are like most people, the biggest hurdle is trust. Trust that God will actually provide for your needs if you begin to tithe. Trusting that God has plenty of resources to take care of you. Pray and ask God to give you the strength and courage to trust him to take a step like this.

- If you are married, begin talking to your spouse about tithing. You want to be on the same page and be united on something as important as this.

- If you do not have a budget, create one to have a better understanding of where your finances currently go. (See the Spiritual Reading section for organizations that provide budgeting forms.) The key is to have your tithe be the first, not last, item that you list as an expense. The Bible refers to this as giving your *first fruits*. This will help you determine what you have left to live on after being faithful to God, rather than deciding what you can give to God after you have taken care of all of your needs. *This may result in some significant changes to your lifestyle.*

- If you have debt, this is an important area to address, because it is a key way to free up funds for giving, as well as saving. Explore the organizations listed in the Spiritual Reading section to get started.

- Take the plunge! It will probably never feel completely comfortable when you begin tithing. This is true whether you have a small or large income. At some point, you have to step out in faith (trust) and go for it. Although it may be scary for you, it will also be one of the most exciting times in your journey, as you begin to see God's faithfulness in very concrete ways. He cares about you, and he will honor your obedience.

If you have been in the practice of tithing for awhile, it may be time to be stretched by God again in your giving. Begin to pray and ask if there are new ways he would lead you to give beyond the tithe. This may be to your church, a ministry, individuals in need, or something else. What would not only help others, but also continue to grow your giving "muscles" so that you are forced to rely on God and see his trustworthiness in action?

A Few Questions

There are often a few specific questions that come up related to tithing. Did the command to tithe continue in the New Testament? Although there are no specific commands in the New Testament, many Christian scholars and leaders note the following: Christians who were also Jews most likely assumed the tithe; Jesus appears to affirm the tithe in Matthew 23:23; in the places that giving is encouraged in the New Testament, it appears that great sacrifice that most likely went beyond the tithe is encouraged. In addition, it would seem strange that God would ask us to trust less in our giving (as compared to the Old Testament command of tithing), rather than the same or more.

Another question that often comes up is whether we give our whole tithe to the church we are a part of or divide it amongst the church and other organizations or individuals. Different leaders and individual Christians have varying opinions on this. The most common encouragement is to bring the tithe to the local church and any offerings above the tithe to other organizations and individuals. This keeps the church financially healthy to be able to serve those within the church and the broader community. This also follows the command in the Old Testament of bringing the tithe to the "storehouse" (the temple).

Lastly, people will ask whether they are to tithe on their gross or net income. Again, there are different views on this, but God asks for our *first* fruits. This would seem to point toward basing our tithe off of our gross income.

At the beginning of this course we talked about the importance of disciples going on to disciple others. In fact, it is part of the definition of being a disciple. You may not feel ready to take this next step of leading a discipleship group—that is a common feeling! In essence, however, you are simply continuing your own discipleship process.

By leading a group, you will have the opportunity to go deeper in the topics you have explored during this course. You will not be required to have all the answers. You are simply someone who is willing to provide an environment for people to learn from one another as they begin to establish a foundation for their life with God.

This session is designed to help remind us of Jesus' passion for discipleship and how he went about choosing and guiding his disciples. This is covered in both the reading as well as the Scripture passages we will look at. This session also includes practical details on taking your first steps with potential disciples and some reminders about some of the key aspects of the discipleship process, this time looking at these keys through the eyes of a leader.

The good news is that none of this is new information. You have been experiencing this process for months now, including opportunities to lead. It is simply a matter of trusting God to help you find the right people and getting started. Get ready, you are in for an exciting journey!

Soaking in Scripture

The timing of this passage is important. These are some of Jesus' last words to his eleven disciples before returning to heaven, which of course gives it even more weight. As you read, reflect on how important this idea of discipleship is to Jesus.

Matthew 28:18-20

¹⁸Then Jesus came to them and said, "All authority in heaven and on earth has been given to me. ¹⁹Therefore go and make disciples of all nations, baptizing them in the name of the Father and of the Son and of the Holy Spirit, ²⁰ᵃand teaching them to obey everything I have commanded you. ᵇAnd surely I am with you always, to the very end of the age."

- Paraphrase vv. 19-20a in your own words.

- Circle each verb in the passage you just paraphrased. Which of these seem significant to you, and why?

- What difference do Jesus' words in vv. 18 and 20b make to you as you think about discipling others?

- Spend some time asking Jesus to help you with any concerns you might have related to discipling others.

Digging into Scripture

This week, we will look at two passages that help us understand how important personal discipleship is to Jesus and what his approach to it is. Both passages are concerned with the same event: Jesus' selection of the twelve apostles.

Some questions to consider as you read:
- What do you notice about how he goes about selecting the twelve?
- What do you notice about what they will be doing?
- What do you notice about who they are?

Luke 6:12-16

¹²*One of those days Jesus went out to a mountainside to pray, and spent the night praying to God. ¹³When morning came, he called his disciples to him and chose twelve of them, whom he also designated apostles: ¹⁴Simon (whom he named Peter), his brother Andrew, James, John, Philip, Bartholomew, ¹⁵Matthew, Thomas, James son of Alphaeus, Simon who was called the Zealot, ¹⁶Judas son of James, and Judas Iscariot, who became a traitor.*

Mark 3:13-19

¹³*Jesus went up on a mountainside and called to him those he wanted, and they came to him. ¹⁴He appointed twelve that they might be with him and that he might send them out to preach ¹⁵and to have authority to drive out demons. ¹⁶These are the twelve he appointed: Simon (to whom he gave the name Peter), ¹⁷James son of Zebedee and his brother John (to them he gave the name Boanerges, which means "sons of thunder"), ¹⁸Andrew, Philip, Bartholomew, Matthew, Thomas, James son of Alphaeus, Thaddaeus, Simon the Zealot ¹⁹and Judas Iscariot, who betrayed him.*

Observation

Interpretation

Application

Spiritual Practice
Discipling Others

Taking the step to disciple others is both exciting and stretching. It is normal to feel a bit nervous at first (maybe even quite a bit nervous!). Hopefully, between the information below concerning the discipling process and the support of the person discipling you now, you can move forward with confidence.

Choosing a Disciple

This might be a good time to review the Bonus section from Session 21. That section discusses what to look for in potential disciples. The key again is to prayerfully ask God to show you the two or three people he would want you to disciple. Also, be looking for those who have made a decision to follow Christ, but do not have a strong spiritual foundation and are eager to develop that foundation, even if it means a significant investment on their part.

After your final session together, it is recommended that your current group continue to meet every other week until you have established new groups. At that time, your current group may want to meet once a month for a period of time to support one another.

Getting Started

Here are some details for your first few meetings with potential disciples. These do not have to be followed precisely, but serve as a guide. The first meeting would take place after an initial contact with those you feel God has been leading you to. You would ask them if they would like to meet to hear more about a personal discipleship opportunity that you have recently experienced. If they are interested in meeting, set up a time (an hour or so), and then proceed as follows:

- **First Meeting** (individually or with both potential disciples)

  - Ask them to share what interests them about the possibility of being personally discipled. This will help you get an idea of how interested and eager they may be at this time.

  - Give a brief overview of what's involved in the discipleship process: use the course overview and a sample week of the materials to give them an idea of what's involved and share about your own experience. Review the covenant agreement as a way to let them know what the specific commitment would be and as a way to review what has been discussed.

  - If meeting individually, share that there will be a third person joining you (share about that person or ask for their ideas if you haven't invited a third person yet).

  - Ask them to look over the overview and covenant and pray about their decision during the coming week, even if they feel that they want to do it.

  - It is important that the investment required is not downplayed. They need to know that it will be a significant investment of time and energy, but that there are also significant rewards. This is a good opportunity for you to share about your own investment and what you have gotten out of the process.

  - Schedule a second meeting.

- **Second Meeting** (with one or both disciples)

  - Ask them to share about their decision-making process. If they are ready to make the commitment, ask them to sign the covenant agreement.

  - If both disciples are present and ready to move forward, then share about your spiritual journeys as a way to begin to get to know one another. If not, inform the person to be praying about the third person.

  - If both disciples are there and ready to go, give them the materials and ask them to complete Session 1 for your next meeting. Decide on a regular meeting day/time.

- **Third Meeting**

  - This will be your first "regular" meeting.

  - Personal sharing: continue getting to know one another and sharing about your week. As mentioned below, model open sharing for the group as it feels appropriate at this time.

  - Make sure to discuss results from the Spiritual Practice section to identify areas to focus on in future weeks, as well as discussing the rest of the session.

  - Pray for the group. In future weeks, it is good to begin having group members pray for each other. This is a good way to help them become more comfortable with group prayer. The sessions on prayer can be a good time to start this if you haven't already by that time.

Things to Remember

Here are a few things to remember once you get into the discipling process.

- *You are not alone.*

  The first thing to remember is that you are not doing this on your own. The person who has been discipling you will transition into being your coach. This is the person to go to when you have questions or when you run into situations you're unsure how to handle or when the people you are discipling have questions you are not sure how to answer. As mentioned above, early on you may want to meet with your current group once a month for support. Of course, you can also talk at other times as needs arise. Over time, you may transition into meeting on an as-needed basis.

- *You set the pace.*

  - **Modeling personal sharing:** Hopefully, throughout your own process you have experienced the benefits of a group who shares openly about the joys and challenges of life and how God is working in your life through all of it. As a leader, it is important to know that you set the pace in being relationally open. As you share openly about what is going on in your life, including the struggles, the others in your group will most likely follow your lead.

  - **Modeling preparation:** In addition to personal sharing, the second key aspect of the group time is discussing the materials for the week. As a leader, it is important that you model the consistent use of these materials during your time with God each week. In other words, the group is seeing that you spend regular time with God using the discipleship materials, rather than cramming the night before. This will encourage them in developing their own regular time with God.

  - **Modeling commitment:** You are the "keeper of the covenant." This is the covenant agreement that is signed by each group member at the beginning of the discipleship process. Part of the covenant is the two elements just mentioned above. Another commitment is making the group a high priority and attending the group on a consistent basis. At times, the group may become less consistent due to illness, holidays, life challenges, work schedule changes, etc. As the leader, it is your role to not only be consistent yourself, but to ensure that the group remains consistent. This may require reviewing the covenant and discussing the need for meeting consistently or discussing a different meeting time/ day. Not being able to meet on some days is inevitable. It is when this becomes a pattern that the discipleship process breaks down.

- *Emphasize multiplication from the beginning.*

  As a leader, it is important to discuss early on the expectation that the new disciple will go on to disciple others at the end of the discipleship process. This is included in the covenant agreement as well as the discipleship overview. They will most likely feel nervous about that idea, but you can assure them that it will be a while before they take that step and that they will be supported in that process when the time comes.

  Begin rotating leadership after three to four months of meeting so that they begin to get the feel for leading a group in the future. After one of the group members leads, ask them about how the experience was for them. Provide positive feedback as well as small amounts of adjustments you would recommend.

Following the Spirit

Hopefully, these first steps and reminders will be helpful to you as you get started. In the end, however, the most important thing is to follow the Holy Spirit as he guides you. Your willingness to seek God for guidance and your genuine concern for those you are helping are the most important elements. Remember that this step of discipling others is part of your own discipleship process. With that in mind, give yourself plenty of grace and room for learning, including making mistakes. This is a normal part of the process. Your Father is pleased with you for venturing out on this adventure to help others as you have been helped!

Jesus' Strategy

Let's pretend you are on a reality show called *World Changers!* You are competing with other contestants to come up with the best plan—the best strategy—to alter the spiritual landscape of the area you live in: to dramatically change the world for Christ in your community. You can come up with any strategy; the only rule is that the plan can only take three years or less to implement. Change your area in three years or less—how would you do it?

This was Jesus' challenge, except it wasn't a reality show. He had three years from the time he started his ministry until he died, was resurrected, and returned to heaven. Three years to implement a strategy that wouldn't just change an area, but would change the world. What was his strategy?

This is an important question, because it's not a reality show for us, either. Do we know Jesus' strategy, his plan, and are we following it?

We know that Jesus spoke to large crowds of people. He healed, cast out demons, and taught in synagogues. But what did he spend the majority of his time doing?

We saw it in our Digging into Scripture passages this week. He chose twelve men out of the larger group of disciples, and then he poured his life into them. It says he chose them to "be with him." A large majority of his time was spent with these twelve men.

Let's think about that for a minute. He has three years to set something in motion that will change the world, and his main strategy is...twelve guys. Not even twelve "stars." Later, some of the Jewish leaders will remark that these were unschooled and ordinary men. Fishermen. A tax collector. A political zealot.

This is a remarkably counterintuitive strategy. Why would Jesus choose this approach? Because he knew a secret. He knew that this strategy had explosive possibilities. He knew this truth: when people are personally and deeply impacted by another person, they often go on to impact the world around them in amazing ways.

This is exactly what happened with these twelve men (okay, things didn't go too well with Judas Iscariot). They were so deeply impacted and shaped by Jesus that they went on to spread his message across the world. They were so committed to him that ten of the eleven would be martyred for their faith (and the eleventh, John, was just exiled to an isolated island in his old age—no big deal). They discipled others who would go on to make disciples, and the "Jesus movement" began to ripple out throughout the known world like a tsunami. They were obedient to Jesus' final command to go and make disciples.

Key Elements

What were the key elements of how Jesus discipled these twelve men?

Teaching

First of all, he taught them. He passed along the key knowledge they needed about who the Father is and what it means to follow him. He did it in a way that was personal. They were able to ask questions and dialogue about a range of topics. It wasn't just one-way communication. And it was comprehensive. Over this two to three year period, Jesus covered a lot of theological ground with them.

Compare that with the experience of some Christians today. Someone comes to follow Christ, and they hear messages on Sunday morning. Some of these connect with them, some don't. There's not a chance to ask questions or to understand how it applies to their particular context. The messages are helpful, but incomplete without someone to personally help them.

In addition, some people only experience a piecemeal approach. They hear a topic on a Sunday, something different at a group or class, maybe a thought on the radio. It's kind of hit or miss, with the hope that over time they will learn what they need. When we follow Jesus' example, we mentor people in a way that is thorough, comprehensive, and personal.

Training

In addition to teaching the twelve, we see Jesus training them. These are skills they needed to know in order to grow in their relationship with the Father and minister to others.

One day, when Jesus finished praying, the disciples asked him to teach them how to pray. They wanted him to get very practical and explain how he prayed and related to the Father. It's not that they had never prayed, but they wanted to know how *he* prayed. They saw something in the way he prayed, and they wanted that.

At one point, Jesus decided it was time to send them out to do the things he had been doing. We looked at this passage during our session on the cost and adventure of being a disciple. He gave them instructions and the opportunity, whether they wanted it or not, to begin preaching, healing, and casting out demons. This was hands-on stuff.

Today, people are in great need of others who can come along and help them in similar hands-on ways. Many people feel inadequate in prayer, and even more so when it comes to reading or studying the Bible or in sharing their faith with others. Again, they need a place to ask specific questions about these areas and many others.

Modeling

The last way that Jesus discipled them could easily be overlooked. He simply gave them the opportunity to be with him. They had the chance to be with him and watch him day in and day out. To see the little things: how he talked about the Father in casual conversation, how he interacted with people from all walks of life, and seeing the things that brought him delight and made him laugh.

Have you ever noticed how much you can tell about people from brief interactions they have with others? Maybe it's the kind way they treat a waitress at a restaurant or the playful way they interact with a friend's child. In these small moments, we can tell a lot about—and learn a lot from—someone.

This is an area of discipleship today that is often left out. We may help people learn knowledge and even help them gain some needed skills. But people need to see what it means to follow Jesus lived out, up close and personal. Ideally, they could watch someone to see what it looks like to follow Jesus as a father or mother, husband or wife, student or employee. To hear from someone who has, through challenging times in his or her life, seen God be faithful.

This requires time together. If possible, it means doing regular life together. It's being in their houses and seeing how they interact with their spouses or kids. It's hearing about how they live out their faith in work environments. It's observing how they handle challenges or decisions in their lives. This is how people can pick up on the nuances of following Jesus—the ins and outs of faith.

We often are helping people grow even when we don't realize it, because they are seeing or hearing about our lives in ways that are helpful to them. We shouldn't underestimate the significance of this.

When we put all three together—teaching, training, and modeling—we have a great mix for discipleship. This is what we see in Jesus' approach, and he seemed to be pretty effective!

The Power of Impacting a Few

Do you want to change the world? Most of us would love to do that, but it's a pretty overwhelming thought. How could little old me do that?

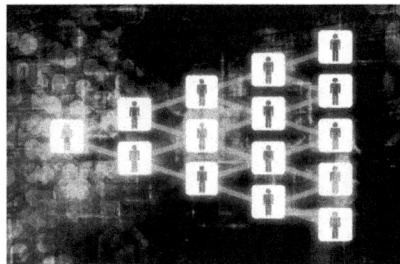

The great news is that, by deeply impacting a few people in your lifetime, you can touch many, many people. Let's say during your lifetime you were able to disciple twelve people through something like *Foundations* or in other ways (*Foundations*, of course, is only one way to disciple or mentor someone). Regardless of the approach, you were able to teach, train, and be a model for a dozen people. If you think about the people they would in turn touch—their spouses and children, friends, coworkers, neighbors—you could impact hundreds of people's lives through them. Some of these would be people that your twelve would go on to directly disciple and many more that they would influence in numerous ways.

Remember the study passage from the first session? It was the parable of the sower. Jesus finishes the parable by describing the seed that falls on good soil:

Matthew 13:8

"Still other seed fell on good soil, where it produced a crop—a hundred, sixty or thirty times what was sown."

What we have been discussing is what Jesus was getting at. When the heart and message of Jesus has been deeply imbedded into our lives, especially through the nurturing of mentors, we can then turn and nurture that seed in others' lives. At the end of our lives, we will be able turn around and see thirty, sixty, even a hundred or more lives impacted, because we intentionally invested deeply into a few people during our lifetimes.

Questions for Reflection and Discussion

- What makes sense to you about using the three elements of discipling that Jesus utilized: teaching, training, and modeling?

- Is there someone in your life who has personally helped you in your spiritual life in one or more of these ways?

- What excites you about the potential of getting to disciple others?

- During your prayer time, talk to God about your excitement and concerns related to discipling others in the future.

Sometimes people miss it, but if you take a closer look at Scripture, you will notice that God loves to celebrate. In the Old Testament, for example, he set up annual festivals to help his people remember and celebrate the highlights of their history together and to remember that he was at the center of if it all. He loves it when his people remember what he has done for them, when they remember his greatness and his great love for them.

With this in mind, this week we will look back at what God has done in our lives through this discipleship process. We will reflect on what we have learned, how we have grown, and the ways he has used the others in our group to impact our lives. We will remember both for our sakes, so we can see how far we have come, and to give thanks to God.

We will also look forward. We will look at the areas in which God may want to take us deeper in the near future. As we have been discussing, God will continue growing us through the discipling of others.

Two sections will be key to this reflection: the Soaking in Scripture and Spiritual Practice sections. Be sure to complete these sections and use your responses for discussion during your group time as a way to reflect and celebrate as a group.

As was mentioned in last session's Spiritual Practice, groups are encouraged to keep meeting on a bi-weekly basis to continue supporting one another until new disciples have been identified and new groups begun. At that time, the type and frequency of support can be discussed. A monthly time together of support might be a good place to start.

God is good, isn't he? Just think: this is only the beginning!

Soaking in Scripture
Stopping to Celebrate

Sometimes we get going so fast that we forget to stop and celebrate what God has done. We just move on to the next thing. It is good to set aside time to just celebrate.

In the Old Testament, we see a key leader of Israel, Nehemiah, doing just this. Nehemiah led the people in rebuilding the walls of Jerusalem, which was a huge task in the face of surrounding enemies. This rebuilding, along with restoring God's laws, meant that they could become the people of God once more. This was something to celebrate!

Nehemiah 12:27-43 describes the mass gathering of singers, dancers, instruments, and all the people having an all-out party.

> **Nehemiah 12:43**
>
> *And on that day they offered great sacrifices, rejoicing because God had given them great joy. The women and children also rejoiced. The sound of rejoicing in Jerusalem could be heard far away.*

- When was a time as a child or as an adult that you remember celebrating with others? This might have been a group, a team, an organization, church, or company you were a part of.

- As you think back over this discipleship experience, what are some of the things that have happened for you or others in your group that you celebrate?

- What are you grateful to God for as you think about the people in your group?

Spiritual Practice
Looking Back, Looking Forward

When you have been on a long journey of any kind, it is often good to look back and take stock of where you have been and how you have grown. This discipleship process certainly qualifies as a long journey. We may not even realize how much God has done in our lives over the past number of months. To help us, we will do some simple reflection exercises to help us look back. Discuss your responses below during your group time to reflect on your experience.

What Have I Learned?

Take some time to look back over the list of topics we have covered (these are listed in the table of contents at the front of your materials). Choose the top three to five areas or topics in which you feel you have learned the most and write them below. Add a brief description of how this has helped you in your relationship with God. Example: Prayer—I now am aware of more ways to express myself to God, which makes my time with God richer.

My top areas and how I have been impacted:

Practices to Explore

During this course, we explored a number of different practices or disciplines in the Spiritual Practice sections. The aim was to try out different practices to see which ones we might want to use more regularly to help us grow closer to God and others.

Take a look at the list below and check off the practices you were drawn to or enjoyed. Make a note of how you might pursue these practices in the future. Examples: Journaling—*I would like to write my prayers at least once a week*. Fasting—*I would like try fasting one or more days when I face a major decision in the future*.

- Picturing Scripture
- Using biblical tools, such as concordances, indexes, online tools
- Inductive Bible Study
- ACTS method of prayer
- Journaling prayer
- Listening in prayer by using the Listening Circle
- Using the 5 guidelines for key decisions
- God reminders
- Watching movies about Jesus/biblical themes
- Using past, present, future reflection for communion
- Getting baptized
- Reflecting on your funeral
- Reflecting on your day: the yesterday exercise
- Fasting
- Sabbath
- The practice of secrecy
- Researching grace
- Praying for potential disciples
- Sharing the gospel message
- Learning about injustice
- Praying for your church
- Creation walk
- Exploring your gifts and passion
- Practicing your listening skills (pictures, words, dreams)
- Taking thoughts captive
- Tithing and beyond
- Discipling others

Practices I will use and how I will use them:

Looking Forward

This discipleship process is designed to establish a strong foundation and to act as a launching pad to go deeper in the areas we have covered. Choose one or two things your group has covered in which you feel drawn to go deeper in the near future and think about what that might look like. This may be something you listed in your top three to five choices above or something different. Examples: Evangelism/Connecting to the world—taking the step to meet more neighbors. God's perspective on money—joining a Crown group.

Ways I want to go deeper:

Digging into Scripture

As we take time to look back on our experiences, it seems appropriate to look at an encounter that brings up the topic of gratitude. As we have done several times before, this is another good opportunity to first picture this scene unfolding. Read through the passage and then try to imagine the encounter. What might the men be thinking and feeling? What might Jesus be thinking and feeling? What might this mean for you?

Afterward, make your observations, interpretation, and application. Spend some time in prayer discussing whatever application comes up for you.

Luke 17:11-19

11Now on his way to Jerusalem, Jesus traveled along the border between Samaria and Galilee. 12As he was going into a village, ten men who had leprosy met him. They stood at a distance 13and called out in a loud voice, "Jesus, Master, have pity on us!"

14When he saw them, he said, "Go, show yourselves to the priests." And as they went, they were cleansed.

15One of them, when he saw he was healed, came back, praising God in a loud voice. 16He threw himself at Jesus' feet and thanked him—and he was a Samaritan.

17Jesus asked, "Were not all ten cleansed? Where are the other nine? 18Has no one returned to give praise to God except this foreigner?" 19Then he said to him, "Rise and go; your faith has made you well."

Observation

Interpretation

Application

▣ Spiritual Reading
Our Joyful God

In a recent TED talk, Nigerian novelist Chimamanda Adichie discussed the danger of having a "single story." What she means by that is having one story—one way—of viewing a person or culture. She offered herself as an example.

Adichie grew up in a middle-class Nigerian home and was exposed to music, movies, and other influences from various western cultures. When she was nineteen, she moved to the U.S. to attend college. Her new roommate was amazed that she spoke English (English is the first language in Nigeria). She then asked her to share some of her "tribal" music. Her roommate was a little disappointed when she put on a CD of Celine Dion.

Adichie's roommate had a single story of African people: they lived in tribes in small villages, speaking a strange tongue and listening to exotic tribal music.

Many people seem to have a single story of God. One picture. That picture, among other things, is one of a very serious God: intense, often angry, frequently disappointed. This is the default picture many hold in their minds.

Here is a different description of God I read recently: God is the happiest being in the universe. Have you ever considered that? That God could be radiating with joy and happiness? That, although he has a full range of emotions and may be upset or disappointed at times, he is also full of life, joy, creativity—that this is his default?

Think about Jesus, who is God in flesh, the One we can most relate to. He had to say difficult things and correct and challenge people. But think of how people were drawn to him, especially those who were less religious, who were not compelled to follow out of religious duty. People are not typically drawn to a dour, lifeless, angry figure.

Think of the One who created the world around us. Does this look like the work of a cranky old man? Think of the unbelievable variety, the breathtaking beauty, the seeming whimsy behind some of his creations (I think of flamingos, for example).

I love this description of what God's approach to work would look like if he weren't a supremely joyful being, taken from *The Life You've Always Wanted: Spiritual Disciplines for Ordinary People*, by John Ortberg.

> *In the beginning, it was nine o'clock, so God had to go to work. He filled out a requisition to separate light from darkness. He considered making stars to beautify the night, and planets to fill the skies, but thought it sounded like too much work; and besides, thought God, "That's not by job." So he decided to knock off early and call it a day. And he looked at what he had done and he said, "It'll have to do."*

> *On the second day God separated the waters from the dry land. And he made all the dry land flat, plain, and functional, so that – behold – the whole earth*

looked like Idaho. He thought about making mountains and valleys and glaciers and jungles and forests, but he decided it wouldn't be worth the effort. And God looked at what he had done that day and said, "It'll have to do."

And God made a pigeon to fly in the air, and a carp to swim in the waters, and a cat to creep upon dry ground. And God thought about making milllions of other species of all sizes and shapes and colors, but he couldn't drum up any enthusiasm for any other animals – in fact, he wasn't too crazy about the cat. Besides, it was almost time for the Late Show. So God looked at all he had done, and God said, "It'll have to do."

And at the end of the week, God was seriously burned out. So he breathed a big sigh of relief and said, "Thank Me, it's Friday."

Aren't you glad God is not like that? Ortberg also points out something I had never thought about. Yes, God experiences sorrow and anger at times, but this is his response to a fallen world. One day, when the world is made right and those who love him are with him in his kingdom, sorrow will be banished, and he (and we) will be free to fully experience who he is: a joyful God.

A Glimpse

To get a taste of this, I would like to take us back to one of the first passages we looked at in this discipleship process. In the parable of the prodigal son, Jesus tells about a young son who takes his share of his inheritance and squanders it. He wastes the money his father worked so hard to earn over the years. Worse than that, he has hurt his father by leaving him, breaking relationship with him. The sorrow and disappointment the father must have felt, each day sitting in front of his home, watching to see if his son might return.

Then one day, he sees him. Far in the distance, the father sees his son. What does he do, this father who has experienced pain and sadness? He takes off running. Running to his son. Bursting with joy and relief, he gives his son a huge bear hug and kisses his face. And then what does he do? He throws a party. He celebrates, because his son is home with him. Everything is as it should be. He can now experience the fullness of his joy.

Celebrating You

Today, your Father is celebrating you. Your desire to know him better through this discipleship process has brought him great joy. Your desire to continue following him in your life and to disciple others brings him great joy as well. He loves you and has deep affection for you. You bring him tremendous joy.

One day, we will lock eyes with our loving, joy-filled Father—and he will come running.

Questions for Reflection and Discussion

- What has your picture of God been in the past? Has it been a "single story"?

- How easy or challenging is it for you to picture God as a joyful being?

- During your prayer time, praise God for his joyfulness and creativity. Imagine what words of joy he might want to say to you as you finish this discipleship process.

www.ingramcontent.com/pod-product-compliance
Lightning Source LLC
Chambersburg PA
CBHW050457110426
42742CB00018B/3283